Journey *of the* Spirit

Trevor Hudson with Morton Kelsey

Journey *of the* Spirit

Meditations for the spiritual seeker

PAULIST PRESS
New York/Mahwah, N.J.

Cover design by Morris Berman Studio

Copyright © 2000 by Trevor Hudson and Morton Kelsey

Published by arrangement with Struik Christian Books Ltd., a division of Struik New Holland Publishing (Pty) Ltd., South Africa.

Scripture quotations taken from the Holy Bible, New Revised Standard Version, copyright 1973, 1978, 1984 by the Division of Christian Education of the National Council of Churches of Christ in the U.S.A. Reprinted by Permission.

Library of Congress Cataloging-in-Publication Data

Hudson, Trevor, 1951-
     Journey of the spirit : meditations for the spiritual seeker / Trevor Hudson and Morton T. Kelsey.
     p. cm.
    ISBN 0-8091-4053-5 (alk. paper)
     1. Spiritual life—Meditations. I. Kelsey, Morton T. II. Title.

BV4501.2 .H767 2001
242—dc21
                                               2001019890

Published by Paulist Press
997 Macarthur Boulevard
Mahwah, New Jersey 07430 USA

www.paulistpress.com

Printed and bound in the
United States of America

*This book is dedicated
with much love and thankfulness
to Debbie, Joni and Mark,
whose warm and caring companionship
enrich my life beyond measure*

and

*Morton and Barbara Kelsey,
whose lives have taught me
so much about the gospel.*

Contents

Acknowledgments

Books are hardly ever written alone, and this one is no exception. Several people inspired and encouraged me during the writing process and I am in much debt to them.

I would like to thank Rhonda Crouse and Fiona Lee for their belief in the initial idea underlying this book, and for their continued support from the first line until the last. Also a warm word of thanks to Inge du Plessis for her editorial expertise.

I'd also like to thank Bill Meaker, who spent countless hours reading each meditation, for all his comments in red ink that greatly enhanced the clarity of this bit of writing. The attention that he gave the manuscript was a gift of grace.

A special word of thanks must go to Lyn Meyer for her extraordinary efficiency and good humor in deciphering my squiggles and typing them onto the computer.

I am also fortunate to live and work among a special group of God's people at Northfield Methodist Church and am very grateful for our life together. Thank you too to Northfielder Debbie Joubert and her mother Noeleen de Beer for their proofreading skills in the final preparation of the manuscript.

Among the many who have been my teachers in the faith, I need to express my deep appreciation to Dallas Willard for all he has meant to me over the years.

Finally, I am very grateful to all my close friends and family for their many expressions of faithful love and caring concern. Thanks especially to Debbie for being there in sunshine and in storm, in joy and in struggle, and also to Joni and Mark for letting me share in their lives.

Without all of you this book would not have seen the light of day.

Foreword

There has been a great resurgence of spirituality and interest in the spiritual life and practice as we verge upon the 21st century. At the same time, many scholarly theologians have declared that human beings cannot know God or the risen Christ or have visions of another dimension of reality. Yet many books have recently appeared attesting the reality of such experiences.

One of the most impressive testimonials of personal religious occurrence is Henri Nouwen's description of his near-death experience and encounter with the risen Christ in his book *Beyond the Mirror*. His writing is a religious jewel. As a matter of fact, experiences of this dimension are not uncommon. Morton Kelsey wrote the foreword to G. Scott Sparrow's *I Am with You Always*. As a psychotherapist, Sparrow has listened to people sharing their deepest experiences of life. Many people do not recount experiences of the divine because they are shy about sharing what so many consider utter nonsense.

Morton and I met in the mid-eighties and discovered that we had much in common. We visited each other and corresponded across the ocean, sharing our deepest thoughts on spirituality. Both of us had written books on how to deepen spiritual life, and we realized that we did not disagree on how this could be achieved. In fact, we found that the experiences and practices of the one deepened, filled in and enriched the other. We combined to describe, in a simple and practical way, the many paths we can follow and need to follow if we are going to be whole. We also did not know of any writing that shared what we have learned about the Christian journey.

This book is the result of this collaboration. The Christian path is an eternal journey, and all of us can share in what Morton and I have experienced.

We welcome you to travel with us on this spiritual road, along with other pilgrims on the same quest.

Trevor Hudson
Morton Kelsey

Introduction

This book is a celebration of a friendship. I first came across the name of Morton Kelsey when I was studying for the pastoral ministry in the mid-seventies. One of the set books for my theological studies was his *Encounter with God*. Reading it turned out to be far more than a mere intellectual exercise. It spoke to the spiritual longings and yearnings of my heart. Not only did it give me a theological base for understanding how I could experience the reality of Abba God, it also offered me some practical guidelines about how I could go about opening my life more deeply to the risen Christ and his Spirit.

I began to read other books that Morton had written. What intrigued me was that he addressed issues other Christian writers tended to avoid. He wrote about subjects like dreams and healing, discernment and evil, meditation and prayer, death and the afterlife. Throughout all his writings I sensed his deeply personal relationship with the risen Lord. Most importantly for me, I came to appreciate his central conviction that compassionate caring lay at the heart of the Christ-following life.

In the mid-eighties I invited Morton and his wife Barbara to come to South Africa. His visit took place at a very dark time in our nation's history. He spent a great deal of his time while he was in the country in conversation with those who had suffered most painfully at the hands of apartheid. I was struck by his humility, sensitivity and willingness to listen. I also found his commitment as a caring husband and father a great personal challenge. Some years later he made it possible for Debbie and me to spend ten days with Barbara and him at their home in Gualala, California. Again it was a time of deep sharing and connection.

One day over breakfast the idea of this book was born. I suggested to Morton that I take some of his key ideas and put them in meditation form. In the process of doing this I would also integrate some of my own thoughts and reflections. He was happy for me to do this and some months later sent out to me copies of the sermons he had preached while he was in pastoral ministry. I went through some of my sermons and began to identify those themes that both of us emphasized.

For the past twelve months I have been working with Morton's material and it has been a deeply enriching time for me. However, this past year has also been one of the more difficult periods of my life. I have faced challenges in my relationships and in my vocation that I have not faced before. Again and again, I found encouragement and strength in working with Morton's insights. I hope that they will nourish your faith as much as they helped mine.

Trevor Hudson
Benoni, South Africa
December 1999

Suggestions on How to Use this Book

This collection of fifty-two meditations is designed to be a companion for your spiritual journey. Each meditation is accompanied by seven daily Bible readings, a question to explore, a carefully chosen quotation and a prayer. This material can be used in a number of ways.

You can use the book for your daily devotions. If you do, read one meditation per week. Read it slowly, meditatively and repeatedly. Follow the order laid down in the book. In addition, spend a few moments each day meditating on the daily Bible verse. Consider what God may be saying to you and end your time with prayer.

Another way of using this book would be in a weekly small group. Remember that a group can start with only two people. Preparation for the weekly meeting would then involve reading the week's material and doing the suggested journal exercise. When you come together, each person can share what he or she has learned from the meditation.

A third way of using the book would be to dip into it at any point that seems most relevant. Should you choose to do this, I still hope that you will reflect on the Bible verses and quotations, and keep some kind of journal in which you record your inner responses and reactions to what has been written. Much more will happen in you if you do not rush from one to the other, but take time to live with each one.

SECTION ONE

New Beginnings

WEEK 1

Getting Connected

When electricity first became available to farmers living in the northern parts of England, there were varied responses. Some property owners refused to have powerlines on their land. They preferred their kerosene lamps and lanterns to all the marvelous benefits of electricity. What intrigued me when I heard these stories, however, was the response of one elderly woman. She used the electricity, but each month when the meter was read, the amount she owed was very small. The local municipality installed another meter, but with much the same results. It was only later in conversation with her that the secret came out:

"Electricity is really wonderful," the lady said to the municipal official, "and I use it every night. When it gets dark I switch on the lights, find my matches, light my candle and then switch the lights off again!"

Although amusing, this story illustrates a sad fact about many of our lives. The "electricity" of God's gracious presence and loving power surrounds us and interpenetrates the entire universe. Some choose not to put up power lines and prefer to remain unconnected. Others only want to use a little bit of the divine electricity to light their tiny candles and then switch it off again. Very few, it would seem, want to connect up fully to receive God's available love and power in their lives on a continual basis. Consequently, they never fully experience "the kingdom of electricity."

Agnes Sanford, well known for her involvement in the Christian healing ministry and a close friend of Morton's, sometimes made a similar point quite dramatically when she lectured. She would suddenly stop, turn to her audience, and say, "Could someone please hand me a hymn book?" Three or four people would usually come forward and offer her their books. Ignoring their offers, Agnes would again ask for a hymn book. Then she would explain, "When we ask for something, we have to be willing to receive it. It's exactly the same in our spiritual lives. If we want to be connected with God's love and power, we need to make the necessary arrangements to accept it into our lives."

Against this background, will you consider again the incredibly good news that Jesus brought? It was a simple yet startling message, which was to change human history forever. "Repent," he cried out to the seekers of his day, "for the kingdom of heaven has come near" (Matt 4:17). In other words, he was saying, think again about your whole way of life in the light of the fact that God is now totally accessible to every human being. How wonderfully different this message is from that popular song, "From a distance God is watching us...." In fact, it is the very opposite. The eternal realm of God has drawn near in the person of Jesus and everyone is welcome to get connected.

As Jesus proclaimed this message, ordinary people from all walks of life flocked to hear him. His words brought life and light and hope, especially to those who lived on the margins of respectable society. They could hardly believe what they were hearing. The presence of the Holy One was now freely available and accessible to all, no matter who they were or where they came from. God was now accepting people and welcoming them into the divine kingdom. Many heard Jesus' message gladly. And to their joyful amazement they discovered that, as they followed him and put his words into practice, they entered a new relationship with God as their real and immediate companion and friend.

But Jesus did not just preach this message; he lived it as well. His treatment of people was totally in harmony with his words. He healed the sick, cast out demonic fear, fed the hungry, welcomed the outsiders and gave people reason to live again. In a nutshell, he renewed their confidence that the God of Israel really cared for each of them. Through actions like these he showed the true nature of the kingdom of heaven. Even though he was betrayed and crucified, he rose again, showing once and for all that evil and death do not have the final word. The good news today is that through the crucified and risen Christ, who is present throughout the universe, the kingdom continues to be available as sheer gift to whoever wants to receive it.

Neither Morton nor I found it easy to accept this good news in our own lives. Morton's father was a fine person, but he was an engineer who did not believe that there was a spiritual realm—or at least that humans had any contact with it. When Morton was twenty-one, his mother died. He felt as if he had entered a dark abyss. It was providential grace that led him to a friend, who took him to a Jewish counselor who had survived the holocaust in Nazi Germany. This man knew from personal experience that God and heaven were real. He also believed that the New Testament was a factual account of Jesus' ministry and that the Holy One could still save people today. Through a close friendship with this man, Morton began opening himself to the reality of the kingdom of heaven and began learning how he could seek it today.

As for myself, I had no formal church background as a child. Had it not been for my friendship with a fellow pupil during my high school years, I may never have embarked on a pilgrimage of faith. Even after I decided to become a Christ-follower during my sixteenth year, I struggled with the existence of an unseen spiritual realm that could affect our lives today. During my thirties I was introduced to the writings of Morton and later spent time with him. His personal testimony, as well as his faithful friendship, encouraged me to step out actively on a spiritual journey. Today, this seeking carries on and I find myself continuing to grow in faith as I learn how to interact with God and the realities of the divine kingdom.

So, although we live in different parts of the world and come from very different backgrounds, both of us know what it means to be caught up in a materialistic world view where there is little place for the spiritual. Both of us can identify with those who struggle to believe in God as a living, relational presence. We know what it means to be blinded by what we can touch and see. We realize how experiences of darkness and tragedy and evil can sometimes mock the message of Jesus. Nonetheless, from personal experience, we have both come to share a common conviction that our lives can be touched and transformed by God's love and power, especially when we seek practical ways of building our relationship with the "electricity" of God's kingdom.

How does this connection begin? Perhaps, as you read these words, you are feeling totally alone and isolated from God. Why not give the idea that we are surrounded by the "electricity" of God's loving presence a chance of being a real possibility? This idea was the basic assumption of Jesus' message and ministry. This kingdom of heaven is so freely available that anyone who calls out from their depths to the risen Jesus will receive it. Furthermore, as we learn to follow him, our connection with God will grow stronger with each passing day. In these next weeks we will explore together how we can live with Jesus in this kingdom, now and forever. But the first thing we need to do is to get connected.

DAILY MEDITATION TEXTS FOR THE WEEK

Day 1   "From that time Jesus began to proclaim, 'Repent, for the kingdom of heaven has come near.'" (Matt 4:17)

Day 2   [For] "in him we live and move and have our being…" (Acts 17:28)

Day 3   "There is…one God and Father of all, who is above all and through all and in all." (Eph 4:6)

Day 4 "Your kingdom is an everlasting kingdom, and your dominion endures throughout all generations." (Ps 145:13)

Day 5 "We look not at what can be seen but at what cannot be seen; for what can be seen is temporary, but what cannot be seen is eternal." (2 Cor 4:18)

Day 6 "For the kingdom of God is not food and drink but righteousness and peace and joy in the Holy Spirit." (Rom 14:17)

Day 7 "Therefore, since we are receiving a kingdom that cannot be shaken, let us give thanks, by which we offer to God an acceptable worship with reverence and awe; for indeed our God is a consuming fire." (Heb 12:28–29)

SUGGESTION FOR JOURNALING

Describe one experience that filled your life with a sense of awe and wonder and mystery. Could this have been an awareness of God's presence?

QUOTE FOR THE WEEK

We cannot be sufficient unto ourselves. We are created for the connection with others, for the connection with the cosmos, for the dynamic connection among ourselves and God. When we ask for connection, we are often met by silence. But if we listen, the silence sings to us.

Jeffery Burton Russell
A History of Heaven

PRAYER

Pray slowly, meditating on these words as you say them:
Open my eyes that I may see
The Presence that is all about me.

Open my ears that I may hear
The Voice that is quiet yet very near.
Open my heart that I may feel
The love of my God close and real.
Open each sense, make me aware
Of the Power and Peace always there.

David Adam
The Eye of the Eagle

WEEK 2

Acting As If

In a *Reader's Digest* article published many years ago, the Rev. Samuel Shoemaker, a prominent figure in the beginnings of Alcoholics Anonymous, introduces what he calls "the experiment of faith." He does this by describing an encounter between himself and a searching skeptic who found himself in a state of spiritual emptiness and personal crisis. After listening to his struggles, Shoemaker asked him if he was willing to try an experiment. He answered, "I don't even believe in God, you know."

"Well," answered the pastor, "there is something that seems to help people who do. And I believe that God will help you if you let him. Would you be at all willing to risk kneeling down with me and saying exactly how you feel?"

"Well," mused the skeptic, "I certainly am in a jam. I'll try anything once." He got down on his knees, half laughing at himself, and said aloud, "O God, if there be a God, send me help now because I need it." As he climbed back into his chair somewhat sheepishly, he said, "I don't feel any different."

Rather bluntly, Shoemaker told him that he didn't especially care how he felt, but that he was interested in what he was going to do. "I suggest that you read a chapter from the New Testament each day. Come to church on Sunday and see whether you can catch anything from the faith of other people. And keep sharing with God whatever is honest about yourself and your situation. I think that you will slowly begin to feel that your prayer is being answered."

In the rest of the article the Episcopalian priest describes how his friend resolutely kept to the experiment of faith. His deep need prodded him to keep going even when he wanted to give up. The faith of other people encouraged him. Finally, he admitted that something was helping him, for his life began to come together in ways beyond his understanding. It was a wonderful moment when, some months later, the skeptic was baptized and became an active member in Shoemaker's congregation.

Can you see how this seeker came to know God as a living and active reality in his life? Quite simply, by acting as if he had faith until, indeed, there was given to him an inner conviction that God really was real. Genuine belief nearly always begins with risk and action. To believe something means acting as if it were so. Accordingly, faith in God grows as we accept the possibility of God's available presence and begin to act as if the kingdom of heaven were real. Action is more important than intellectual certitude. If we believe we must be absolutely sure about God's kingdom before we consider trying it out, we may wait forever and never experience its power in our lives.

In our search for living faith we can learn much from the scientists of our time, who operate in a pragmatic rather than purely intellectual way. They realize they don't fully understand our physical, material world, and they try one path, then another until they discover an answer that leads to another question. In its beginning stages, the process of finding real faith can follow a similar path. We entertain a hypothesis that God is real, try it in our own personal experience and then consider the results. As the skeptic discovered, a real experiment of faith, entered into with an open and honest attitude, can be a gateway to truth.

This was the experience of the very first Christ-followers. When Jesus proclaimed that the kingdom was available to all, they accepted this proclamation. However, this acceptance was not merely intellectual. When they heard the wonderful news that God was now accessible to ordinary human beings, they took deliberate action. They responded to Jesus' call to discipleship and began putting into practice the things he taught them. Even though there were moments of doubt and unbelief, they gradually became convinced about the gospel message. After Jesus' resurrection and ascension, these disciples trained others to believe and live in the kingdom. Soon, many dynamic, excited, transformed Jewish apostles of Jesus traveled all over the Roman Empire and proclaimed the freedom, love and victory that Jesus Christ had preached and lived.

Few people come to know God by reason or logic alone. But we can experience God through taking part in the experiment of faith, acting as if God were real and seeing what happens. As we embark upon this adventure with expectancy, what we receive will not necessarily be blinding lights and immediate change in our life situations, but rather a sense of added strength, greater sanity and peace of mind, and a realization that we are connected with a power from beyond ourselves. This has been the testimony of countless Christ-followers, from New Testament times right into the present.

Are you willing this coming week, and perhaps for the rest of your life, to consider seriously the good news that Jesus brought? If you are, begin acting as if God is very near. Tell him honestly what is in your heart. Ask specifically for what you need. Read a portion of the New Testament each day. Find kindred spiritual seekers who also want to grow in the spirituality of genuine prayer, love and service, and join them in their search. Worship together with other Christ-followers and explore the possibilities of regularly receiving communion.

You, too, may come to discover how the experiment of faith can turn into an experience of God.

DAILY MEDITATION TEXTS FOR THE WEEK

Day 1   "So faith comes from what is heard, and what is heard comes through the word of Christ." (Rom 10:17)

Day 2   "And without faith it is impossible to please God, for whoever would approach him must believe that he exists and that he rewards those who seek him." (Heb 11:6)

Day 3   "Faith by itself, if it has no works, is dead." (Jas 2:17)

Day 4   "And this is the victory that conquers the world, our faith." (1 John 5:4)

Day 5   "For we walk by faith, not by sight." (2 Cor 5:7)

Day 6   "For in it [the gospel] the righteousness of God is revealed through faith for faith; as it is written, 'The one who is righteous will live by faith.'" (Rom 1:17)

Day 7   "The apostles said to the Lord, 'Increase our faith!'" (Luke 17:5)

SUGGESTION FOR JOURNALING

Write out a prayer expressing your desire to act each day as if God's presence is very near.

QUOTE FOR THE WEEK

The leap of faith is not the admission of credulity but of a kind of courage. We really believe only when we have found sufficient evidence. The first steps of faith consist of looking for the evidence. And the greatest evidence of all is a first-hand experience of God.

Samuel Shoemaker
*Act As If—The First
Step Toward Faith*

PRAYER

*Lord, thank you for the good news that God is close.
Help me to live today as if this were really so.
Grow in me a real and living faith so that I may come
to know your living presence and loving power.
Amen.*

WEEK 3

Discovering What God Is Like

There is a story about a mother who constantly served stewed prunes to her family. She had a young son who thoroughly hated them. When he refused to eat the prunes, as he was prone to do, she would say, "God won't like that. God doesn't like little boys who don't finish their prunes. God will punish you." One night at dinner, looking at the last two prunes in his bowl, the boy had finally had enough. He would not eat the prunes however angry God became. His mother sent him off to his room. A few minutes later, there was a violent thunderstorm—lightning dashed across the sky, thunder clapped, and wind and rain hammered his bedroom window. His mother thought that he would be terrified. When she got to his room, he was standing with his face pressed against the windowpane saying, "My, my. Such a fuss to make over two prunes."

Sometimes we think of God as someone who "makes a fuss over two prunes." We believe that if we put one foot out of line, God will punish us. Not surprisingly, God comes to be feared as a heavenly tyrant, always ready to pounce on us. This negative perception of God prevents us from building up a personal relationship, based on confidence and intimacy. It is almost impossible to entrust ourselves wholeheartedly to such a vengeful and fickle Deity. Yet this is the distorted understanding of God that some of us carry in our hearts and minds. Then, when some crisis or disaster strikes, we cry out spontaneously, "What have I done to deserve this from God?"

How, then, do we find out what God is really like? This is also what Philip, one of the first disciples, wanted to know. He approached Jesus one day and asked to be shown the Father. Jesus' answer crystallizes the wonderful news of the Christian faith. Listen again to the answer that came from his lips: "Have I been with you all this time, Philip, and you still do not know me? Whoever has seen me has seen the Father" (John 14:9). In these words we have summarized the breathtaking affirmation of the Christian faith that if we want to know who the real God is, we must look more closely at Jesus.

Now, according to Jesus, God can best be understood as an incredibly loving and devoted parent. He spelled out this good news in that well-known parable about the waiting father and his two sons (see Luke 15:11–32). Sadly, we may have become so familiar with this story that we are no longer amazed by its scandalous extravagance, its reckless mercy. Read it again with fresh eyes and an open heart. See how the father runs down the road to embrace his returning son, receiving him back without a word of criticism. Watch how the servants, following their master's orders, bring out the best robes for the repentant son. Notice that even toward the self-righteous elder brother, the father is openhearted and caring. Instead of reprimanding him for only being interested in justice, he begs him to come to the party and join in the rejoicing. This, we are told, is the kind of God we discover when we call out to the risen Christ for that divine reconnection that we all need.

All these words about God being like this loving father may sound too good to be true. Please remember, however, that Jesus lived the love that he spoke about. Throughout his life he consistently reached out to those around him. In his company people from all walks of life felt accepted, valued and welcomed. But it was especially in his death on the cross that Jesus gave us reason to believe the story he told about the father's love. For when we look into the face of the crucified Christ, we catch a glimpse of the divine love that never lets us go, no matter what we do. Apostle Paul puts it so well: "Indeed, rarely will anyone die for a righteous person—though perhaps for a good person someone might actually dare to die. But God proves his love for us in that while we still were sinners Christ died for us" (Rom 5:7–8).

Morton often uses a moving illustration to underline that the love which Jesus spoke about, he also lived. He describes how, in the Chapel at Notre Dame, on the one side of the altar, there is a statue of the prodigal son with head buried in his father's bosom. This is the story that Jesus told. On the other side of the altar there is a monumental marble statue of Mary holding the body of her crucified son in her arms. This is the story that Jesus lived. The message proclaimed by these two statues is clear. The way Jesus lived is a powerful illustration of the story he told.

If God is truly like Jesus and like the wonderfully loving father in the parable, there are a host of practical implications for the way in which we relate to the Holy One. Rather than reaching out to some vague impersonal force, we can now approach God like small children who need their parent and call out, "Abba Father." As we share our hearts in prayer, we can know that we are speaking with someone who knows completely what it means to walk on this earth. When we ask Abba for what we need, we can do so expecting guidance and help and wisdom. We can know too that, like the father in the parable, God gives us the freedom to choose our way through life. Most importantly, in our relationships with those around us, we can begin learning how to treat people in the same way that we have been treated by our heavenly Father.

Believing in Jesus' God makes an immense difference to the way we go about our spiritual seeking. If we believe that God "makes a fuss over two prunes," we will continue to keep God at arm's length. Whatever relationship we may have with God will be characterized by mistrust, fear and suspicion. On the other hand, if God is Christlike, our relationship with the Holy One will be marked by intimacy, deep sharing and honesty. It is a wild gamble to believe that God is like Jesus, but what do we have to lose? On the other hand, we have everything to gain!

Daily Meditation Texts for the Week

Day 1   "Jesus said to him, 'Have I been with you all this time, Philip, and you still do not know me? Whoever has seen me has seen the Father.'" (John 14:9)

Day 2   "He [Christ] is the image of the invisible God..." (Col 1:15)

Day 3   "No one has ever seen God. It is God the only Son, who is close to the Father's heart, who has made him known." (John 1:18)

Day 4   "All things have been handed over to me by my Father, and no one knows the Son except the Father, and no one knows the Father except the Son and anyone to whom the Son chooses to reveal him." (Matt 11:27)

Day 5   "Jesus said to him, 'I am the way, and the truth, and the life. No one comes to the Father except through me. If you know me, you will know my Father also.'" (John 14:6–7)

Day 6   "He said to them, 'When you pray, say: Father...'" (Luke 11:2)

Day 7   "Jesus said to them, 'Very truly, I tell you, the Son can do nothing on his own, but only what he sees the Father doing; for whatever the Father does, the Son does likewise.'" (John 5:19)

Suggestion for Journaling

Write down what it would mean for you to begin seeing God like Jesus. How could this view of God affect your relationship with him?

QUOTE FOR THE WEEK

God is Christlike and in him is no un-Christlikeness at all.
Archbishop Michael Ramsay

PRAYER

Abba, Father, thank you for disclosing to us in Jesus both your own self and your eternal love for us, and also the men and women you call us to be.

Thank you that through Jesus you set us free to become our true selves, and so through your Spirit to love and serve the world around us.

Help us to press forward, abiding in Christ, the true vine, by love and prayer now and forever.

Amen.

Mark Gibbard
Jesus Liberation and Love

WEEK 4

Bringing All of
Ourselves to God

Recently I had breakfast with a recovering alcoholic in our congregation. Over eggs and bacon we talked about his difficult drinking days. He told me how, when he went to work, he would take a bottle of brandy with him. Whenever he could, he would remove the bottle from his office desk drawer and sneak a quick sip. However, he always left the brown wrapping paper on the bottle. Intrigued by this little detail, I asked whether this was because he wanted to hide what he was drinking from others. "Oh no," he answered quickly, "I left the paper on because I didn't want to see what I was drinking myself!"

My friend's response illustrates rather humorously our struggle to be honest with ourselves. It is not easy to face ourselves as we are, to admit our faults and to recognize our addictions. We much prefer to see ourselves as decent, respectable and well-meaning individuals. Indeed, our capacity to remain deliberately unaware of our inclinations toward evil can sometimes reach remarkable extremes. As I once heard a preacher say, tongue in cheek, "Denial is not the name of a river in Egypt."

Unless we overcome this and begin to confess the less attractive parts of our lives, we will find it difficult to grow in our relationship with God. Progress along the spiritual pathway requires that we bring all of ourselves, warts and all, into the Divine Presence. God can hardly transform us by the Spirit if we do not willingly reveal the parts of us that most need transformation: our anger, our fears, our critical and gossipy sides, our stinginess, our indifference to our neighbors' suffering, our prejudices, our lustful desires. But when we do bring all of what we are to God, the light of the kingdom, like the light of the sun, will shine deeply into us and bring us growth and freedom.

Perhaps this is why Jesus found himself so much more at home with the outsiders of his day than with the religious leaders and scholars. They were willing to come to him as they were and quite literally throw themselves upon his grace and mercy. There were no pretenses, no masks, no spiritual cosmetics. They simply allowed Jesus to meet them at their deepest point of need. It seems when we come before our Creator in utter honesty, there is a response on the part of God that opens channels of transforming power between the Holy One and ourselves.

This could be why the Bible places such a great emphasis on honesty, on knowing and speaking the truth, on being transparent before God. One commandment tells us not to take the Lord's name in vain. When we swear by God's name we are bound to speak the truth. Jesus goes further and tells us that we should not even have to swear by God's name at all. Simply let your "yes" be "yes," he says, and your "no" be "no." Later Paul encourages the early Christ-followers to speak the truth in love with each other. But it is very difficult to be honest with others until we first seek to be honest with ourselves. And it can take a lifetime to do this fully.

This journey toward a greater self-honesty begins with a few simple steps. We can take some time to be quiet, just by ourselves, and ask God to help us search our hearts. We can reflect on our instant reactions to others, especially those who harm and do damage. We often find in ourselves what we condemn in others. It is also helpful to talk these things over with someone we trust, someone who can look at our lives objectively and see our faults and virtues. It is so easy to deceive ourselves. Our subjectivity can hide our most obvious faults from our own eyes.

This is one reason why, as we shall explore next week, spiritual companionship is so important.

When we have begun to face the truth of who we are, we then need consciously to bring all of ourselves into the Divine Presence. God is infinitely polite and seldom barges into the hidden corners of our hearts until we throw open the doors to our soul room and allow the Spirit in. Knowing that God is like the father in Jesus' parable about the prodigal son gives us the courage to do this. For as the runaway boy was offered those grace-soaked gifts of the robe, the ring and the shoes, so are we. The robe speaks to us of our unconditional acceptance by God. The ring signifies our belonging to God's family. The shoes tell us that we are indeed Abba's beloved children. Picturing ourselves receiving these gifts and putting them on, when we come to God as we are, can be a deeply healing experience.

Deep changes take place inside our lives when we come before God as we are. We can let go of our false images of ourselves, put aside our defensiveness and leave our reputation in God's hands. We don't need to pretend to be anything any longer. We can just be who we are. We can stop trying to earn God's acceptance with our good works. All that matters is that we receive God's gifts of unconditional acceptance and rich mercy and start sharing them with others. In fact, having become more honest with ourselves, we find that we become less judgmental and more compassionate toward others.

Why not begin your own journey this coming week into a deeper self-honesty with God? If you truly want to know God's power in your life, then bring all of yourself to the one who seeks you out. Be assured that nothing you discover within yourself will ever stop God from loving you. Getting truthful with yourself does not distance you from God. Rather, it draws you deeper into the Divine Presence, opens your life to transforming grace and enables you to know the goodness of God. And it all begins by taking off the brown paper wrapping.

DAILY MEDITATION TEXTS FOR THE WEEK

Day 1   "You desire truth in the inward being; therefore teach me wisdom in my secret heart." (Ps 51:6)

Day 2   "When, however, the Spirit comes, who reveals the truth about God, he will lead you into all the truth." (John 16:13, Good News Bible)

Day 3   "Let your word be 'Yes, Yes' or 'No, No'; anything more than this comes from the evil one." (Matt 5:37)

Day 4   "If we say that we have no sin, we deceive ourselves, and the truth is not in us." (1 John 1:8)

Day 5   "Go and learn what this means, 'I desire mercy, not sacrifice.' For I have come to call not the righteous, but sinners." (Matt 9:13)

Day 6   "If we confess our sins, he who is faithful and just will forgive us our sins and cleanse us from all unrighteousness." (1 John 1:9)

Day 7   "But speaking the truth in love, we must grow up in every way into him who is the head, into Christ." (Eph 4:15)

SUGGESTION FOR JOURNALING

Make a note of those instant reactions that cause harm in your relationships. Bring them to God and receive the gifts of a new robe, ring and shoes.

QUOTE FOR THE WEEK

Honesty before God requires the most fundamental risk of faith we can take: the risk that God is good, that God does love us unconditionally. It is in taking this risk that we rediscover our dignity. To bring the truth of ourselves, just as we are, to God, just as God is, is the most dignified thing we can do in this life.

Gerald G. May, M.D.
Addiction and Grace

PRAYER

Search me, O God, and know my heart;
test me and know my thoughts.
See if there is any wicked way in me,
and lead me in the way everlasting.
Amen.

Ps 139:23–24

Finding Spiritual Companionship

Yesterday I had lunch with a fellow Christ-follower. As we enjoyed our meal, we also caught up with each other's lives. He told me what he was going through at the moment. The difficult decisions he was facing at work. The challenges he was experiencing as a husband and father. His struggle to find adequate time to pray and be alone. After listening to him, I spoke about some of the joys and the struggles I was having in my own attempts to follow Christ. At no stage did we try to fix each other up, give advice, or pass critical judgment. We just shared in each other's life journey. However, when I left the restaurant to return to work I felt strengthened, encouraged and nourished in my soul.

We need companions on our spiritual journey. Significantly, when Jesus sent out his disciples he told them to travel two by two. On another occasion he reminded them that whenever they met together in twos or threes, he would be there among them (see Matt 18:20). He took it for granted that his followers would need fellowship if they were going to remain strong in their faith. This has certainly been my experience. Without the faithful friendship of other Christ-followers and the support of the different groups I belong to, I doubt whether I would still be traveling along the gospel path today. This is why I believe so strongly that everyone who is serious about seeking God needs to find spiritual companionship.

Morton tells of an experience of fellowship many years ago when he was serving a large congregation. He attended a weekday communion service every week and noticed that several people came to the service early and lingered around afterward. After a few weeks this small group discovered that each of them wanted to deepen his or her spiritual life. They agreed to get together for an hour and a half after the Eucharist each week. During this time they shared something of themselves and their thinking. They prayed and discussed scripture together. They spent time in silence. Through this group of seekers Morton and Barbara built friendships that have lasted for over thirty years. Such is the immense value of sharing together in vital Christian fellowship.

However, I need to sound some warnings when it comes to selecting spiritual companions or a fellowship group. Only those who are on a pilgrimage of faith themselves can safely companion others on their journeys. The blind cannot lead the blind, otherwise someone is likely to fall into a ditch. Also, many seekers have been deeply hurt by Christians who are authoritarian, legalistic and dogmatic. Perhaps, most importantly, we need to steer clear of those people and groups who believe that they alone possess the final truth.

How, then, do we go about finding spiritual companionship? Real Christian fellowship is like a five-pointed star. Making sure that these points are clear will ensure that our fellowship with other Christ-followers is healthy and meaningful.

The first point is that the risen Jesus needs to be at the center of our fellowship. He is the lens through which we read the scripture, reflect on our traditions and evaluate our experience. God has come among us in Jesus to show us the way. He lived and loved, taught and ministered, died and rose again. His Spirit is with us and within us, closer to us than the very air that we breathe. We look to him always as our living teacher. He is our individual and communal guide as we seek after God.

The second point is that healthy, spiritual fellowship must be open to the different ways in which God relates to people. Some have very dramatic experiences of the risen Christ; others seem to experience God in a more gentle, subdued and quiet way. Some find speaking in tongues helpful; others like to be still and silent. Some like to worship in extroverted, expressive and enthusiastic ways; others prefer a more sacramental, ordered and liturgical approach to God. If we are going to be good spiritual companions, we need to respect these differences. Wonderful things begin to happen among us when we do.

Point three is that genuine fellowship accepts others as they are. We don't need to force people to change. It is helpful to keep in mind that the Holy Spirit is God's primary agent of change. Some of the greatest Christ-followers were once agnostics or atheists who were turned around by the humble, gentle understanding of friends who were simply uncritical, caring, open, compassionate spiritual companions. Most people are closer to God than they think. Concern and caring for them helps them to realize this. Arguing or disagreeing seldom does.

The fourth point is that transforming fellowship seeks to be a safe and sacred space for people to tell their stories. We all have our own stories. Stories of grief and pain. Stories of joy and celebration. Stories of struggle and doubt. When we share these stories and reflect on them in the light of our faith and with others who listen to us, we find ourselves strengthened and encouraged. Our discipleship grows. It is always worth remembering that the Greek word for fellowship, *koinonia,* essentially refers to the sharing of real life at its deepest levels.

The last point for life-giving spiritual companionship is the sharing of the healing mercy of God with one another. We must learn how to share the love and compassion we have received from God in our brokenness with others in their need. That is why it is usually those who have known the depths of their own unworthiness and experienced God's love in spite of it who can best accompany others on their journey with Christ. We must always keep in mind that the church is not a museum for saints;

it is a hospital for recovering sinners. If we forget this, our discipleship can easily become hard, judgmental and legalistic. Many of us long for a genuine experience of Christian fellowship. It is not always easy to find. But when we intentionally search out companions with whom we can share our faith and lives, God has a wonderful way of sending the right people across our path. I hope that this will happen for you. When we find the kind of fellowship where the five-pointed star burns brightly, we experience immeasurable blessing. If you cannot find a group like this, remember that fellowship can begin with just two people. May you find the spiritual companionship that you need for your unfolding journey into the heart of God.

DAILY MEDITATION TEXTS FOR THE WEEK

Day 1   "For where two or three are gathered in my name, I am there among them." (Matt 18:20)

Day 2   "If one member suffers, all suffer together with it; if one member is honored, all rejoice together with it." (1 Cor 12:26)

Day 3   "And let us consider how to provoke one another to love and good deeds, not neglecting to meet together, as is the habit of some, but encouraging one another, and all the more as you see the Day approaching." (Heb 10:24–25)

Day 4   "After this the Lord appointed seventy others and sent them on ahead of him in pairs to every town and place where he himself intended to go." (Luke 10:1)

Day 5   "Faithful friends are a sturdy shelter: whoever finds one has found a treasure. Faithful friends are beyond price; no amount can balance their worth." (Eccl 6:14–15, in the Apocrypha)

Day 6   "Faithful friends are life-saving medicine, and those who fear the Lord will find them." (Eccl 6:16, in the Apocrypha)

Day 7 "So we, who are many, are one body in Christ, and individually we are members one of another." (Rom 12:5)

SUGGESTION FOR JOURNALING

Write down the names of those men and women who are your spiritual companions. Make a note of what they mean to you and give thanks to God for them.

QUOTE FOR THE WEEK

A person becomes a person through other people.
African proverb

PRAYER

Lord, give me insight into my friendships. Help me to see your gifts in them. And help me too, Lord, to be a faithful friend to others, loyal and generous and kind. Amen.

WEEK 6

Learning to Pray

How do we learn to speak with God? This was the concern of the little girl who, when asked by her mother to pray before the family and some guests at a mealtime, became tongue-tied and shy. "But I don't know what to say to God," said the girl.

"Come on," the mother tried to persuade her, "just say what I said this morning before breakfast."

"Dear God," prayed the little girl, "why did I have to ask all these people for lunch? Amen."

Many surveys done during recent years show that spiritual seekers, rather like this innovative little girl, want to know how to pray. Recently, one of the largest denominations in southern Africa asked its members to indicate their needs. After sifting through the responses of more than twenty-five thousand members, the desire to know how to pray came out on top. If we generalize this experience of one denomination on the grounds that it widely represents a diverse population, it shows that countless ordinary people yearn for a firsthand relationship with God. Lacking perhaps a vital sense of the Eternal in their lives, they want to know how to communicate with God.

Long ago, the early disciples wanted to know the very same thing, so they asked Jesus how to pray. Significantly, this was the only time they ever asked Jesus to teach them something. He gave them simple instructions, which have been widely misunderstood. For example, many people assume that if they say the words of the Lord's Prayer, they are praying, but this is far from the truth. These words need to be prayed, not just said. Let us look at how we can pray some of the central themes of the Lord's Prayer (see Luke 11:1–4).

The first suggestion that Jesus made was to address God directly and personally. He said we must turn toward God and say, "Father." Except for one desolate occasion, the cry of dereliction from the cross, Jesus constantly used this form of address in relationship to the Holy One. Throughout his life on earth he spoke directly to God in Aramaic, addressing him as "Abba," meaning "my own dear father." Never before had anyone dared to pray as intimately as this. Imagine the astonishment of the disciples when they were invited to pray as Jesus did. They were being offered the privilege of coming to God in the same way that Jesus did.

When we call God "Abba, Father," the image that immediately comes to mind is the father in Jesus' parable of the prodigal son. So it can be helpful when we begin praying to see ourselves as prodigals returning home, having messed up our lives in various ways. We can imagine the Father there with open arms and gifts that go beyond our wildest imaginings. Here is God accepting us as we are, assuring us of our belonging and welcoming us home. When we hold this picture before us, we realize that there is nothing that we cannot talk about with God. We can be totally open, transparent and honest.

Next, Jesus invites us to pray, "Your kingdom come." With these words we ask that God's way of compassion, concern and sacrificial caring will come among us just as it fills heaven. Clearly, this prayer is rather hypocritical if we pray it only on behalf of others but not for ourselves. So we need to ask that God's will be done in our lives as well. Praying this part of the Lord's Prayer genuinely, therefore, involves us meaning something like this:

God, here is my life which I offer to you. May I know what you want for me and how best I can extend your kingdom in my life, in my relationships and in the wider community.

Please give me the knowledge and power I need so that I can show your love toward myself and others around me.

Third, Jesus tells us to ask for our "daily bread." Asking for daily bread makes us mindful of those basic necessities that we all need for a full human life. We ask for safety and warmth, for food and clothes, for inner strength and peace of mind, as well as for physical sustenance and protection. We ask for what we need so that we can go out and do his will. And we are urged to make these requests daily—not once a week or when we are in need, but daily. We ask not only for ourselves, but also for all humankind:

Give us this day our daily bread.

But there seems to be one condition. Jesus insists that as we ask for forgiveness we also seek to forgive others. In praying like this we acknowledge that there is so much that we need to have forgiven, so many follies and stupidities and even some loveless and downright mean actions. And we can be forgiven everything, if only we are willing to embark upon that difficult road of forgiving those who have hurt us. So in this petition we are asking,

Lord, forgive me and help me to forgive. Please give me your Spirit so that I am able to forgive and open myself to your forgiveness. Then free me Lord, please, of my guilt and inner anguish and pain.

And finally, we ask that God may guide and protect us. Jesus clearly believed in the reality of an evil one, a personal and intelligent force for corruption and evil in this world, a force bent on spoiling human life from within and beyond. And so we ask that we may be protected from evil striking against us in the outer world, or striking within us in discouragement and darkness, or striking through us with hatred or with a loose or vicious tongue.

How much we need this protection. We cannot stand alone depending on our own resources against the evil one. None of us can, so we ask for the protection that God wishes to give us.

Can you see how the Lord's Prayer serves as a pattern for our prayer? When offering these petitions, Jesus was saying in effect, "If you want to learn how to pray, here are the essentials. Use each petition as a point from which to begin your conversation with God." It takes less than a minute to recite the Lord's Prayer, but it takes much longer when we use it in the way Jesus intended. And when we do, we will discover that the love and power and protection of God gradually begin to enter our lives and transform them. Wouldn't you like to be open to that?

DAILY MEDITATION TEXTS FOR THE WEEK

Day 1   "He was praying in a certain place, and after he had finished, one of the disciples said to him, 'Lord, teach us to pray…'" (Luke 11:1)

Day 2   "He said to them, 'When you pray, say: Father, hallowed be your name.'" (Luke 11:2)

Day 3   "Your kingdom come." (Luke 11:2)

Day 4   "Give us each day our daily bread." (Luke 11:3)

Day 5   "And forgive us our sins, for we ourselves forgive everyone indebted to us." (Luke 11:4)

Day 6   "And do not bring us to the time of trial, but rescue us from the evil one." (Matt 6:13)

Day 7   "For if you forgive others their trespasses, your heavenly Father will also forgive you; but if you do not forgive others, neither will your Father forgive your trespasses." (Matt 6:14–15)

SUGGESTION FOR JOURNALING

Describe the effects of praying the Lord's Prayer more meditatively and leisurely, as suggested in this week's meditation.

QUOTE FOR THE WEEK

To pray the Lord's Prayer as Jesus intended is to pray for life as God intended. To live the Lord's Prayer is to live in the will of God.

Everett Fulham
Living the Lord's Prayer

PRAYER

Dear Father always near us, may your rule be completed in us—may your will be done here on earth in just the way it is done in heaven.

Give us today the things we need today, and forgive us our sins and impositions on you as we are forgiving all who in any way offend us. Please don't put us through trials, but deliver us from everything bad.

Because you are the one in charge, and you have all the power, and the glory too is all yours—forever—which is just the way we want it!

Amen.

Dallas Willard
The Divine Conspiracy

Finding Out God's Will
for Our Lives

When I committed my life to Christ as a teenager, I was constantly told by my new Christian friends to let God guide me. They would tell me how God had spoken to them and led them when they had to make decisions about their lives. Listening to their confident comments usually left me feeling a little on the outside looking in. God certainly did not seem to speak to me that clearly. At the same time, while I knew that I could learn from the Bible what God thought about many life issues, there were also many everyday choices not covered by the Biblical witness. How would I find out God's will in these areas of my life?

Over the years I have wrestled deeply with this question. I knew that I would need to be careful in finding an answer. People who have claimed to know God's will have often imposed great misery on the world. Those who engaged in religious wars often got their will and God's will mixed up. Today, we look with horror at the Crusades and the wars between Catholic and Protestant in Europe. Was either side really doing God's will or were they merely indulging human prejudice, intolerance and hatred? Even those who trapped and murdered Jesus believed they were doing God's will. These examples warn us that when it comes to discerning God's will, we are always beginners and must take great care.

My starting point is the belief that God has a good purpose for the life of every human being. Consider briefly these striking words in the New Testament: "For we are what he has made us, created in Christ Jesus for good works, which God prepared beforehand to be our way of life" (Eph 2:10). God has a specific calling for you and me through which we can grow and contribute in a significant way to God's kingdom on earth. There is a God-designed place for everyone in this universe. This is how important we are to our loving Creator. What we have to do is to find out what it is and to pray and work toward making it a reality.

But how do we do this? The answer is really quite simple. Achieving it is more difficult. Here is a threefold formula that I have personally found helpful. First, I stop, then I listen, then I reflect and make my decision. It is nearly impossible to discern God's will for our lives unless we stop. As long as we are speeding down the freeways of life we have little time to check the car in which we are traveling or make any change of direction. Many people live their whole lives without ever actually stopping to think who they are and where they are going. They just go, unconsciously keeping on, missing out on what God wants for their lives. So the first step in finding God's will is to cease our business, quiet ourselves and come to a halt.

Morton discovered the importance of stopping some forty years ago when he was going through a time of great spiritual crisis. As the pastor of a large Episcopalian parish he was constantly on the go—preparing sermons and preaching, teaching, visiting, counseling and writing. His deepest problem was that his life and ministry lacked a real sense of God's immediate and interactive presence. One day, during this period of his life, he complained to a Jewish psychologist-friend about the struggle he was having with insomnia. His friend listened and then smiled and said, "Has it ever occurred to you, Morton, that someone might be trying to get through to you? Don't you remember how God called Samuel in the night?" This question struck a deep chord in him and forcibly reminded him that if he was really going to hear God speaking, he was first going to have to stop. And when he did so it proved to be the key to a profound renewal in his life and ministry.

The second step is to listen. Once we stop and ask God for guidance, we need to be attentive to what is happening in our lives and minds and hearts. When we do this we will find that there is a clamor of different intuitions and desires, thoughts and feelings, longings and hopes within us. It is a good habit to write down such things so that we can later reflect on them. When God does speak to us, the divine voice usually takes the shape of one of these inner promptings. So unless we stop and listen to what is happening within us, we can easily miss the whisperings of the Spirit.

Third, we need to reflect. Here we need to take all that we have become aware of within ourselves, all the inner responses to life as it happens around us, and carefully sift through them. Responsible faith thinks. We must not act impulsively. Rather, we must mull over what is going on inside of us in the light of all that we know from the scriptures about God's way as it is revealed in Jesus Christ. This is why knowing the scriptures, especially the gospels, is so important. If we sense God speaking to us, we must always ask, "Is what I am hearing in accordance with the life and teachings of Jesus?" If not, we can be reasonably certain that it is not God's still small voice we are hearing.

Another way of reflecting involves the use of our imagination. We can picture ourselves coming to Jesus and saying, "Lord, here is the situation in which I find myself. Please show me your way forward for me." We see him in our mind's eye walking into our particular situation in our place. We try to imagine what he would say, what he would do, how he would respond. It's amazing what insights are gained as we do this. Some of the great Christ-followers in history have prayed like this when trying to discern God's will for their lives.

After we have followed these three steps it is also useful to discuss the whole situation with some mature associates of Jesus.

Other people's objectivity can help us see the overall picture of our lives more clearly and give us perspective on the steps we need to take. This is one reason why we need companions on the spiritual journey. The Holy One often speaks to us through the words of those around us. Significantly, on one occasion when the early New Testament church was faced with a choice, they prefaced their decision with the words: "For it seemed good to the Holy Spirit and to us…" (Acts 15:28, NKJV).

Eventually, there comes the moment when we decide to act. If our stopping, listening, and reflecting has shown us a particular path we need to follow, we should not claim infallibility for our decision. Phrases like "the Lord has told me" are usually not helpful. It is far better to take personal responsibility for our actions and to leave open the possibility that we may be wrong. On the other hand, should no clear guidance be forthcoming, we can assume that God wants us to use the intelligence he has given us to decide what to do. By using our common sense and reason, we can then try to discern how best to live in the faith, hope and love of Christ. What is all important is that we seek daily to know and do the will of God. Only then shall we grow up into the people that God wants us to be.

DAILY MEDITATION TEXTS FOR THE WEEK

Day 1   "For we are what he has made us, created in Christ Jesus for good works, which God prepared beforehand to be our way of life." (Eph 2:10)

Day 2   "But the wisdom from above is first pure, then peaceable, gentle, willing to yield, full of mercy and good fruits, without a trace of partiality or hypocrisy." (Jas 3:17)

Day 3   "Let the same mind be in you that was in Christ Jesus." (Phil 2:5)

Day 4   "Therefore Eli said to Samuel, 'Go, lie down; and if he calls you, you shall say: Speak, Lord, for your servant is listening.'" (1 Sam 3:9)

Day 5   "Teach me to do your will, for you are my God. Let your good spirit lead me on a level path." (Ps 143:10)

Day 6   "The human spirit is the lamp of the Lord, searching every inmost part." (Prov 20:27)

Day 7   "He calls his own sheep by name and leads them out. When he has brought out all his own, he goes ahead of them, and the sheep follow him because they know his voice." (John 10:3–4)

SUGGESTION FOR JOURNALING

Describe one current situation or concern for which you are seeking God's guidance. Write out fully some of your inner responses toward it and reflect prayerfully upon them.

QUOTE FOR THE WEEK

Christians believe in a God who speaks. Ours is not a silent God, a God who sits, sphinx-like, looking out unblinking on a world in agony....He speaks because he loves. Love always seeks to communicate.

Donald Coggan

PRAYER

My Lord God, I have no idea where I am going. I do not see the road ahead of me. I cannot know for certain where it will end. Nor do I really know myself, and the fact that I think I am following your will does not mean that I am actually doing so.

But I believe that the desire to please you does in fact please you. And I hope I have that desire in all that I am doing. I hope that I will never do anything apart from that desire. And I know that if I do this you will lead me by the right road, though I may know nothing about it.

Therefore I will trust you always though I may seem to be lost and in the shadow of death. I will not fear, for you are ever with me, and you will never leave me to face my perils alone.

Thomas Merton
Thoughts in Solitude

WEEK 8

Reading with Our Heart

During a Bible Society distribution campaign in Zimbabwe some years ago, one of those who was offered a Bible gave a rather antagonistic response. "If you give me that New Testament, I will roll the pages and use them to make cigarettes," the young man told Gaylord Kambarami, the General Secretary of the Bible Society of Zimbabwe.

"Do what you like with it," Gaylord replied, "but will you promise to read slowly the page of the New Testament before you smoke it?" With that request Gaylord gave the man a New Testament, and that was the last he saw of him—until recently.

While Gaylord was attending a Christian convention in Zimbabwe, the speaker on the platform suddenly pointed to him in the audience, and said, "This man doesn't remember me, but fifteen years ago he gave me a New Testament. When I told him I would use the pages to roll cigarettes, he asked me to read the page before I smoked it. Well, I smoked my way through Matthew, I smoked my way through Mark and I smoked my way through Luke. But when I came to John 3, verse 16, and read about God loving the whole world, I stopped smoking. At that moment God spoke to me and my life began to move in a different direction."

This dramatic conversion story reveals the life-changing wisdom and spiritual power of the Bible. Countless people have found their lives changed by reading it. They have become contagiously different. I have never known a mature Christ-follower who wasn't nurtured by a regular reading of the scriptures. Indeed, it is hard for me to see how we can progress along the spiritual way unless we read the Bible. It is almost impossible to know Jesus, and the God he reveals, without learning from the biblical witness. However, its greatest benefit lies in its ability to bring us into a living encounter with the speaking God, provided we read it with our heart and not only with our head.

What do I mean by this? Well, there are two entirely different kinds of reading. There is an intellectual reading of a text that aims at analyzing, picking apart, and comparing it with other literature. This is reading with our head. Reading with our heart is more meditative, leisurely, receptive. When we read with our heart, we open ourselves to what is before us, listen to its deep undertones, and let its important truths strike home. We pause to reflect upon its meanings and explore the mood and power of what is written. If we only read the Bible with our head, we will not experience these transforming effects. If we read it with our heart, God speaks to us and we find ourselves gradually changing.

Reading the Bible with our heart requires that we first settle down, become quiet and get into a receptive mood. One of the best preparations for this is to spend a few minutes in silence before we read. We put aside our pressing concerns, and ask for the help of the Spirit of God. In the silence, we ask for the same attitude and faith of those who first wrote the words. We try to become teachable, expectant and nondefensive. We resolve not to fight what we read, but rather to let the words make their home in us. We will always be spiritually safe in our use of the Bible if we read it with a readiness to surrender all of our preconceived plans and opinions.

A second general rule for reading with our heart is to "read little and ponder much." Our modern methods of speed-reading are fine for novels and daily newspapers, but they are all wrong for the Bible. When we read fast we do not allow the passage time to soak in. So when we come to a word or phrase that strikes us, we need to pause, mull it over, taste its flavor, relate it to our lives and relationships. Baron von Hugel, one of the great spiritual directors of the 20th century, would often compare this kind of reading to the way a cow grazes. The cow does not rush around the field from one tuft of grass to another; it stays in one place, eating slowly, ruminating what it has taken in and chewing repeatedly.

Lastly, if we are going to get anywhere with our Bible reading, we need to plan our reading carefully. If we don't have some definite plan about this, we simply won't get to it. We don't have to read much at one sitting. Maybe we have been told to read the Bible through every year, and we can ensure this by reading three chapters a day. If we do this we may enjoy the reputation of being one who reads the Bible through on a regular basis, and we may congratulate ourselves on this achievement. But have we been transformed by our reading? Have we become more loving human beings, more filled with the life and power of God? It is far better to have a few verses take root in the substance of our lives than to know all the scriptures but be unchanged in character and outlook.

There are a number of ways to begin reading the Bible with our heart. One suggestion is to start with those passages that already mean a great deal to us, such as Psalm 23, the Lord's Prayer, 1 Corinthians 13 and Romans 8. When we return to these passages and meditate on them, we find ever new depths opening up to us. Memorizing these passages and carrying them with us in our daily lives further deepens their influence on us. Another starting point can be to begin with one of the gospels and to read a passage each day until something strikes us. We then pause and turn the words over and over in our heart, asking, "Lord, what are you saying to me here?" These are small beginnings, but remember, our aim is not to become scholars or to impress others with our Bible knowledge. We simply want to nourish our souls and encounter God in a way that is real and meaningful.

Countless Christ-followers through the ages have testified to the incredible value of reading the Bible with our heart. They tell us that when we read the scriptures in this way we find a new dimension to life. A new power. A new joy. A new love. A new hope. A deeper and richer faith. Furthermore, we start to know Jesus, and the God he shows us, more personally and more intimately. Is there anyone reading these words, who doesn't want this experience? Begin reading the Bible with your heart!

Daily Meditation Texts for the Week

Day 1   "I treasure your word in my heart, so that I may not sin against you." (Ps 119:11)

Day 2   "Your word is a lamp to my feet and a light to my path." (Ps 119:105)

Day 3   "This book of the law shall not depart out of your mouth; you shall meditate on it day and night, so that you may be careful to act in accordance with all that is written in it. For then you shall make your way prosperous, and then you shall be successful." (Josh 1:8)

Day 4   "Simon Peter answered him, 'Lord, to whom can we go? You have the words of eternal life.'" (John 6:68)

Day 5   "If you abide in me, and my words abide in you, ask for whatever you wish, and it will be done for you." (John 15:7)

Day 6   "But he answered, 'It is written: One does not live by bread alone, but by every word that comes from the mouth of God.'" (Matt 4:4)

Day 7   "Indeed, the word of God is living and active, sharper than any two-edged sword, piercing until it divides soul from spirit, joints from marrow; it is able to judge the thoughts and intentions of the heart." (Heb 4:12)

SUGGESTION FOR JOURNALING

After you have spent some time reading a biblical passage with your heart, write a paragraph beginning with the words, "As I read the scriptures today, it became clearer that…"

QUOTE FOR THE WEEK

The Bible is…God's gift to the world through his Church, not to the scholars. It comes through the life of his people and nourishes that life. Its purpose is practical, not academic. An intelligent, careful, intensive but straightforward reading— that is, not one governed by obscure and faddish theories or by a mindless orthodoxy—is what it requires to direct us into life in God's kingdom.

Dallas Willard
The Divine Conspiracy

PRAYER

O send thy Spirit, Lord, now unto me,
That He may touch my eyes and make me see,
Show me the truth concealed within Thy word,
And in Thy book revealed, I see the Lord.

Mary Ann Lathbury

WEEK 9

———

Girding Ourselves with Persevering Patience

Several years ago Morton introduced my wife and me to one of his favorite places—the redwood forests of the northern parts of California. It was an unforgettable experience. These giant trees only mature after three or four hundred years, and many live well beyond two thousand years. They have withstood earthquakes, fires and floods. As I stood in the shade of these towering monarchs of the forest and thought about their incredible persistence, I was filled with awe. They are magnificent symbols of the need for patience and perseverance.

Jesus certainly emphasized this truth for those who wanted to know God. Think for a moment about the story of the man who kept knocking on his neighbor's door in the middle of the night until he got an answer. The widow who constantly nagged the judge until he gave her justice. The pearl merchant who was constantly on the lookout for the finest pearl and, when he found it, sold everything so he could buy it (see Luke 11:5–13, 18:3–8; Matt 13:45). Parables like these are powerful reminders that if our spiritual quest is spasmodic or erratic we will not get very far in our exploration of the realm of the Spirit.

This challenge to gird ourselves with persevering patience has a profound and timely relevance. We live in an instant society where we are encouraged from an early age to seek out the quick and easy solutions. When it comes to relating to God, many of us want to reach up to a shelf and take down our spiritual maturity in a package. We want one dramatic encounter with

God that will solve all our problems, instantaneously reduce the hunger inside and change us overnight. But real relationships with God do not come in this way. They grow slowly. God can and does give us intense spiritual experiences, but they do not transform us at once into the people we are meant to be. Our conversion is a lifelong journey that unfolds step by step, little by little, until our personality has been recreated by God. Real spirituality, like a redwood tree, matures over many years.

The life story of Paul the Apostle is an excellent example of persevering patience. He had a frightening and profoundly transforming experience of the risen Christ on the Damascus road, and another at the hands of Ananias. Undoubtedly, Paul was deeply touched by God and filled with the Holy Spirit. However, soon after these experiences he went into seclusion for three years. This prolonged period of reflection gave Paul the opportunity to unlearn some of his former ways and integrate the implications of his new faith into his life. Only after this time of hidden preparation and inward integration of his Damascus road experience was he ready to become a spiritual guide to others (Acts 9:1–30).

By contrast, we sometimes make the mistake of thinking that we can come to know God in a single experience, or in an hour on Sunday morning or by reading a book or two. We forget that God is the deepest and richest, the most marvelous and beautiful, the greatest and most boundless reality that there is. When we relate to God we are dealing with an inexhaustible Mystery. There are no limits to the depth we may plumb or the riches we may find, or the new aspects of relationship that we may discover when we come to God. If, after twenty years of marriage, I am still discovering new things about my wife, whom I can see, how much more is there to discover about God and that dynamic, unseen realm of divine reality in the midst of which all of us live? Indeed, how can we ever pretend to be more than apprentices in our relationship with God and the kingdom of heaven?

More than any other reason, people fail to mature spiritually because they don't exercise the patience to learn and grow. Too many contemporary congregations persist in offering a microwave faith that promises quick-and-easy shortcuts to spiritual growth. The earliest Christ-followers would turn in their graves at the thought of such assurances. For the first three hundred years of the church's existence, those who wanted to be counted among the Christians needed to attend three years of instruction and be tested in a host of ways before they were baptized. They knew their faith. They knew their Bible. They knew their God. The church of those times was alive, precisely because it was a community of people who knew what it meant to seek God with persevering patience. And for that reason it also had an unbelievable power, which outlived, outthought and overcame the ancient world.

The message is clear. One of the things required of you and me, if we want to experience a truly transforming relationship with God, is persevering patience. God is a wise and loving parent who wants to mature his sons and daughters. But if we do not keep at our spiritual journey with grit and endurance, we will not grow up to become the people God wants us to be. No one becomes spiritually mature overnight. Spirituality that comes quickly usually goes quickly. Nothing can take the place of slow, steady growth in coming to know God and being enlightened by the Spirit. Let me end with a challenge for each one of us:

+ How much do you really want to know God?
+ How much do you want your life to reflect the character of Christ?
+ How much do you want to discern and do the will of God?
+ How much do you want a real meaning to your life?
+ How much do you want your life to be filled with the Holy Spirit?

If you truly desire these things and are prepared to seek them with persevering patience, they will be given to you. Those who pursue God consistently, faithfully, determinedly, and don't give up will not be disappointed. They will come to know the reality of God in their own experience and many other good things besides. May the message of the redwood trees become a powerful symbol for you as well.

DAILY MEDITATION TEXTS FOR THE WEEK

Day 1   "So I say to you, 'Ask, and it will be given you; search, and you will find; knock, and the door will be opened for you.'" (Luke 11:9)

Day 2   "When you search for me, you will find me, if you seek me with all your heart." (Jer 29:13)

Day 3   "But strive first for the kingdom of God and his righteousness, and all these things will be given to you as well." (Matt 6:33)

Day 4   "[Love] bears all things, believes all things, hopes all things, endures all things." (1 Cor 13:7)

Day 5   "My brothers and sisters, whenever you face trials of any kind, consider it nothing but joy, because you know that the testing of your faith produces endurance; and let endurance have its full effect, so that you may be mature and complete, lacking in nothing." (Jas 1:2–4)

Day 6   "The kingdom of heaven is like treasure hidden in a field, which someone found and hid: then in his joy he goes and sells all that he has and buys that field..." (Matt 13:44)

Day 7   "By contrast, the fruit of the Spirit is love, joy, peace, patience, kindness, generosity, faithfulness, gentleness and self-control." (Gal 5:22)

SUGGESTION FOR JOURNALING

Express in written words your response to the closing challenge outlined in the meditation.

QUOTE FOR THE WEEK

Stick-to-it-iveness. Perseverance. Patience. The way of faith is not a fad that is taken up in one century only to be discarded in the next. It lasts. It is a way that works. It has been tested thoroughly.

Eugene Peterson
A Long Obedience in the Same Direction

PRAYER

Lord, there are times when I want to give up. The way seems too difficult and I feel that I'm getting...nowhere. When these moments come, remind me that you never give up on me and breathe into my life the spirit of persevering patience. Amen.

Putting on the Whole
Armor of God

I recently preached a sermon about the reality of the evil one. What struck me was the varied responses I received. Some said that there was no place for a "personal" force of evil in a contemporary world view. On the other hand, many felt that they could identify with what I had said. They said they, too, had experienced some aspect of this evil power that bedevils our society and personal lives. One of the teachers at a local school raised a significant point. "If we are really engaged in a conflict with the evil one," she asked, "how can we live more victoriously?"

It's a question that deserves careful thought. If we fail to take it seriously, we can become very vulnerable to the devices of the evil one. Before we know it, we find ourselves yielding to temptation more often. Our standards drop. We begin behaving in ways that spoil our lives and the lives of those around us. Perhaps most significantly, we lose our sense of the importance of growing spiritually and end merely going to church, learning a few moral rules and adding a little perfume to our outwardly respectable lives. When we think and live this way, the subtle tentacles of evil have begun to tighten their grip. And from here it can get much worse.

I am often sick at heart when I think about how lightly many churchgoers, including myself, take these matters. We seem to have no real sense of urgency. We live with an inadequate understanding of the deviousness of evil. Nor do we have a deep awareness of God's strength and his resources, which are available to us. As a result, we fail to be effective agents of the love, peace and justice of God in those social structures that make up our communities. Because of our lack of spiritual nerve and commitment, we actually contribute to the rapidly rising levels of darkness and despair around us. Little wonder that our society reflects what the present pope calls a "culture of death."

How does this happen? I can suggest one reason. It is because we don't take the reality of the evil one seriously enough. We think that we are wrestling only with flesh and blood. We fail to realize that our real struggle is with demonic forces of unbelievable cunning and power. This is why we must take the question asked by my teacher-friend seriously. Thankfully, the apostle Paul's concluding words in his letter to the Ephesians give us a clear and practical starting point for our response (see Eph 6:10–18). We need to read this passage with open hearts and minds and allow it to become an integral part of our thinking. Unless we strengthen ourselves to be overcomers in this engagement with evil, our lives and communities will continue to be disrupted and oppressed.

We begin by equipping ourselves with the belt of truth. Our postmodern world laughs and asks with Pilate, "What is truth?" The powers of darkness smile and say there is no truth. But truth does exist. And if we are to have any real hope in the battle against evil, we must make sure we live by the truth. Paul's image of the belt is helpful here. Belts support and hold things up so we are able to move freely. When we know more about the truth of God, the truth about the world and about ourselves and live by this truth, we find that we are able to break free from many of our bondages. We also live more victorious lives and are set free to fight for what is right and true.

Many of us are actually afraid of knowing the truth. We shy away from looking at the ugly truth about the hatred, the back-biting, the selfishness, the cruelty and the inhumanity of this world. We switch off the TV when something is shown about the holocaust, or when we are reminded of the atrocities that have taken place in our own society, because we do not want to be upset by the frightening evil around us. Sometimes, we also close our eyes to the truth about ourselves because we cannot admit that the demonic forces can be found right inside us. Until we are prepared to face ourselves as we really are, and stop blaming others for faults that are just as much our own, we cannot have any real hope for victory over evil.

Then we put on the breastplate of righteousness. This means learning to live in an honest relationship with God, with others and our world. We find this difficult to do. We are sometimes ashamed to stand up for what we believe and so we try to make other people think that we are less principled than we really are. We like to be part of the crowd, even when they do things that break God's heart. The powers of darkness have infiltrated our society so deeply that it is no longer popular to live as God's children. Indeed, our contemporary media send out a clear message that to be a righteous person is rather dull, boring and unexciting. After all, how many people today would want to watch a TV series called *Miami Virtue* instead of *Miami Vice*? Against this background, we need all the righteousness, all the moral courage that we can muster, or we are lost.

Our feet are so important. They take us to where we need to be. They take us to work, they take us home, they take us to the dinner table, they take us to bed. The same is true of our feet as spiritual instruments. It is with our feet that we follow Jesus, step out on the gospel way, and walk more closely with God. Wherever we go we are called upon to take the peace of Christ with us. When we shoe ourselves with concern and thoughtfulness and nonviolence—essentials of the gospel of peace—we halt the spread of evil in our midst. Moreover, our feet are kept in good condition so that we are able to keep moving to those places where God needs us most. Soldiers whose feet are torn and broken cannot do much.

The shield of faith is also part of our basic equipment. Ensuring that our faith is strong enables us to ward off the fiery darts of the devil. Many allow themselves to be drawn into cynicism and despair because they do not take the trouble to deepen their faith and acquire this crucial piece of armor. On the other hand, when we strengthen our faith, when we know that we are God's beloved and believe that nothing can separate us from the divine love, we find ourselves able to stand firm in the midst of deep spiritual conflict. This is why it is so important always to have the shield of faith at hand.

With the helmet of salvation we protect our heads and hearts. The evil one always tries to influence the way we think. Have you noticed how easily destructive thoughts pop into our minds? We find ourselves doubting God's goodness, or wishing someone dead, or thinking that we are worthless. When we put this helmet on, we defend ourselves against these attacks. We do this by accepting the risen Lord into our lives, filling our minds with his message about God and then living as though it were really true. As we do this, we discover that Jesus imparts to us a new vision and fresh understanding that eventually transforms our whole lives.

Finally, we take into our struggle against evil the sword of the Spirit, which is the word of God. No good soldier goes into battle unarmed. As Christ-followers, we do not engage the evil one depending upon our own strength and cleverness. If we do, we fail again and again. Rather, we rely upon the living word and spiritual power of the risen Lord. These are the weapons that enable us to overcome. When we put into practice those things that God says to us—perhaps in the words of scripture, in a sermon, in the counsel of a friend, or in that "small still voice"—we are empowered and guided by the Spirit. Jesus himself promised that our commitment to follow his words would bring the living reality of his spiritual presence into our lives (see John 14:15).

During the week after my sermon, our family met with other

families in our small group. Together we spoke about the various pieces of equipment in God's armor and how to apply them in our daily lives. When I suggested that we choose one piece of equipment to put on, the youngest member of our group, an eight year old, chirped, "What good is one piece? We need to put them all on if it is going to do us any good." No wonder Jesus drew attention to the spiritual wisdom of children. Won't you try, this week, to put on the whole armor of God? Nothing less will do.

DAILY MEDITATION TEXTS FOR THE WEEK

Day 1   "Put on the whole armor of God, so that you may be able to stand against the wiles of the devil." (Eph 6:11)

Day 2   "Stand therefore, and fasten the belt of truth around your waist, and put on the breastplate of righteousness." (Eph 6:14)

Day 3   "As shoes for your feet put on whatever will make you ready to proclaim the gospel of peace." (Eph 6:15)

Day 4   "With all of these, take the shield of faith, with which you will be able to quench all the flaming arrows of the evil one." (Eph 6:16)

Day 5   "Take the helmet of salvation, and the sword of the Spirit, which is the word of God." (Eph 6:17)

Day 6   "Finally, be strong in the Lord and in the strength of his power." (Eph 6:10)

Day 7   "Therefore take up the whole armor of God, so that you may be able to withstand on that evil day, and having done everything, to stand firm." (Eph 6:13)

SUGGESTION FOR JOURNALING

Describe one way in which you experience yourself as a tempted human being.

QUOTE FOR THE WEEK

The pilgrim, if he/she is honest, will have to take seriously the mystery of evil, and more important, will have to encounter the awful possibilities of evil within himself/herself.

Alan Jones
Journey into Christ

PRAYER

Affirm this Celtic prayer every day of this week, using your imagination if you find it helpful:

I put between me and all evil
The saving power of God.
I put between me and all darkness
The saving power of God.
I put between me and all weakness
The saving power of God.
I put between me and all terror
The saving power of God.
I put between me and all destruction
The saving power of God.
I put between me and death
The saving power of God.
Amen.

SECTION TWO

*Learning Ways of
Living Love*

WEEK 11

Letting in God's Love

This week I want to invite you to let God's love into your life more deeply. My reason for this is simple. Over the next nine weeks we will be exploring ways of living this love in our daily lives. But before love can flow through us, we need to be filled by it. It is only when we really open ourselves at a personal level to the love of God that we are more able to love those that cross our path.

Now, you may be wondering how we can do this. Let me describe a way that Morton taught me. It's a simple meditation based on that famous painting by Holman Hunt, *The Light of the World*, which shows the crucified and risen Christ standing outside a door. There is no latch on the outside. He stands there knocking, a lantern in his hand. This is a picture of how God comes to each one of us. The Holy One waits, always ready to enter our lives, but rarely stepping over the threshold until we open the door. The meditation that follows shows how we can do this and consciously allow the living Lord and his love into our lives. After reading how I use this exercise in my devotions, you may like to try it yourself.

I start by imagining myself leaving the busy streets of my everyday life and finding my way to my own little soul-room. I enter this inner place, shocked by its untidiness. The chairs are overturned. The dirty dishes are stacked high on the kitchen counter. The refuse bin is overturned. As I sit down in this mess, I hear an accusing voice whispering, "Trevor, look at your life. It's such a mess. You're not much good at living for God. Why don't you give up? You'll never be an effective instrument of God's love."

As I listen to this voice I know that it does not come from God. It's a lying, destructive, deceiving voice. So I summon all my courage, reject the message this voice brings and say with all the strength I can find, "Be still. You are not speaking the truth." Then I hear someone knocking on the door. The negative inner voice whispers that I should ignore the knocking, that it is just an illusion. However, I ignore the dark voice and move over to the other side of the room. The knocking continues, gentle, persistent, determined. It's amazing how much the sound of a knock reveals about the one who is knocking. I go toward the door and call out, "Come in." A voice replies softly, "I cannot. The door is locked on the inside."

I look at the bolt. It is rusty. So are the hinges. I draw it back and open the door. Standing before me in the doorway is the figure of the crucified and risen Jesus, lantern in hand. The other hand raised to knock. A crown of thorns is pressed onto his head. Quietly, he says: "Look at me. I stand at the door. I knock. If you hear me call and open the door, I'll come right in and sit down to supper with you" (Rev 3:20, *The Message*). Falling to my knees, I cry out that I'm not worthy that he should enter my room. It's in too much of a mess. He speaks to me again. This time there is a note of harshness in his voice. "How dare you call yourself unworthy when I died for you. Even if you had been the only human being I would have given my life for you. I want to share my love with you more than you will ever know. This is why I have been knocking on your door from your very beginnings." As he speaks he takes me by the hand and lifts me up.

He enters through the door. Light from his lantern radiates warm rays of hope into the shabbiness around me. He leads me to a table in the center of the room on which there is bread and wine. He invites me to share my thoughts with him. I pour out my anguish, my hopes, my joys, my fears. All of me. He listens. Then he takes bread, breaks off a piece and gives it to me with the words, "This is my body broken for you." He also takes the cup of wine, blesses it, and shares it with me, saying, "This is my blood shed for you." As I receive these sacraments of divine love my heart begins to glow again. I know myself to be loved, accepted, forgiven.

Before he leaves the room, he asks me to tell him about the people in my life. I tell him about my wife Debbie and my children, Joni and Mark. I tell him about my mother, my sister and her family. I also speak of those whom I love, but who have died, my friends and acquaintances, and those I know who are in pain and grief. As I speak, I lift each of these people into his light and love. Then he says to me, "Thank you for letting me come into your life and allowing me to give you my love. I will always be with you. Now go out and bring my love to those you are with. Remember that no matter how messy your life may be, I will never give up on you."

Over the years I have used this biblical image countless times. It's a picture that helps me relate to the loving God who wants my fellowship more than I will ever fully know. Going through the full meditation usually takes about twenty minutes. But I sometimes only use parts of the exercise when I need to. This usually happens when I feel that I have failed to be an effective witness for God's love. Then I like to stop for a few moments, turn inward and again open myself to the risen Jesus whose love never gives up on me. In whichever way I use this meditation, I usually get a renewed sense of peace and desire to reach out in love to other human beings.

Some may say that this meditation is just wishful thinking. Morton and I would disagree. By using our God-given imagination in this way, we place it in the service of our faith. Of course the image is not the reality, but the image deepens our participation in the reality it seeks to describe. When we imagine something we find ourselves more deeply involved in what we are thinking about. Perhaps this is why that great London preacher Leslie Weatherhead once said, "Faith is imagination all grown up."

As we set out on the adventure of loving these next few weeks, let us not try to do it on our own. We simply do not have the necessary reserves. We need to be filled with a constant supply of divine love if we are to have the reservoir of caring that we need. Hence our first task, and our constant task, is to keep ourselves open to the love of God who stands patiently, knocking at the door of our lives. This we do by regularly turning toward the risen Christ in prayer and meditation and allowing his love to flow into us. Only then are we ready to explore ways of living this love in our daily lives.

DAILY MEDITATION TEXTS FOR THE WEEK

Day 1   "Listen! I am standing at the door, knocking; if you hear my voice and open the door, I will come in to you and eat with you, and you with me." (Rev 3:20)

Day 2   "God's love was revealed among us in this way: God sent his only Son into the world so that we might live through him." (1 John 4:9)

Day 3   "In this is love, not that we loved God but that he loved us and sent his Son to be the atoning sacrifice for our sins." (1 John 4:10)

Day 4   "Beloved, since God loved us so much, we also ought to love one another." (1 John 4:11)

Day 5   "No one has ever seen God; if we love one another, God lives in us, and his love is perfected in us." (1 John 4:12)

Day 6   "God is love, and those who abide in love abide in God, and God abides in them." (1 John 4:16)

Day 7   "We love because he first loved us." (1 John 4:19)

SUGGESTION FOR JOURNALING

Describe how you experienced this week's suggested meditation.

QUOTE FOR THE WEEK

God waits to dwell in us and to fill us with yet more grace, more love, more wholeness and with his own fullness. But the God of the Bible never bulldozes his way into a person's life. He loves us enough to wait until, out of our own free will, we invite him to come to us.

Joyce Huggett
Open to God

PRAYER

Lord, thank you for wanting to enter my life.
I open the door of my heart and ask you to come in.
Please make my heart your home, now and forever.
Amen.

Cultivating the Fine Art
of Liking Ourselves

For nearly thirty years I have followed the call to be a pastor. One of the most special privileges this vocation has brought me is the opportunity to get close to people. Over the years I have been able to share God's love with men and women from all kinds of backgrounds. In these encounters I have discovered that many people struggle to really like themselves. And it is strange that when people do not like themselves, they usually find it difficult to genuinely like and love others.

I can identify with this struggle. For reasons that I cannot clearly understand, I have sometimes found it difficult to value myself as someone who is deeply cherished and loved by God. One memory from my young adult years stands out clearly. I was at a Christian conference where the speaker asked us to repeat the sentence, "Because God loves me in Christ, I can now love myself as I am." I found that I could not say these words and mean them. In fact, I even remember arguing with the speaker that such a thought was self-centered and unchristian.

Since those early days I have slowly learned the importance of liking myself. I now see that when we are on good terms with ourselves, we are more free to like others as they are. Accepting ourselves "warts and all" enables us to accept more graciously others with all their weaknesses and faults. It can also prevent us from being threatened by their successes and strengths. When we have a genuine regard for ourselves, we don't need to defend ourselves by drawing attention to the faults of others or by putting them down when they do well. Instead, we can reach out to them with the acceptance, affirmation and love that we ourselves have received from God. Jesus was certainly right when he said, "Love your neighbor as yourself." This commandment clearly implies that we cannot love our neighbor until we have loved ourselves.

But how on earth do we go about cultivating this delicate art of liking ourselves? It's one thing to accept with our heads the gospel truth that God loves us. It's quite another to feel this "belovedness" in our hearts. A few simple steps have helped me to move this good news from my head to my heart. I offer them to you and hope they will also make it easier for you to find a greater measure of self-acceptance and self-love.

The first step is to see yourself through the eyes of God. Let me describe a way of doing this imaginatively. We can start by picturing ourselves as children cooped up in one small room of a big house. We do not feel good enough to live in the whole house, so we sneak off and hide in a tiny cell of self-abasement. From here we call out to God to come and help us. And the living Lord comes and says, "Leave this little room and inherit your vast mansion. This is only a cellar. The whole place is yours." But we raise our eyes and reply, "Oh, Lord, I am not worthy." The Holy One gets annoyed and says sternly, "How dare you call unworthy someone for whom I had died. You are worthy because I made you, and I came to give my life for you. Let go of your proud unworthiness. Come with me and inherit the kingdom I have prepared for you from the foundation of the world."

You see, when we do not acknowledge our proper value, we are telling God that it was a waste of time for Jesus Christ to give himself for us. It is as if we think we know better than God. But the mystery of our faith proclaims this incredible truth. We are worthy and valuable to God. As we noted last week, God loves each one of us and would have died on the cross even if you or I had been the only human on earth. This is how much we mean to our Creator. How dare we, then, refuse to like ourselves when God values us in such an extraordinary way.

The second step is to accept forgiveness. This is not always easy. Sometimes it can be easier to forgive others than to receive forgiveness ourselves. When a good friend of Morton's offended him deeply he forgave him. Even so, they drifted apart. One day, while they were talking, Morton realized that his friend was unable to accept his forgiveness. Somehow he had felt unworthy of Morton's friendship and had withdrawn. Clearly, one has to value oneself in order to accept forgiveness. Then, in accepting forgiveness, one develops a deeper understanding of this valuing of self.

Sometimes the forgiveness we need to receive can only come from God. All of us have done things that have broken God's heart. These actions also make us feel guilty, ashamed and unworthy. The only way to move beyond our self-rejection and self-hatred is to receive the forgiveness that Christ freely offers us. This forgiveness sets us free to live and love in a renewed way. In fact, have you ever realized that the whole Christian church was built on people who had accepted forgiveness and then loved the Lord even more? There was Peter who denied him, John who fled from him, Thomas who demanded proof, Paul who persecuted his followers. Yet, each one of them accepted the forgiveness of God and became the foundation of Christ's church.

The third step is to take the risk and relate to other human beings even when they let us down. This is exactly what Jesus did. We must work to forge real relationships with people around us. And this will involve accepting and being accepted; forgiving and being forgiven; loving and being loved. We cannot sit on our own and come to an acceptance of ourselves. It has to be worked out in living relationships. The miracle of self-acceptance happens when there is interaction between human beings. Those who stay aloof from relationships seldom come to like themselves. Only as we have the courage to be our real selves with others does there grow within us a proper appreciation of ourselves. This is always risky but it is always well worth it.

Ideally, the church should be the place where we can do this. It should be a fellowship filled with the compassion, understanding and friendship of Christ. If we could find genuine friendship in our local congregation, there would be far less need for the professional care of secular psychologists. However, the sad fact is that many people experience greater acceptance and warmth in a therapist's office than they do in a church. But, perhaps, beginning with your and my efforts, this situation could right itself. If that day comes, the church will become, to use a delightful Quaker phrase, "a society of friends."

It is clear that genuine love for another human being is seldom possible unless we cultivate the fine art of liking ourselves. When we love ourselves, as God does, we find that we have far more to give to others. We can then forget about ourselves and give our total attention to others. May this meditation lead you into a deeper self-love and self-acceptance. Above all, as you go on this journey, stay close to the risen Christ who totally accepts and loves you, no matter who you are or what you do. Remember just how precious and valuable you are to God.

DAILY MEDITATION TEXTS FOR THE WEEK

Day 1   "But God proves his love for us in that while we still were sinners Christ died for us." (Rom 5:8)

Day 2   "But the steadfast love of the Lord is from everlasting to everlasting." (Ps 103:17)

Day 3   "Bless the Lord...who forgives all your iniquity." (Ps 103:1, 3)

Day 4   "For you, O Lord, are good and forgiving, abounding in steadfast love to all who call on you." (Ps 86:5)

Day 5   "Welcome one another, therefore, just as Christ has welcomed you, for the glory of God." (Rom 15:7)

Day 6   "Forgive each other; just as the Lord has forgiven you, so you also must forgive." (Col 3:13)

Day 7   "Are not two sparrows sold for a penny? Yet not one of them will fall to the ground apart from your Father. And even the hairs of your head are all counted. So do not be afraid; you are of more value than many sparrows." (Matt 10:29–31)

SUGGESTION FOR JOURNALING

Write down one characteristic that you really appreciate about yourself.

QUOTE FOR THE WEEK

> *The Bible does not say, "Love your neighbour instead of yourself," but "Love your neighbour as yourself." Self-love is thus the prerequisite and criterion for our conduct toward our neighbour. It is the measuring stick for loving others which Jesus gives us.*
>
> Walter Trobisch
Love Yourself

PRAYER

> *Dear Lord, help me to love myself*
> *with the love that you have for me.*
> *I make this request in Jesus' name.*
> *Amen.*

WEEK 13

Learning to Listen

I remember once walking down a Johannesburg street with my family when we were suddenly surrounded by a group of zealous Christians. Without any introduction they began talking about the claims of the Christian faith. They spoke nonstop about Jesus and urged us to accept him into our lives. I tried vainly to get a word in. All I wanted to say was, "Guys, we're on the same side as you," but they would not give me a chance. At no stage did they try to find out our names, where we were from or how we were. Through their lack of listening they failed to show us the divine love they were talking about.

I often reflect on that encounter. I do not want to pass judgment on those young Christ-followers. Too often I have also failed to listen well, especially to those closest to me. Nonetheless, over the years, I have become increasingly aware of the importance of listening in our spiritual life. Listening lies at the heart of a genuinely loving life and of all ministry in the name of Jesus. Perhaps most significantly, I have come to understand that it is only when we learn to listen to other human beings that we are able to begin listening to God. After all, how can we listen to someone who we cannot see if we do not listen to those we can see? If listening is as critical as this, I'm sure you will agree that we need to learn what it is and how it should be done.

Consider for a moment this helpful definition. Listening is being silent with another person in an active way. In other words, it is silently bearing with the other as they share their story. Unfortunately this kind of listening is in short supply. Have you noticed how people are sometimes silent but not really present?

Their eyes become empty or glazed. They are either not interested in what you are saying or they are thinking about what they are going to say. You realize that although your companion may be silent, no real listening is taking place. In contrast to this, true listening means actually tuning in to the other person in an attentive, concerned and creative way.

Learning to listen is a difficult and demanding discipline. Few activities require as much effort and concentration if we are going to listen well. Morton remembers a time when a woman came to see him in his office. He asked how she was. She answered that she was quite well. He replied that he was happy that she had no serious problems because he was tired from his day's work. Their time together continued pleasantly but at a superficial level. Then the woman left. Several years later he visited her in the hospital and found out that she had come laden with problems that day. Her daughter was pregnant and not married, and she had come from the doctor's office where she had learned that she had cancer. Morton realized that in thinking only about himself, he had failed to listen to someone in deep need.

How do we go about learning to listen? First of all, we need to stop talking. It is hard for some of us to halt our chatter. Our tongue seems to have a life all of its own, far beyond our rational control. On a recent retreat that I led on the subject of addiction, one brave lady acknowledged that she was addicted to talking. We all need to check whether we talk too much. Interestingly, James points out that if we are not able to control our tongues, our religion is useless (Jas 1:26). It is only when we take control of our tongues that we are able to start listening.

We must be silent, however, not only with our lips. We also need to become quiet in our inner being. When we truly listen to others, we are silent inside. This requires a certain inner security. When we are secure in ourselves we can listen to others, even when they express ideas with which we disagree. It means that we no longer become easily upset or shocked by what is said. We simply listen openly, allowing the other person to be who he or she is. Listening gives freedom and does not need us to control or censor what is said.

Second, listening demands patience. When we hurry people along to say things or to get them to come to the point, they usually close up. People need to reveal themselves at their own pace and in their own way. We may first have to listen to many superficialities before being trusted with deeper matters. Again and again, I have found that when I am able to bear with the superficial beginnings of another person's story, I am eventually admitted into the deeper and more intimate levels. Being patient while another person is sharing his or her deepest feelings communicates true concern and care.

Third, creative listeners do not always remain silent. Sometimes there is a need to clarify what the other person is saying. We may ask for more detail or for greater clarity, but always with the intention to understand better what the other person is trying to say. By asking appropriate questions, our listening becomes warm, interested and concerned. It seeks to know in order to care. One of my earliest mentors in pastoral ministry would often say to me, "Trevor, the greatest gift you can give to another person is the knowledge that you are really trying to understand what he or she is saying."

Fourth, good listening usually requires a quiet and private place. Few people will talk about their deepest feelings unless there is privacy and time. I enjoy going out with my wife and children separately so that I can give them uninterrupted time to share themselves. It also gives me space to share some of my concerns and struggles with them. Few practices have enriched my family relationships more than this one. It gives us a leisurely opportunity to share and listen. When I recommend this to other families in counseling interviews, I am frequently surprised how few have thought of making such an arrangement.

Lastly, good listeners seldom offer quick or easy answers to problems. Glib responses could cut off those who are speaking and keep them from discussing the real issue. A good rule of thumb is never to give advice unless we are asked for it. When we speak too soon and jump to conclusions, we usually jump to the wrong ones. Creative listening, more often than not, involves holding our own conclusions in check until others have come to theirs. The value of this kind of listening goes beyond words. All genuine human relationships have this at their heart. Indeed, true communication and fellowship are totally impossible without it. How can we care about and deal creatively with a person we do not know? And how can we ever come to know someone to whom we have not listened? The ability to listen, therefore, is a prerequisite to love. We simply cannot love others without first learning to listen. All deep relationships begin with listening. Then they continue with actions of thoughtfulness and care.

This week I invite you to embark on a spiritual adventure of learning how to listen. Begin by listening to your children, your spouse, your neighbor, your friends, your colleagues at work. Let listening become a way of life, an everyday habit, a spiritual discipline. You will find, as both Morton and I have, that listening opens up not only our human relationships, but the whole realm of the Spirit as well.

DAILY MEDITATION TEXTS FOR THE WEEK

Day 1   "You must understand this, my beloved: let everyone be quick to listen, slow to speak…" (Jas 1:19)

Day 2   "Guard your steps when you go to the house of God; to draw near to listen is better than the sacrifice offered by fools; for they do not know how to keep from doing evil." (Eccl 5:1)

Day 3   "For everything there is a season, and a time for every matter under heaven…a time to keep silence, and a time to speak…" (Eccl 3:1, 7)

Day 4   "Then Job answered: 'Listen carefully to my words, and let this be your consolation. Bear with me and I will speak…'" (Job 21:1)

Day 5   "Morning by morning he wakens—wakens my ear to listen as those who are taught." (Isa 50:4)

Day 6   "When words are many, transgression is not lacking, but the prudent are restrained in speech." (Prov 10:19)

Day 7   "If any think they are religious, and do not bridle their tongues but deceive their hearts, their religion is worthless." (Jas 1:26)

SUGGESTION FOR JOURNALING

Describe one moment in your life when you felt "listened to." How did the other person give you the assurance that he or she was really listening?

QUOTE FOR THE WEEK

Many people are looking for an ear that will listen. They do not find it among Christians, because Christians are talking when they should be listening.

Dietriech Bonhoeffer
Life Together

PRAYER

Lord, you are so willing to teach me how to listen. May I be willing to have my ears opened. Help me to listen to those who cross my path today, and give me a desire for them to be helped towards greater wholeness. Amen.

Living the Prayer
of St. Francis

Several years ago Morton was flying home after a conference on the spiritual life. Alone on the flight, he took out his journal and began to reflect on the things which had happened during the week. With his open journal on his lap he asked God, "Lord, what did you think about my presentations at the conference? Were the messages relevant? How did I do?"

As he thought quietly, the silence became deafening. Suddenly it dawned on him that he was flying very close to the home of his only brother. They were not on good terms. It also struck Morton that, unless he took some initiative, there was no real hope for the relationship. These reflections seemed to Morton like a strange answer to the questions he had posed to the Spirit.

Then he realized that the next leg of his journey would fly him over the home of his father and stepmother, with whom he was also not on good terms. When Morton had sent his dad a copy of his newly published book there was no response. His father did not ever seem to value what Morton did. Communication between the two had broken down and Morton had ceased trying to relate to him in any significant way.

And then a third realization came to his mind. He had planned a stopover in Phoenix, where his daughter Myra was at college. This relationship, too, had been very strained. He felt that things could perhaps improve if he visited her on her own turf. Later he learned that when his daughter heard about the proposed visit, she had remarked to her best friend, "What on earth am I going to do with Dad for five hours?"

As he wrote down these thoughts in his journal they hit him hard. Here he was leading a conference on developing your relationship with God; yet some of his closest relationships were in a bad state. He had talked about God's unconditional love, but he had not shown it to his own family. And then, out of the blue, the following words bubbled into his mind from somewhere deep inside him, and he wrote them down as well:

O Divine Master
grant that I may not so much seek
to be consoled—as to console
to be understood—as to understand
to be loved—as to love.

They spoke deeply to him. He knew that they were meant for him. However, he did not know the source of the words and could not remember having ever heard them before. When he returned home he tried to find them in the Bible but they were not there. Eventually he learned that they came from a prayer attributed to St. Francis of Assisi.

When the plane landed at Phoenix, he asked God to help him to give rather than expect to receive. From his side, he would try his best to focus his entire attention on his daughter and give her a real experience of his unconditional love. They went shopping together, even though that wasn't his favorite pastime. He took her to lunch at her favorite restaurant. He listened to her plans and hopes for the future. The visit proved to be a turning point in their relationship. He realized just how much he really cared about her. She came to realize that her father could also be interested in her. No longer was it, "What will I do with Dad for five hours?" but "Why don't you come more often and stay longer?"

Living the prayer of St. Francis can be life changing. Most of us are more interested in being taken care of, being loved, being consoled and being understood than in giving these as gifts to others. This is sometimes even the case in our own families. How often do we want those closest to us to satisfy our needs for affection and sympathy? How frequently do we complain about how little attention others give to us? We end up being so easily hurt and feeling sorry for ourselves. A lot of this complaining would cease if we took seriously the words of this prayer. Our wounded feelings cannot persist if we are less concerned with ourselves and more intent on bringing consolation and understanding to others.

Praying this prayer draws us deeper into the loving heart of God. God pours out unconditional love on each one of us. Our task is to be open to this love and then to share it with those around us. It is seldom easy. We cling to our desires for attention and satisfaction. In fact, when we give up this desire, something radically new is born in us. As Jesus says, we must lose our lives in order to gain them. As we put the prayer of St. Francis into practice, we die to self and we rise again. We begin to go the way of the cross and the resurrection. When we try to live by this simple prayer, the whole gospel opens up with new meaning and comes to life. The way of Christ begins to make sense and takes root in our daily lives.

But there is also something else that happens. We become instruments of God's peace in our world.

Where there is hatred, we sow love
Where there is injury, we bestow pardon
Where there is doubt, we bring faith
Where there is despair, we bring hope
Where there is darkness, we shed light
Where there is weakness, we inspire strength
And where there is sadness, we bring joy.

All this flows from within a life that seeks to give rather than receive. Such a life spreads the kingdom of heaven. Inevitably!

And, inwardly, when we live this way, we are renewed, cleansed, and given a deeper experience of God's kingdom ourselves. For it is in giving that we receive, it is in pardoning that we are pardoned, it is in dying that we are born to eternal life.

I long from the deepest of my being to live in the spirit of this prayer. I fail so often to do so. When others don't give me what I feel I need, I tend to withdraw my own love and care. I have found it helpful to have this prayer near me all the time. Perhaps you may as well. You can find it on cards or in framed plaques in most bookshops. Put one in your office at work, or on your bedside table, or on the fridge, or in your Bible. Stop, often, to meditate upon it. Let your spirit drink from it. Allow your actions to be shaped by the words. Perhaps, then, when we do this, we may become these words in heart and mind and deed.

DAILY MEDITATION TEXTS FOR THE WEEK

Day 1   "Blessed be the God and Father of our Lord Jesus Christ, the Father of mercies and the God of all consolation." (2 Cor 1:3)

Day 2   "When the cares of my heart are many, your consolations cheer my soul." (Ps 94:19)

Day 3   "Give, and it will be given to you. A good measure, pressed down, shaken together, running over, will be put into your lap; for the measure you give will be the measure you get back." (Luke 6:38)

Day 4   "You are the salt of the earth; but if salt has lost its taste, how can its saltiness be restored? It is no longer good for anything, but is thrown out and trampled under foot." (Matt 5:13)

Day 5   "I am giving you these commands so that you may love one another." (John 15:17)

Day 6   "Above all, maintain constant love for one another, for love covers a multitude of sins." (1 Pet 4:8)

Day 7   "Those who say, 'I love God,' and hate their brothers or
sisters, are liars; for those who do not love a brother or
sister whom they have seen, cannot love God whom
they have not seen." (1 John 4:20)

SUGGESTION FOR JOURNALING

Write out as honestly as you can your response to the prayer of
St. Francis.

QUOTE FOR THE WEEK

*We are put on earth for a little space that we may learn to
bear the beams of love.*

William Blake

PRAYER

*Lord, make me a channel of thy peace
That where there is hatred I may bring love,
That where there is wrong I may bring the spirit of forgiveness,
That where there is discord I may bring harmony,
That where there is error I may bring truth,
That where there is despair I may bring hope,
That where there are shadows I may bring thy light,
That where there is sadness I may bring joy.
Lord, grant that I may seek rather
To comfort—than to be comforted;
To understand—than to be understood;
To love—than to be loved;
For it is by giving that one receives;
It is by self-forgetting that one finds;
It is by forgiving that one is forgiven;
It is by dying that one awakens to eternal life.*

St. Francis of Assisi

WEEK 15

Loving Those
Who Love Us

I wonder if you have heard that delightful story about the farmer who had been married for twenty years. His wife constantly complained that he never told her that he loved her. One Sunday after church at dinner she complained again. He rose from the table, stood up straight and said, "My dear, when I married you twenty years ago, I told you that I loved you. If anything changes, I will let you know."

When I tell this story at weddings there is always a burst of laughter. But the laughter betrays the sad fact that this kind of atmosphere actually exists in many marriages and homes. Those closest to us, be they our spouses, our children, our parents or our brothers and sisters, often need to know that we really love them. They long to feel valued, cherished, noticed. So often we seem more able to share our negative and hostile feelings than our positive and loving ones. In fact, one reason why it is so hard to bear anger and criticism from our loved ones is that these feelings are sometimes the only ones that are ever expressed. We must therefore find ways of also expressing our love to those who love us.

There is another reason why we should give attention to this. Few things are more hypocritical than caring for distant neighbors at the expense of our own families. Yet, it is a sad fact that sometimes our acquaintances and friends find us more caring and compassionate than the people we live with. Recently, a newly married woman shared with me her anger about the fact that her husband seemed more concerned about others in their church than about her. He would spend hours away from home, giving large doses of attention and concern to fellow church members, but he had very little left over when he came home. One sure sign that we need to stop and reexamine our priorities is when serving others begins to spoil our close relationships.

How do we express our love to those closest to us? We can begin with simple acts of kindness and thoughtfulness. There is no child who does not appreciate a little gift from Mom or Dad returning home from a trip. Little gifts are as important as hugs. In my pastoral counseling I often hear spouses say that they feel taken for granted. I hear comments like, "I'm nothing but a bank account," "All I'm good for is cooking the meals and doing the washing," "It wouldn't matter if I wasn't around." Remarks like these remind us that we all need small displays of affection and interest from our loved ones to give us a sense of value and worth. That is why just stopping to think about each other or doing little acts of caring can do wonders for our close relationships.

I think of the small, thoughtful things that my wife did for me today. When I was leaving for work I found a small packet at the door with some sandwiches, a banana and my favorite chocolate. During the afternoon she phoned to ask how the day had gone and reminded me that she loved me. A few moments ago, while I was writing this, she popped in to my study and asked whether she could make me a cup of warm milk before she went to bed. These simple and thoughtful gestures of kindness touch me deeply. They tell me that I am loved, special and appreciated.

Another way of expressing love to those nearest and dearest involves spending time alone with them. The times that the family spends together on outings and holidays are of immense value, but if we really care about someone or want to care for them, we will also try to spend time alone with each of them. Time spent with a spouse or child or partner in the presence of others does not have the same value as time spent alone with them. Family members often end up feeling rather used when we take what they give us but deny them the time that is needed for genuine sharing. This hit Morton in a very dramatic way some years ago. Coming home after a full day's work, he had to make two calls at the hospital before supper. His seventeen-year-old daughter asked if she could drive him there. Clearly, there was something on her heart that she wanted to share. Nearing the hospital she turned and said, "Dad, when are you going to treat my mother like a human being?" She said it quietly, but it struck him like a bullet. Morton was dumbstruck. His daughter had put her finger on a painful reality that his business was preventing him from seeing.

Later that evening Morton sat down with Barbara to talk. He admitted that he had become so busy that they had seldom enjoyed prime time together as a couple. They almost never had time alone. He made a tentative suggestion. He offered to take her out once a week. Depending on finances they would either have a meal or simply a cup of coffee. More importantly, they would spend time with each other. For the last thirty-five years this weekly practice has became a wonderful means of renewal in their marriage. Together they have discovered that love cannot be expressed or grow without making quality time for the person we love.

A third way of showing love to our families or intimate friends involves the power of touch coupled with words. Of course, touch that is forced on another or is inappropriate is not acceptable. Neither is crude or belittling language. However, it is significant that in Jesus' ministry of healing love, he often combined these two ways of communication. Touch can have a wonderful way of conveying real care and affection, whether it be a touch of the arm, a squeeze of the hand or a hug. It can mean so much. Whether they are spoken or written, words also communicate a deep assurance of our love. Can you imagine a couple or a family living together who really love each other and yet never speak of it or touch one another? Word and touch are two of the simplest and yet most profound ways of sharing our loving feelings. We need to use these two ways of expressing love every day. I invite you this week to reflect on your relationships with those closest to you. Is there any particular person in your family or friendship circle that needs your loving attention? What thoughtful and kind action would best express the love you feel? In what way can you reach out and touch? Are there words that you may need to speak? Our journey into the genuinely loving life begins with these kinds of practical steps. From there it stretches out to embrace those other acquaintances and strangers who cross our paths. I hope you will be guided into the loving ways of the Spirit right where you live.

DAILY MEDITATION TEXTS FOR THE WEEK

Day 1   "If I speak in the tongues of mortals and of angels, but do not have love, I am a noisy gong or a clanging cymbal." (1 Cor 13:1)

Day 2   "And if I have prophetic powers, and understand all mysteries and all knowledge, and if I have all faith, so as to remove mountains, but do not have love, I am nothing." (1 Cor 13:2)

Day 3   "If I give away all my possessions, and if I hand over my body so that I may boast, but do not have love, I gain nothing." (1 Cor 13:3)

Day 4   "Love is patient; love is kind; love is not envious or boastful or arrogant or rude." (1 Cor 13:4)

Day 5   "It does not insist on its own way; it is not irritable or resentful." (1 Cor 13:5)

Day 6   "It does not rejoice in wrongdoing, but rejoices in the truth." (1 Cor 13:6)

Day 7   "Pursue love and strive for the spiritual gifts." (1 Cor 14:1)

SUGGESTION FOR JOURNALING

Describe one close relationship which is struggling at the moment. Write out one act of kindness and thoughtfulness that you can do on this person's behalf.

QUOTE FOR THE WEEK

Never be afraid of your petty selfishness when you try to achieve love, and don't be too alarmed if you act badly on occasion. I'm sorry I cannot tell you anything more reassuring. A true act of love, unlike imaginary love, is hard and forbidding. Imaginary love yearns for an immediate heroic act that is achieved quickly and seen by everyone.

People may actually reach a point where they are willing to sacrifice their lives, as long as the ordeal doesn't take too long, is quickly over—just like on the stage, with the public watching and admiring. A true act of love, on the other hand, requires hard work and patience, and, for some, it is a whole way of life.

But I predict that at the very moment when you see despairingly that, despite all your efforts, you have not only failed to come closer to your goal but, indeed, seem even farther from it than ever—at that very moment, you will have achieved your goal and will recognize the miraculous power of our Lord, who has always loved you and has secretly guided you all along.

Father Zossima in
Brothers Karamazov

Prayer for the Week

Dear God, thank you for those loved ones
with whom I share my life.
Please forgive my failures in loving
as God would like me to.
And empower me by your Spirit
to love them more deeply this coming week.
For Jesus' sake,
Amen.

WEEK 16

Showing Love in the Marketplace

After worship services I often stand at the door to say goodbye to people as they leave. Usually there is a brief exchange of words. One comment I am never sure how to respond to is when someone says, "Well, Trevor, thank you for the service. But now it's back to the real world." Somehow this throw-away remark seems to imply that when it comes to our everyday lives in the "marketplace," the message of God's love has little relevance.

Jack Smith (that's his real name) would disagree. Jack was a director of a medium-sized manufacturing plant that employed about seventy people. The business had been started by his father and, when it became too much for him, was handed on to Jack. For reasons beyond his immediate control, things did not go well for Jack. One day, in the midst of an intense labor conflict, he went into his office, sat down and said to himself, "I'm not running this business well and I don't know what to do. I guess I can either get drunk or I can pray." He thought a little longer and then reflected quietly, "Nothing will probably change if I pray. But if I get drunk, nothing will change either, and I'll have a hangover. And if I pray and nothing comes of it, I can always get drunk later on." With this strange logic and tiny seed of honest faith he put his head down on his desk and he prayed, "Okay Lord, I can't run this business on my own. What should I do?"

He sat in silence for a few moments. Suddenly these words came into his mind: "Create the conditions in which individuals can develop to the maximum of their capacities within the

102 JOURNEY OF THE SPIRIT

opportunities available." He was thunderstruck and said out loud, "What was that, Lord?" This time the same sentence spoke itself again in slow, measured words in his mind. He found his notebook and wrote them down.

Before I continue with Jack's story you may like to think about that sentence yourself. It suggests an excellent way to show love and caring toward employers, employees, committee members, acquaintances, or in any group where we have influence. Our task is to try to provide a climate in which other people can grow to their maximum potential. I know of no better way to love those in the groups and organizations to which we belong.

Jack was deeply moved by this experience. He did not know at the time that this insight was a principle many management theorists recommended. He decided that if God did still speak, he ought to take the New Testament more seriously. He began reading it more intentionally. In fact, he read it through from start to finish seven times. When he had done so, he began to realize that the answer to his prayer made a lot of sense. His company was little more than the people who worked there. If all of them were working, thinking, creating at their highest potential, the company would grow. His task, as the main influence in his company, was to develop an environment in which each human being could grow.

But how was he to establish such a climate among his employees? For many months he allowed his new insight to percolate in his thinking. He continued to pray. He listened to his employees. Gradually he came to the conclusion that he had to try to apply as many of Jesus' teachings to the everyday running of his business as he could. He felt that this would be putting the love of Christ into practice in the marketplace. One day as he was thinking about how to accomplish this goal, eleven guidelines emerged from the depth of him just as his original insight had come to him. Here they are:

+ Serve those who you expect to serve you.
+ Consider no person inferior, but recognize his or her limitations.
+ Lead others by action and example.
+ Be humble in speaking about accomplishments.
+ Teach and be prepared to be taught.
+ Attack unfairness from any quarter.
+ Believe that your employees must prosper if you are to prosper.
+ Seek the truth no matter who may get hurt.
+ Pray for God's guidance when you must make a decision affecting the life and future of any person.
+ Make your own decisions based on your own best judgment only after careful consideration has been given to all the facts.
+ Forgive honest mistakes where the person making the mistake is honestly self-critical.
+ If people are not self-critical, they must learn to be or they can never successfully supervise others or develop to the best of their abilities.

These guidelines became his personal manifesto as company director. As you will see from the Bible verses for this week, these guidelines are also solidly rooted in the teachings of Jesus and the New Testament. They provide a very helpful base for living God's love in the different groups and organizations to which we belong. In Jack's case, these principles actually did create an atmosphere in the business that helped both the employees and the company to grow.

But this is not just a business success story. The important moral of this story is that consciously opening ourselves to the voice of God, and trying to apply caring values, can change the spiritual and moral climate of any group of which we are a part. This is God's calling for our lives in the marketplace.

Will you, this week, think about these eleven guidelines? Which one speaks most to your own Monday-to-Friday world? Of course, they need to be varied and adjusted to suit different situations. Nonetheless, they do represent one man's genuine attempt to take seriously the values of the gospel in his working life. As such, they can provide a helpful starting point for us to do the same. If they do so, you may well discover the deep relevance that Christ's way has for the real world.

DAILY MEDITATION TEXTS FOR THE WEEK

Day 1 "You call me Teacher and Lord—and you are right, for that is what I am. So if I, your Lord and Teacher, have washed your feet, you also ought to wash one another's feet." (John 13:13–14)

Day 2 "For by the grace given to me I say to everyone among you not to think of yourself more highly than you ought to think, but to think with sober judgement, each according to the measure of faith that God has assigned." (Rom 12:3)

Day 3 "And whatever you do, in word or deed, do everything in the name of the Lord Jesus, giving thanks to God the Father through him." (Col 3:17)

Day 4 "And all of you must clothe yourselves with humility in your dealings with one another, for 'God opposes the proud, but gives grace to the humble.'" (1 Pet 5:5)

Day 5 "So then, putting away falsehood, let all of us speak the truth to our neighbors, for we are members of one another." (Eph 4:25)

Day 6 "Do not lag in zeal, be ardent in spirit, serve the Lord." (Rom 12:11)

Day 7 "Bear with one another and, if anyone has a complaint against another, forgive each other; just as the Lord has forgiven you, so you also must forgive." (Col 3:13)

SUGGESTIONS FOR JOURNALING

Select one guideline from the list outlined in the meditation and write out how you would like to practice it in your "market-place."

QUOTE FOR THE WEEK

> *Holiness and devotion must now come forth from the closet and the chapel to possess the street and the factory, the school-room and boardroom, the scientific laboratory and govern-mental office.*
>
> *Instead of a select few making religion their life, with the power and inspiration realised through the spiritual disci-plines, all of us can make our daily lives and vocations be "the house of God and the gate of heaven." It can—and must—happen.*
>
> Dallas Willard
> *The Spirit of the Disciplines*

PRAYER

> *Give me this day, O God,*
> *The energy I need to face my work;*
> *The diligence I need to do it well;*
> *The self-discipline which will make*
> *me work just as hard,*
> *even if there be none to see*
> *and none to praise, and none to blame;*
> *The self-respect which will not stoop*
> *to produce anything which is less*
> *than my best;*
> *The courtesy and the considerateness,*
> *which will make me easy to live with*
> *and easy to work with.*

*Help me so to live today that I
may make this world a happier place
wherever I may be;
Through Jesus Christ my Lord.
Amen.*

William Barclay
*More Prayers for the
Plain Man*

WEEK 17

Making Strangers Feel at Home

Several years ago a suicide took place at the University of Notre Dame where Morton was lecturing. It deeply shocked the staff and students. Being a Catholic college, students were taught that suicide is not an acceptable option. Furthermore, this university had an excellent structure of pastoral care and crisis support. Dormitories were supervised by priests, nuns or trained lay people in residence in each of them. Obviously, the Director of Students was deeply troubled. He decided to get to the cause of the tragedy. He called in all the students who had attended classes with the suicide victim. He spoke to all those who had shared the same dormitory floor with the student. He wanted to know what kind of person this student was. What he found out was that no one ever knew him. Small wonder this young man took his own life.

This story gives us a penetrating glimpse into our contemporary world. There are many people today who live in big cities surrounded by swarms of people yet have no real friendships. When we have no genuine fellowship with other human beings it's easy to feel like we are strangers. This disconnection can also happen in our places of work, our church communities and even our homes. People can be colleagues for years, or sit next to each other in the pew week after week, and never connect. In a counseling interview with a middle-aged man struggling in a difficult marriage, I heard these haunting words, "I feel like a stranger in my own home."

Significantly, Jesus and the New Testament writers placed incredible emphasis on loving the stranger. In Matthew 25 we find these words: "Come, you that are blessed by my Father, inherit the kingdom prepared for you from the foundation of the world; for…I was a stranger and you welcomed me" (verses 34, 35). We find similar emphasis in the letter to the Hebrews, where the author encourages his readers: "Do not neglect to show hospitality to strangers, for by doing that some have entertained angels without knowing it" (Heb 13:2). Not only are we encouraged to make strangers in our midst feel at home, but we are also reminded that Jesus and the kingdom of heaven come closer when we do.

Clearly, if we are going to live as Christ-followers, reaching out to the stranger has to take a more prominent place in our lives. It is a basic ingredient of the genuinely loving life and a gospel spirituality. Realizing the immense human and spiritual value of such an action is the first step in moving us toward the stranger in our midst. As I write these words I realize that I have become deeply conscious that I have never in thirty years of preaching spoken on this theme, nor have I ever heard someone challenging me to become more aware of those strangers that cross our paths each day.

The second step is to actually look out and see the stranger. This may sound quite simple, but it is not as easy as it sounds. In order to notice the stranger, we must be aware enough to look beyond ourselves. Our eyes must be opened so that we are not always thinking of ourselves and our circle, our clique, our reactions, our desires. Frequently when we are in a group we gravitate to our own friends and start talking about the latest thing of common interest to our circle. How seldom do we pause and look around and say to ourselves, "I wonder if there is someone here who is new or lonely, a person who needs me to take an interest in him or her."

Sadly, this sometimes happens in churches, especially large churches. When Morton and his wife first began to work in the cathedral in Phoenix, Arizona, they tried an experiment. Barbara did not tell anyone that she was Morton's wife. She quietly attended the early service every Sunday morning. It was two months before anyone spoke to her, a stranger. In many churches the gospel statement "Many are called, but few are chosen," could well be parodied, "Many are cold, but few are frozen." Sometimes one can be more warmly welcomed at the local pub than the local congregation!

The third step is to start reaching out to the stranger. This may be difficult for those of us who tend to be more introverted. However, there are three simple questions that will help conversation to flow. Where are you from? What brings you here? Do you have any family? Asking such questions after we have introduced ourselves can help to unlock conversation. People nearly always like to talk about home. When asked why they are here, they get an opportunity to talk about their lives at whatever depth they choose. And if they are separated from family and loved ones, they often relish the opportunity to tell us about them. These three questions can lead into a dozen others, and before very long we are no longer strangers.

Finally, this reaching out to the stranger must be backed up with action. We could invite them around to our homes for a meal. We could have coffee together. We could introduce them to some friends of ours who have a common interest. We could ask them to come to a church group. It is important that we are not too pushy and that we do not promise more than we can deliver. Reaching all the strangers who need our care requires more than individual effort. It also demands in most churches some structure. When my wife and I worked in a city-center congregation, Debbie was part of the hospitality ministry. Every Sunday this group would consciously be on the lookout for newcomers, show interest in them and try to provide practical care.

Won't you try this week to become aware of the stranger in your midst? She or he may be a recently appointed colleague at your place of work; the person sitting next to you at church; the neighbor who has moved in down the street; the new member of your sports club. Risk taking the initiative. Reach out with an extended hand or word of greeting. If it seems appropriate, ask the three suggested questions and see where the conversation leads. Remind yourself that making strangers feel at home is another part of the complex picture of Christian love. And you may find yourselves entertaining angels without knowing it!

DAILY MEDITATION TEXTS FOR THE WEEK

Day 1   "Do not neglect to show hospitality to strangers, for by doing that some have entertained angels without knowing it." (Heb 13:2)

Day 2   "Whoever welcomes one such child in my name welcomes me, and whoever welcomes me welcomes not me but the one who sent me." (Mark 9:37)

Day 3   "I was a stranger and you welcomed me." (Matt 25:35)

Day 4   "See that none of you repays evil for evil, but always seek to do good to one another and to all." (1 Thess 5:15)

Day 5   "And a harvest of righteousness is sown in peace for those who make peace." (Jas 3:18)

Day 6   "Be at peace among yourselves." (1 Thess 5:13)

Day 7   "And this is love, that we walk according to his commandments; this is the commandment just as you have heard it from the beginning—you must walk in it." (2 John 6)

SUGGESTION FOR JOURNALING

Remember one past experience when you were a stranger, and describe what it was like.

QUOTE FOR THE WEEK

Into this world, this demented inn, in which there is absolutely no room for him at all, Christ has come uninvited. But because he cannot be at home in it, because he is out of place in it, and yet he must be in it, his place is with those others for whom there is no room.

His place is with those who do not belong, who are rejected by power because they are regarded as weak, those who are discredited, who are denied the status of persons, tortured, excommunicated. With those for whom there is no room, Christ is present in this world.

Thomas Merton

PRAYER

Lord, bring into my life this week someone who is on the outside, whom I can welcome in your name. Amen.

Deepening Our Capacity
for Loving Our Enemies

When we begin to get to know the Jesus of the gospels it isn't long before we are struck by his emphasis on loving enemies. Not only did he teach this aspect of love, he also demonstrated it in his own life and called his followers to do the same. Surely this must be one of the most difficult challenges of the spiritual way. It seems almost absurd to try to love those who have hurt us or someone that we love, and those who belittle us, damage us or say evil things about us. And yet, if we really want to go the way of love, the way of Christ, we need to face this challenge and work out what it means in real life.

One popular way of side-stepping this tough challenge is to maintain that we can love people without necessarily liking them. This is an often-used cliché in Christian circles. I have never found it convincing. I find it difficult to believe that loving without liking can be love at all. I certainly would not want to be loved by someone who didn't like me. If we want to love the way Christ loved, then our loving and liking need to come closer together. This does not mean approving of everything people do. But we still need to learn genuinely how to "love-like" those whom we consider to be enemies.

How can we move toward this seemingly impossible goal of enemy love? First of all, we have to recognize that we do have enemies. Sometimes we don't want to admit this about ourselves. We want to think that we really love everyone and that everyone loves us. This is highly unlikely. Most of us have people in our lives whom we don't like or who don't like us. Sometimes these enemies pop up right in our family circle. There is a delightful quip that one reason why children and grandparents get along so well is that they have a common enemy!

The second step toward enemy love is to stop doing anything that is unkind to the person we don't like. Letting out our animosity in spiteful actions can never increase our love for our enemy. Yet this is a very common reaction. If our spouse complains about something we have done, then we find some sensitive spot in his or her life and get our own back. If the neighbor sweeps the leaves over into our yard, we'll find some way of retaliation. If colleagues hurt us, we either try to hurt them in return or else we have nothing more to do with them. Active retaliation usually carries deeper undertones of hostility and hatred. Hence this needs to be stopped if we are going to make any progress in trying to love our enemies.

Third, we must stop our gossip. Few of us find this easy. At times the tongue seems to have a life all its own. Especially when someone we don't like, or who has hurt us, is under discussion. And then before we know it, we hear ourselves adding another juicy morsel to the conversation. Such gossip is usually an expression of our own maliciousness, arrogance and pride. It certainly pushes us away from our goal of loving others. Indeed, I have come to realize that there can be no real growth toward becoming a loving person until we control our tendencies to gossip and stop talking maliciously behind people's backs.

I know of only two valid reasons for saying something unkind or critical about another person. In the first case, in order for us to find healing from some hurts, there are times when it is entirely appropriate to share them, even if this means naming particular people. Such sharing may happen with a confidential friend, a family member, a counselor or in a relevant professional setting. The other reason is when we believe that the actions of certain people will bring harm to others and themselves. In this case, we would do well to follow the detailed instructions given by Jesus in Matthew 18 starting at verse 15.

The fourth step concerns praying for our enemies. This kind of prayer works in two ways. First, it discourages us from saying or doing anything nasty to those we dislike. It would be sheer hypocrisy for us to pray, "Lord, please bless John, while I fix him here below." And second, there is real power in prayer. As we pray for the person we dislike, real changes often begin to occur in our relationship and attitude. Morton remembers praying for a woman who he found very unpleasant and almost impossible to like. After holding her in daily prayer for three weeks, he received a phone call from her. She wanted an appointment. When she came into his office she flopped down in a chair and began to cry. She said she realized what a difficult person she was, but that she wanted those at the church to know how much she appreciated them. At that moment Morton realized that she suffered as much being the person she was as he did being himself. They became good friends, and he realized again the truth that everyone carries a heavy burden.

The fifth step is to examine the life of the person we dislike and find something that we can genuinely appreciate. I have discovered that with some effort I can find something admirable in everyone. With some people it does take a little longer, though. But there are redeeming qualities in all people. And then, when the opportunity comes, we can make known the positive quality we have seen. The effects of this action can be quite startling. Try it for yourself. If you find yourself in a group where the tongues are wagging about a particular person, just throw in your positive tidbit and see what happens. Often the atmosphere changes and the conversation takes on a whole new direction.

The last step is to do something kind for the person who is difficult to love; something that will make him or her happy. We can watch them, see what would bring them joy and then perform the action. Our gift may be a small act of thoughtfulness, like baking a cake, or something that requires greater effort. It makes little difference as long as our action brings joy to them. They don't even need to know that we had anything to do with it. The effect on ourselves of doing this is often quite miraculous. We find out that it is very difficult, if not impossible, to dislike those whom we have made happy. This is a deep psychological and spiritual law. If we try it, we may well find that our specific dislike can turn toward love.

Deepening our capacity for enemy love is a journey. I hope that the six suggestions given above will help you find a place to start. As we embark on this adventure, we will begin to realize more and more fully the importance and power of love and our need for it. Someone once asked Morton what happens when we have dealt with all the enemies in our lives. He replied that we don't need to worry. God loves us so much and is so interested in our growth that in his infinite mercy and love, he will always provide us with a few more!

DAILY MEDITATION TEXTS FOR THE WEEK

Day 1   "But I say to you, Love your enemies and pray for those who persecute you, so that you may be children of your Father in heaven." (Matt 5:44–45)

Day 2   "If another member of the church sins against you, go and point out the fault when the two of you are alone." (Matt 18:15)

Day 3   "Do not rejoice when your enemies fall, and do not let your heart be glad when they stumble." (Prov 24:17)

Day 4   "If your enemies are hungry, give them bread to eat; and if they are thirsty, give them water to drink." (Prov 25:21)

Day 5   "But love your enemies, do good, and lend, expecting nothing in return. Your reward will be great, and you will be children of the Most High; for he is kind to the ungrateful and the wicked." (Luke 6:35)

Day 6   "You prepare a table before me in the presence of my enemies; you anoint my head with oil; my cup over-flows." (Ps 23:5)

Day 7   "For if while we were enemies, we were reconciled to God through the death of his Son, much more surely, having been reconciled, will we be saved by his life." (Rom 5:10)

SUGGESTION FOR JOURNALING

Write out a prayer of blessing for someone whom you do not like.

QUOTE FOR THE WEEK

We become what we hate. The very act of hating something drains it to us. Since our hate is usually a direct response to an evil done to us, our hate almost invariably causes us to respond in the terms already laid down by the enemy. Unaware of what is happening, we turn into the very thing we oppose.

Walter Wink
Engaging the Powers

PRAYER

Dear Lord, your challenge to love my enemies seems almost impossible. I cannot do this without your help and power. Please fill my life with your love that I may be able to respond to those who have hurt me in your spirit. I ask this so that your light may shine through me. Amen.

Living Out Our Little Piece of God's Dream

A few days ago a child just a few hours old was found in a city dustbin. Like scores of other babies who are thrown away in Johannesburg each year, this little baby had been thrown away like unwanted trash and left to die. Those who found her phoned the local newspaper and the story was reported the next day. The photograph of the tiny, pink child lying next to a dustbin triggered the compassion of Johan de Villiers, a retired Christian businessman. He and a group of friends decided to show their respect for the abandoned child by organizing a funeral in their church. At the service they named her Elizabeth Precious because, as Johan put it, "every human being has a soul and is therefore precious to God."

This little group of compassionate disciples also tried to reach out to the mother. In a newspaper interview their spokesperson said, "We also pray for the mother. We do not judge her because we do not know whether she was forced into the act, maybe by the father or by other family members. We just pray that she will also feel compassion enough to be able to confess that what she did was wrong and realize that she can be forgiven."

This story challenges me. These concerned Christ-followers put into practice what God calls each one of us to do. When we read the gospels we see that God loves every human being through and through, no matter who they are or what they have done. In the vision of the kingdom of heaven that Jesus brought, each person has a special place in the Divine Heart. God's dream for our world is that every human being will come to know this. As Jesus' disciples, we are called in some specific way to make this vision come true. We do this by helping those to whom we are drawn to realize that God loves them. This is how we can flesh out the astonishing gospel affirmation that all persons have infinite worth and value.

Jesus repeatedly shared this dream with people around him. On one occasion he drew a comparison between people and the birds of the air: "Are not five sparrows sold for two pennies? Yet not one of them is forgotten in God's sight. But even the hairs of your head are all counted. Do not be afraid; you are of more value than many sparrows" (Luke 12:6–7). Imagine the powerful impact these words must have had on the lives of those who listened to him. Without a shadow of doubt they would have known that their lives mattered to Jesus and to the one of whom he spoke.

Jesus also lived out God's dream. Whether it was hugging a little child nagging for attention, touching an outcast leper living on the margins of society, visiting the home of a politically ostracized tax collector, hearing the cry of a blind beggar at the roadside, or affirming a used and abused woman, Jesus acted toward individuals with immeasurable respect and care. His actions enabled each one of them to realize that he or she mattered and was now acceptable to God. Picture the joy and delight!

It is not easy to really live with this gospel truth. I think it was G. K. Chesterton who wrote that the hardest part of the Christian faith to bear was the value it places on the individual. Nonetheless, it is a truth that continues to challenge us. We live in a world filled with suffering neighbors, many of whom have lost all sense of value and worth. How can they ever hear the good news about God's personal love for them unless someone shows it to them? This is the urgent task that has been entrusted to you and me. When we rise to the challenge we keep God's dream alive in our broken and shattered societies.

But where do we begin? Obviously one cannot reach out to all the human need and misery in our midst. We cannot call on all the shut-in elderly, care for all the destitute, get alongside all the sick and bereaved and dying. We cannot minister to all the poor, empower all the homeless, educate all the illiterate, visit all the prisoners. But we can ask God, "Lord, who is part of my particular bundle? Which human cry has my name written on it?" This is what Johan de Villiers did. This is what we must do. Such questions, when accompanied by persistent prayer and purposeful action, carry forward God's dream in our midst.

Usually when we discern the part we need to play in God's dream, we also discover that we cannot do it alone. Then we need to share the concern we feel among those with whom we worship. Others may feel a similar call and decide to join us in a particular ministry. Or we might decide to join an organization or group that is already involved in the area to which we feel drawn. Indeed, one of the most important challenges facing local congregations today is to establish groups who wish to minister to the hungry, call on the sick, follow up the bereaved, befriend the lonely and reach out to those who are hurting. A Christian church that does this becomes a little microcosm of the kingdom of heaven.

One of the best examples of this kind of congregation is the Church of the Saviour in Washington, D.C. Presently it has been restructured into several small congregations, each of which is organized around some specific form of ministry. Every member belongs to what is called a mission group. These mission groups range in purpose from ministering to the addicted, caring for abandoned children, providing shelter for the homeless to running a coffee shop that provides hospitality and friendship in the inner city. In their different ways, members of this remarkable church are reminding their suffering neighbors that they are precious to God. By so doing they are living out God's dream in their community.

Each one of us is called to bring God's love to others through prayer and practical action. As you reflect on the following questions they may provide you with some clues regarding the shape of your own particular calling:

♦ What "human cry" in your community disturbs you the most?
♦ What do you feel most concerned about at the moment?
♦ What people or issues do you find yourself most interested in or drawn to?
♦ What are your own particular gifts and how can they be used to demonstrate God's love?
♦ When you look around your community, what makes you angry?

Stay close to these questions this coming week. Let them get inside you at odd moments during the next days. It could just happen that you discover how to live out a little piece of God's dream where you are.

DAILY MEDITATION TEXTS FOR THE WEEK

Day 1   "Are not five sparrows sold for two pennies? Yet not one of them is forgotten in God's sight. But even the hairs of your head are all counted. Do not be afraid; you are of more value than many sparrows." (Luke 12:6–7)

Day 2   "All this is from God, who reconciled us to himself through Christ, and has given us the ministry and reconciliation..." (2 Cor 5:18)

Day 3   "The spirit of the Lord God is upon me, because the Lord has anointed me; he has sent me to bring good news to the oppressed, to bind up the brokenhearted, to proclaim liberty to the captives, and release to the prisoners..." (Isa 61:1)

Day 4   "Comfort, O comfort my people, says your God." (Isa 40:1).

Day 5   "And the king will answer them, 'Truly I tell you, just as you did it to one of the least of these who are members of my family, you did it to me.'" (Matt 25:40)

Day 6   "Praise be to the God and Father of our Lord Jesus Christ, the Father of compassion and the God of all comfort, who comforts us in all our troubles, so that we can comfort those in any trouble with the comfort we ourselves have received from God." (2 Cor 1:3–4, NIV)

Day 7   "Religion that is pure and undefiled before God, the Father, is this: to care for orphans and widows in their distress, and to keep oneself unstained by the world." (Jas 1:27)

SUGGESTION FOR JOURNALING

Write out your reflections on one of the five questions outlined in this week's meditation.

QUOTE FOR THE WEEK

Each one of us has something beautiful to do for God.
Mother Teresa

PRAYER

God has created me to do him
some definite service.
He has committed some work
to me which he has not
committed to another.
I have my mission.
I may never know it in this life
but I shall be told it in the next.

I am a link in a chain,
a bond of connection between persons.
He has not created me for naught
I shall do good—I shall do his work
I shall be an angel of peace
A preacher of truth in my own place
While not intending it
If I do but keep his commandments.

John Henry Newman

Experiencing the Invincible
Power of Love

Morton tells a profound story about how the invincible power of love healed his relationship with his youngest son, John. At the age of eleven his son was still struggling to read. One day, Morton was called to the school and found himself in the unusual position of sitting on the other side of the table with a psychologist asking him, "Do you have any idea what your child's problem is?" He replied that he didn't know of any reason other than stubbornness and obstinacy. Then the counselor dropped the bombshell. "The problem with your child is that he doesn't think that you really care for him or love him."

Morton protested vigorously. He tried to explain that whenever he attempted to show love, his son pushed him away. The psychologist was not impressed by this explanation. After listening for a while, he continued, "Has it ever occurred to you why he pushes you away? He is testing you to see how much you really do love him."

"At eleven years of age?" Morton asked.

"Even at eleven," replied the psychologist.

Morton made a decision at that moment that he would show John how much he loved him, even if it killed him. Even though Morton acknowledges that he has the manual dexterity of a palsied hippopotamus, he and his son began to do things together, like woodworking and horseback riding. The real turnaround, however, came one day at a motel on the oceanfront at Laguna

Beach. Morton came into John's room one morning and asked if he wanted to go swimming.

"Nah…I'd rather watch television," was the reply he got, in the way that only an eleven year old could say it.

In the past when Morton got this kind of response he would leave feeling rejected. He would then go and do something he would have preferred to do anyway. This time he responded differently. In a playful manner he went over to the TV set and turned it off. His son turned it on. This happened several times until they began to tussle together lightheartedly. They wrestled around the room, out the door, down the stairs, across the sand and finally into the ocean.

There the first miracle took place. As they came out of the first wave, John blew the water from his nose and exclaimed, "Father, I wondered how long it would take you to do this." The psychologist had been right. His son did want his attention. They had a wonderful weekend together. Within six months John's school results had improved. He began to learn to read. However, their new journey together had only just begun.

There were still moments of struggle. One day, when John was nineteen, they were sitting together beside a pool in Arizona. Out of the blue and quite deliberately John spoke to his dad, "Father, you know, I haven't always liked you very much." It wasn't what Morton wanted to hear, but he remembered that he had decided that he was going to try to show love. He replied, "John, I don't blame you. There are many times when I struggle to like myself as well."

Some years later John joined his father at a conference that Morton was giving in Ojai, a hundred miles north of Los Angeles. As part of his lecture Morton decided to tell the story of the miracle that had taken place at Laguna Beach. Afterward, John didn't comment at all. The next morning they both got up early. They were breakfasting when John suddenly initiated the conversation, "Father, did I actually say that at Laguna Beach?"

Morton nodded. His son went on, "Father, I know exactly when I made up my mind never to ask you for anything again in my life."

"When was that?" Morton asked.

"I was seven years old. You had been reading *Tales of Sherlock Holmes* to my brother and me. He went away, but I wanted you to read aloud to me anyway. So I brought the book to you and asked you to read. You said that you were too busy. I brought the book the next night, and you said that you were too busy. The same thing happened on the third night, and I consciously made up my mind never to ask you for anything again in my life."

It was hard for Morton to hear this. His refusal to read the story had struck his son as effectively as if he had wielded a club. Nevertheless, he learned that patient love could even make the desert burst into bloom. Slowly, a deep relationship began to develop between the two of them. Soon, John would minister to his father with as much love, sensitivity and concern that Morton had felt from the finest of counselors.

It happened in January 1981 when Barbara was seriously injured in a dockyard incident. She was sent to a Los Angeles hospital not far from where her son lived. John invited Morton to come and stay with him so that he would be able to visit Barbara regularly. For four months they lived together while Barbara underwent treatment. They spent hours talking. They did the washing-up together. They cooked together. And they became good friends. When the time came for Morton and Barbara to return home, John gave his father a card. On the front were two iguanas facing each other. One was crying. Inside were the printed words, "Iguana miss you." Underneath them his son had written, "It seems strange how we were forced together. You have become my best friend. I love you more than I can say. If you need my help with Mom, you know that I am here."

Their friendship continued to grow. Over time John was able to share some of his deepest hurts. A large part of this pain was caused by his father's absence when he was a child. One day as they walked together through the redwood forests he was able to tell his father just how much he had missed him. The hurt of the fatherless child in John flooded out. Morton could only be silent and listen. That night they dined out together at a special restaurant. It was like having a banquet. The final barrier had come down.

A few years later when John was living in Hawaii, Morton received a call from him. John had come down with an incurable form of encephalitis. He was beginning to be paralyzed and was suffering from repeated blackouts. Each blackout could have been the end. After canceling all their work engagements, Morton and Barbara left immediately. Day and night they took turns to be with him. One day as they sat together, Morton again asked for forgiveness for not having known how to be the caring father his son needed as a child. John replied, "Father, what you are doing now makes up for anything that you didn't do at any other time."

For four months they lived together. During this time Morton and Barbara watched the slow physical and mental disintegration of a handsome and sensitive young man. One morning Morton was sitting by John's bedside when some powerful words flowed into Morton. He wrote the words down. Two days later Morton read the words to John who asked for a copy of the words. When he received it he shared it with a close friend. She later told Barbara that when John read the words to her, he said, "My father understands how I feel."

John eventually died. Wonderfully, however, God had restored the years which the locust had eaten. Such is the invincible power of love. When we step into the stream of real agape-love, the kind that Jesus revealed, we step into the world of God's lifegiving healing. Miracles of the Spirit begin to take place. Our lives and relationships are gifted with transformation and newness. This is what happened for Morton when he made a decision to love. This is what can happen also for you and me if we make the same decision. The choice is ours.

DAILY MEDITATION TEXTS FOR THE WEEK

Day 1   "The only thing that counts is faith working through love." (Gal 5:6)

Day 2   "Little children, let us love, not in word or speech, but in truth and action." (1 John 3:18)

Day 3   "Do not let loyalty and faithfulness forsake you; bind them around your neck, write them on the tablet of your heart." (Prov 3:3)

Day 4   "Love one another with mutual affection; outdo one another in showing honor." (Rom 12:10)

Day 5   "For God did not give us a spirit of cowardice, but rather a spirit of power and of love and of self-discipline." (2 Tim 1:7)

Day 6   "Therefore be imitators of God, as beloved children, and live in love, as Christ loved us and gave himself up for us, a fragrant offering and sacrifice to God." (Eph 5:1–2)

Day 7   "And now faith, hope, and love abide, these three; and the greatest of these is love." (1 Cor 13:13)

SUGGESTION FOR JOURNALING

Write out what you think and feel God may be saying to you through this week's meditation.

QUOTE FOR THE WEEK

There is no greater need than to love and be loved. This need touches the deepest level of the human heart. And the need to love may be deeper and more central than the need to be loved.
Morton Kelsey
Caring

PRAYER

Dear God, strengthen me with power to love through your Spirit in my inner being. Fill my heart with your presence and please do not leave me. Help me to grasp how wide and long and high and deep your love is for me. And, above all, enable me to know this love that surpasses all knowledge so that I may share it with others. Amen.
Based on Ephesians 3:14–21

Spiritual Living in a Material World

WEEK 21

Breaking Free from the Grasshopper Complex

There is a common affliction around today that robs many of us of our power to deal with life. This disease could be understood as both spiritual and psychological. One way of describing it would be to call it the "grasshopper complex." Those who struggle with this inferiority complex often feel that they are worthless. And as a result they don't get what they could out of life. Perhaps you struggle with this affliction yourself. If so, I hope that God will use this week's meditation to bring a greater freedom and zestfulness into your life.

Before continuing, let me explain the biblical origin of the term *grasshopper complex*. This will help us understand the nature of this sickness. It comes from a story in the little-read but very instructive Old Testament book of Numbers. The children of Israel had finally escaped from Egypt. You may remember how they had groaned under the yoke of their oppression and what amazing signs and wonders God had to work through Moses before pharaoh would let them go. Finally, however, he did release them.

After three years of desert wanderings, years full of amazing evidence of God's favor, the children of Israel eventually arrived at the borders of the Promised Land. There Moses chose one man from each of the twelve tribes and sent them into Canaan to spy out the land. They scouted the country for forty days before returning to Moses. In their report-back they all agreed that it was a wonderful land, overflowing with milk and honey.

Two of the twelve, Caleb and Joshua, wanted to occupy the territory immediately. But the others protested vehemently. They had seen giants in the land and were terrified. Furthermore, they said, "…to ourselves we seemed like grasshoppers, and so we seemed to them" (Num 13:33).

"To ourselves we seemed like grasshoppers"—what a sad and tragic admission. These people lacked any sort of self-confidence. Nor did they have a vision of what they could accomplish with God by their side. They had lost the capacity to see the future through the eyes of faith. They were still struggling with the slave mentality of Egypt and had forgotten what God had done for them on the way. Tragically, the way we see ourselves usually determines what we become. And so, because they seemed to themselves like grasshoppers, it manifested in their behavior.

The consequences were disastrous. God was so upset that Moses had to intercede on behalf of the people. It was clear that they were not ready. Because of their grasshopper complex, the whole nation was doomed to wander around for a further forty years until everybody who shared this attitude to life had perished. No one with such a negative self-image can enter into God's Promised Land. The grasshopper syndrome robs us of the real and vital potential of life.

There are striking parallels in our own lives. When we think ill about ourselves, we effectively keep good things from happening to us. In fact, it may be more dangerous to think of ourselves as grasshoppers than to have too high an opinion of ourselves. It is a strange fact that those who truly realize how amazing and mysterious we humans are seldom become inflated or proud. Rather, they tend to become quite humble and awed at being so fearfully and wonderfully made. Life so often whittles down people who overvalue and exalt themselves. But the person with the grasshopper complex simply misses out on life's possibilities.

"Well then," you may be asking, "how does one break the power of the grasshopper complex?" We can begin by realizing that no human being is like a grasshopper. Ponder again the Genesis account of our beginnings. We are made in God's image and are endued with God's breath. As such, we have unlimited potential. God entered into this world and became a human being. He became like us so that we can become like him. And Jesus Christ was certainly no grasshopper! Can you see that when we see ourselves as grasshoppers, we demean not only ourselves but also God and the whole human race?

Another way to defeat the grasshopper complex is to have a real friend. This requires a great deal of courage. But I know from personal experience that when we make the effort and let another person into our life, he or she will find in us hidden depths that we never thought existed. And when we make these discoveries, we begin to see ourselves differently. We discover a life for ourselves that stretches way beyond the existence of a grasshopper: a life of significance and meaning; a life where we make a difference; a life with color, texture and depth. In fact, this is my own testimony when I consider the healing that has come to me through the sacrament of friendship.

Finally, we can let God's love into our lives. Remember a similar meditation that we did along these lines some weeks ago? Someone is knocking persistently on the doorway of our soul. He will not force his way in. If we open the door, we will find the risen Christ there. His one hand is raised to knock. In the other there is a lighted lantern. When we allow him to enter our lives he embraces us with his crucified hands. He tells us that we are loved with a love that will never let us go. In fact, there is nothing in all of creation that can separate us from this divine love. When we receive this assurance in our hearts, we know that we are not like grasshoppers.

You and I can be liberated from the grasshopper complex. Perhaps this week we will take another step on our journey toward freedom. And then, as we experience greater release, we can try to enable others also to break free from this dreadful affliction. There are few greater services we can do for those around us. In fact, the best thing about the grasshopper complex is that no one needs to remain imprisoned by it. Through our loving concern, being friends and sharing our experience of the risen Christ, each of us can help someone else to become free of it.

DAILY MEDITATION TEXTS FOR THE WEEK

Day 1   "O Lord, our Sovereign, how majestic is your name in all the earth! You have set your glory above the heavens." (Ps 8:1)

Day 2   "Out of the mouths of babes and infants you have founded a bulwark because of your foes, to silence the enemy and the avenger." (Ps 8:2)

Day 3   "When I look at your heavens, the work of your fingers, the moon and the stars that you have established; what are human beings that you are mindful of them, mortals that you care for them?" (Ps 8:3–4)

Day 4   "Yet you have made them a little lower than God, and crowned them with glory and honor." (Ps 8:5)

Day 5   "You have given them dominion over the works of your hands; you have put all things under their feet, all sheep and oxen, and also the beasts of the field, the birds of the air, and the fish of the sea, whatever passes along the paths of the seas." (Ps 8:6–8)

Day 6   "Then God said, 'Let us make humankind in our image, according to our likeness; and let them have dominion over the fish of the sea, and over the birds of the air, and over the cattle, and over all the wild animals of the earth, and over every creeping thing that creeps upon the earth.'" (Gen 1:26)

Day 7   "So God created humankind in his image, in the image of God he created them, male and female he created them." (Gen 1:27)

SUGGESTION FOR JOURNALING

Describe one way in which you would like the glory of God to shine through your life.

QUOTE

Our deepest fear is not that we are inadequate. Our deepest fear is that we are powerful beyond measure. It is our light not our darkness that most frightens us. We ask ourselves: Who am I to be brilliant, gorgeous, talented and fabulous?

Actually, who are you NOT to be? You are a child of God. Your playing small doesn't save the world. There's nothing enlightened about shrinking so that other people won't feel insecure around you. We were born to make manifest the glory of God that is within us. It's not just in some of us, it's in EVERYONE.

And as we let our own light shine, we unconsciously give other people permission to do the same. As we are liberated from our own fear, our presence automatically liberates others.

Source unknown

PRAYER

Dear God, may I have the same delight
about my own life that you have for it.
For Jesus' sake,
Amen.

Removing the Logs
from Our Own Eye

One pastoral encounter from the mid-eighties stands out vividly for me. At that time South Africa was in a state of emergency. The townships were burning. Relationships between the different racial groupings had sunk to an all-time low. Feelings were running high. Against this dark background, I remember preaching about the need for those of us who lived in the relative security of the suburbs to stay connected in some way with township dwellers. The day after I received a visit from an irate congregation member. He was very upset by what I had said. He was also angry about the increasing spiral of violence in the townships. "Look at how these people hurt their own," he said angrily. "I want nothing to do with them."

Some months later this man's wife asked to see me. The marriage was in crisis and she wanted to talk about it. We got together in my office. In a trembling voice she poured out the story of their relationship. It was a painful story of vicious abuse, violence, betrayal and deceit. As she spoke, I remembered her husband's remark about township people: "Look at how these people hurt their own." He condemned in others precisely that which he did not want to acknowledge in himself.

We must be careful not to judge this man too harshly. We all tend to judge others for faults that we find in ourselves. Just the other day I reprimanded my teenage son for leaving his homework to the last minute. As I walked away, I realized that I also tend to procrastinate, especially when it comes to things that I don't enjoy doing, such as completing tax returns, taking out the garbage, and arranging important meetings. Here I was, picking on my son for something that is alive and well in my own life. Perhaps you may like to pause a while and think of times when you do this as well.

Jesus addressed this tendency to judge with a striking word picture. He told his followers not to try to remove the speck from their neighbor's eye while there was a log in their own. We must first take the log out of our own eye; then we would be able to see the speck in the other's eye more clearly (see Matt 7:3–5). This image takes on greater significance when we keep in mind Jesus' symbolic use of the word *eye*. Whenever he talks about the eye, he is referring to our inward capacity to discern, our ability to be aware, to understand life and to see it in true perspective. Jesus also said the following words:

> *The eye is the lamp of the body. So, if your eye is healthy, your whole body will be full of light; but if your eye is unhealthy, your whole body will be full of darkness. (Matt 6:22–23)*

We need to reflect on these two gospel statements together. When we fail to remove the logs from our own eye, our eyesight is damaged. Darkness begins to fill us. We become critical, gossipy and judgmental. Our relationships get snarled up in misunderstanding and argument. Seeds of strife start to grow in our hearts. On the other hand, when we begin to get rid of our inner logs, light enters our lives. We get along more easily with others. We stop focusing on other people's problems. We realize our first task is to acknowledge our own logs, face them honestly and try to remove them. If we don't do this, we know that the light within us will grow dim.

We all have a great many logs sticking out of our eyes. As we get rid of one, we often find another and another and yet another. In fact, this can be very discouraging. But I assure you that once we dislodge our own logs, we will smile at our attempts to pick the specks of sawdust out of the eyes of others. They may well have their own logs, but these are generally so well hidden that we don't see them. We seldom see other people's real problems. And once we begin to tackle our own, we realize that we have plenty to do to ensure that our inner eye stays filled with light. We realize that we have no business worrying about anyone else's quirks and foibles. When we come to this point, we move beyond judging or criticizing or gossiping. It just doesn't make any sense at all to do so.

It's also not very pleasant to look at our own logs. Indeed, it can be quite painful. Perhaps this is one reason why we try to forget them by going about searching for specks in the eyes of others. And in whom do we see these specks that must be picked out right away? Well, it is often in those closest to us: our children, our husbands or wives, our parents or in-laws, our brothers and sisters. Or it could be in someone on the other side of the political fence, in our bosses or our employees, or in someone from a different racial group or nationality. It is a popular game today—speck, speck, let's find the speck.

There is only one way to stop the game. It is Jesus' way. We have to stop, take an honest look at ourselves and see what our own problems are. What are the logs in us that threaten to damage our eyes and leave us in darkness? Is there a log of anger or bad temper? Is the biggest one lust or greed? Is it laziness? Or is it too much business? Is it pride, envy or deceit? Or is it perhaps prejudice, racism or hatred?

Let me end with some good news. When we stop to acknowledge our own logs, something beautiful begins to happen in us. In the first place, we become far more forgiving and understanding. Somehow, being more aware of our own problems makes us gentler with the struggles that others may have. Second, the living God becomes a deeper reality in our own lives. When we look at all the logs we need to remove, we find ourselves calling out to God from the very depths of our being. We realize that we are not able to change ourselves on our own. We desperately need the grace and mercy and power of God. And wonderfully, these are precisely the gifts that come to us when we place our logs before the risen Lord. May this be your experience this coming week.

DAILY MEDITATION TEXTS FOR THE WEEK

Day 1   "Why do you see the speck in your neighbor's eye, but do not notice the log in your own eye? Or how can you say to your neighbor, 'Let me take the speck out of your eye,' while the log is in your own eye? You hypocrite, first take the log out of your own eye, and then you will see clearly to take the speck out of your neighbor's eye." (Matt 7:3–5)

Day 2   "The eye is the lamp of the body. So if your eye is healthy, your whole body will be full of light; but if your eye is unhealthy, your whole body will be full of darkness. If then the light in you is darkness, how great is the darkness!" (Matt 6:22–23)

Day 3   "Indeed, God did not send the Son into the world to condemn the world, but in order that the world might be saved through him." (John 3 :17)

Day 4   "But if we judged ourselves, we would not be judged." (1 Cor 11:31)

Day 5   "Search me, O God, and know my heart; test me and know my thoughts." (Ps 139:23)

Day 6   "Therefore do not pronounce judgment before the time, before the Lord comes, who will bring to light the things now hidden in darkness and will disclose the purposes of the heart. Then each one will receive commendation from God." (1 Cor 4:5)

Day 7   "Not many of you should become teachers, my brothers and sisters, for you know that we who teach will be judged with greater strictness." (Jas 3:1)

SUGGESTION FOR JOURNALING

Make a note of the people you cannot stand. Write down the things that you intensely dislike about them—habits, beliefs, attitudes, behavior, traits, and so on. Consider that these may be splinters coming from logs in your own eyes.

QUOTE

Everybody thinks of changing humanity and nobody thinks of changing himself.

Leo Tolstoy

PRAYER

Lord, you said, "Let the person without sin cast the first stone." Show us our own sin and your mercy, so that we may always be gentle and never condemn others in our hearts. We ask this through Jesus Christ, our Lord.
Amen.

Gerard Hughes
Oh God, Why

Handling Our Difficult Feelings Creatively

As a Christ-follower, I sometimes struggle to live with some of my feelings, especially those that seem unchristian and foreign to the way of the gospel. I am thinking of feelings like dislike, hostility and hatred; feelings like envy, jealousy and competition; feelings like lust, desire and greed. Almost every day, emotions like these ambush me and mock my attempts to live as Jesus would have lived. For many years I chided myself for even having such feelings. Today, however, I have come to recognize them as part and parcel of being human. The challenge is not to eliminate them, but to learn how to deal with them creatively and constructively.

There seem to be three different ways of responding to these emotions. First of all, we can simply turn them loose. Though this option is generally frowned on by society, more and more of us seem to take it. And so we give vent to our bitter feelings with vengeful determination, not caring who gets hurt in the process. Or we pursue the object of our attraction and desire even though it may be someone else's husband or wife. Or we allow our envies and jealousies to spill out in harsh criticism and gossip. These things we cannot do, Jesus says, if we want to live as citizens of the kingdom of heaven. Besides, common sense tells us that there would be chaos if everyone were to give free reign to feelings like these.

Of course, it does not help us, either, to keep a lid on our feelings and then fantasize about them day and night. If we keep our hatreds or forbidden desires alive by mulling over them, the chances are that sooner or later we will give in and express them in action. Our imaginations are more powerful than we think. What we desire and contemplate with enough imaginative fire often has a way of happening.

Now we can see why Jesus insisted that the only safe object to pursue wholeheartedly in contemplation is God. God alone is the center of wholeness and reality. Everything else is only partial, and total devotion to anything partial leads to trouble. When we give way to our feelings, we are generally giving way to the spirit of domination and power and self-centeredness. We then either take what that spirit wishes, or we dwell on its object, hoping to obtain it. Then it isn't long before our feelings begin to control us. Can you see why it is so dangerous always to yield to what we feel?

The second response toward these feelings is to deny them entirely. Christ-followers who follow this option simply refuse to acknowledge that they have any hostile or negative feelings. They say things like, "I love everyone I meet," "I never get angry," or "I don't hate anyone." Thinking this way can be dangerous for two reasons. On the one hand, when we refuse to acknowledge certain feelings, they hide in a corner of our hearts where they operate on their own, autonomously, and with no chance for our conscious personalities to control or direct them. They often build up in these hidden places of the soul, and then suddenly explode in uncharacteristic behavior and speech.

This happened to a church member whom I counseled. Brought up in a strict Christian home, she was taught from an early age to "always be nice." She explained to me how she had carried this instruction through into her adult years. Whenever she felt a twinge of spitefulness or hostility, she would push it away and pretend that it didn't exist. People around her would constantly speak of her as considerate, kind and gentle. But something happened one day that shocked her and made her seek counseling. Out of the blue she had smacked a work colleague across the face. She couldn't believe what she had done. As we spoke together, she came to recognize how she had stuffed down into the cellar of her life all kinds of hostile feelings. Now suddenly they exploded, reminding her that they were still an undeniable part of her.

Denying our feelings can be dangerous for another reason. Mental health professionals warn us that bottled-up emotions often turn against our bodies and begin to destroy them with psychosomatic illnesses. These insights point us toward the many destructive diseases that come about because of unresolved feelings like anger and resentment. The denial of feelings, it would seem, denies life itself.

So where do we go from here? No one can live without feelings, and no one can live creatively by letting feelings control his or her life. Is there a third alternative? Yes, there is. We can befriend our difficult feelings, confront them lovingly, place them honestly in God's presence and then decide what we are going to do with them. You may feel this is too difficult and time consuming. Besides, it can also be painful. But did Jesus ever say that the spiritual journey would be easy? Remember what he said to his followers on one occasion:

> *If any want to become my followers, let them deny themselves and take up their cross and follow me. (Matt 16:24)*

We don't have to go through the world looking for crosses. They are built into the very fabric of our being. Learning to live spiritually in a material world will always carry a certain cost. Seeking the way of the Spirit in our physical natures usually involves some kind of inner crucifixion. Let me try to explain. We are not expected to deny our physical natures. We must look at them with love, and at the same time control and bring their feelings into line with the purpose God has for them. This is the gospel way. It is not the way of indulging every whim or of denying our instinctual beings. Rather, this way stretches us out upon life as

Christ was stretched out on the cross. Out of this, the Spirit brings creativity and well-being and deep joy.

One practical way of going down this third route is to bring our feelings into our daily conversations with God, however unchristian or unloving they may be. We do this by first identifying and naming the feelings we have: "This is what I am feeling at the moment—my anger, my hostility, my lust, my envy.' Then we turn toward the Lord and express our feelings aloud to him: "Lord, today I am feeling..." Finally, we can reflect on these feelings with the risen Christ and ask him to show us how best to live with them. Building this honest sharing of feelings into our daily prayers has a wonderful way of channeling the energy within our feelings into creative action.

This is not an easy solution, which is why we will always need help. Thankfully, God offers the living Spirit of the risen Christ to all who ask. God wants to help us handle our feelings creatively. We cannot help what we feel. Our feelings are real. They happen to us, and this is beyond our control. But we can help what we do with them. And with Christ empowering and guiding us, we can discover that we are able to direct our feelings in a healthy way. In learning to do this, we share more fully in the eternal life which God has for each of us.

DAILY MEDITATION TEXTS FOR THE WEEK

Day 1   "Then Jesus told his disciples, 'If any want to become my followers, let them deny themselves and take up their cross and follow me.'" (Matt 16:24)

Day 2   "When you are disturbed, do not sin; ponder it on your beds, and be silent." (Ps 4:4)

Day 3   "Let us test and examine our ways, and return to the Lord." (Lam 3:40)

Day 4   "Those conflicts and disputes among you, where do they come from? Do they not come from your cravings that are at war within you?" (Jas 4:1)

Day 5   "And he said, 'It is what comes out of a person that defiles.'" (Mark 7:20)

Day 6   "For those who live according to the flesh set their minds on the things of the flesh, but those who live according to the Spirit set their minds on the things of the Spirit." (Rom 8:5)

Day 7   "But you are not in the flesh; you are in the Spirit, since the Spirit of God dwells in you. Anyone who does not have the Spirit of Christ does not belong to him." (Rom 8:9)

Suggestion for Journaling

Write out a prayer that brings one of your difficult feelings into God's presence.

Quote

> *Emotional maturity is not about becoming dispassionate but rather living in the fullness of my God-given humanity, discovering and owning my emotions and learning to express and share them appropriately.*
>
> Anne Long
> *Listening*

Prayer

> *Search me, O God, and know my heart;*
> *test me and know my thoughts.*
> *See if there is any wicked way in me*
> *and lead me in the way everlasting.*
>
> Psalm 139:23–24

WEEK 24

Keeping Hope Alive

I enjoy a good movie. One of the best I have seen is *The Shawshank Redemption*. It tells the story of a banker who was jailed for a crime he didn't commit. It describes vividly his struggle to keep hope alive in the midst of soul-crushing conditions. In spite of repeated humiliation, he refuses to give in to despair. In one moving scene he says to a fellow prisoner who has succumbed to hopelessness, "In this life you are either busy living or busy dying. The difference is hope."

I keep this sentence close to my heart. It's easy today to lose hope. Social evils that range from rampant crime and spiraling violence to the widening gap between haves and have-nots constantly threaten to tear our society apart. As we look around us, it sometimes feels as if we are living in the midst of a gathering darkness. Even in the microcosm of our personal lives, we can become down and discouraged. A stuck marriage, a struggling business, a grieving heart, a terminal illness, a wayward child—all these experiences, and others like them, can bring about a sense of paralyzing desperation. When this happens, we start running out of hope and our lives fall apart.

Yet we have to keep hope alive. It is one of the most important characteristics of our faith. It is central to some of the great passages of the New Testament. I think especially of the key place it has in Paul's magnificent thirteenth chapter of his letter to the Corinthians. He places the word right between two other vitally important cornerstones of real Christian faith. "And now," he writes, "faith, hope, and love abide..." (1 Cor 13:13). Hope must be very important to be wedged in between the famous twins, faith and love. And it really is! As a friend of mine constantly reminds me, "Where there is hope, there is life."

What, then, is hope? Hope is faith in action. Christ-followers lay claim to many hope-filled beliefs. We believe, for example, that we are unconditionally loved, accepted and forgiven. We believe that God has decisively defeated the forces of evil and death on the cross. We believe that God wants to help us overcome difficult situations. We believe that God is tirelessly seeking to bring light and life where there seems to be only darkness and death. Above all, we believe that God is always present with us. These convictions are part and parcel of the message that Jesus brought. Furthermore, they are backed up by his life, death and glorious resurrection. When they find expression in our daily lives we keep hope alive.

This can mean different things for different people. It can mean focusing on the ray of light in every situation rather than on the shadows. It can mean refusing to become paralyzed by worry and dread, or starting again after a disastrous failure. It can mean reaching out for a dream in spite of the odds against us, or working for those things that will make our lives happy and whole. Hope is ultimately more realistic than pessimism and worry. These attitudes seize on all the negative aspects of an event and magnify them. Hope does the opposite and knows that in the end, when all the chips are down, it will be justified.

Keeping hope alive is vital for a number of reasons. First of all, it makes us much happier. Worry and anxiety breed darkness, depression and unhappiness, even in the midst of fairly favorable circumstances. What psychosomatic medicine tells us about these two attitudes should make us want to avoid them like the plague. They slowly destroy the human body, with the digestive system, cardiovascular system and nervous system all going to pieces. Hope, on the other hand, brings light and strength, even in the midst of the worst calamity. It oils the whole body for smooth and efficient operation.

Second, by some mysterious chemistry of the spirit, hope often creates its desired object. Those who believe in their hope and work toward its fulfillment have their hopes fulfilled more often than those who live without hope. People who constantly worry sometimes bring the object of their fear on themselves. Everyone I know who has given worry and hope an equal try, has finally admitted to the truth of this. The power of constructive, faith-centered, positive thinking cannot be overestimated, and hope is the essence and core of such thinking.

Third, hope is a crucial distinguishing mark of the Christ-follower. Paul the apostle writes that "…in hope we were saved" (Rom 8:24). By some strange perversion of the modern mind, worry and pessimism have gained a certain sophisticated approval. Few sincere people of faith would ever boast of a lack of love or faith or of hate and disbelief. Yet we often parade our worries and our visions of a bleak future before others. It is almost as grievous a fault to be without hope as it is to be without love or faith.

Writing these words challenges my own patterns of thinking and living deeply. However, hope has not been the most prominent characteristic of my life. Until a few years ago, my wife would often call me "Mr. Pessimism." The demons of worry and dread occupied far too much space in my mind. Then I began to pray that God would make me a more hopeful and positive person. As I have sought to keep hope alive in me, two things have become clear.

On the one hand, if we are going to keep hope alive, we need to have a growing relationship with the risen Christ. He is the foundation of our hope. As we seek him with all of our being, we get to know the God "…who is above all and through all and in all" (Eph 4:6). Then a little of the Divine Presence will shine through every situation, every emergency, and even every tragedy, if only we will see it. We begin to realize that this world's evil, though very real, will be defeated in the end. It is only at the end of time that we will understand the meaning of tragedy. There is no answer to the "why" question. Hope is impossible unless it is based on God and eternity.

On the other hand, we need to realize that hope doesn't just fall from heaven. It doesn't mean sitting around and doing nothing. It comes only as we work hard at it and constantly struggle to possess it. This takes determination and choice. We must courageously and resolutely set our faces away from worry and fear and choose to be people of hope, even if we are otherwise inclined. We can do this in a number of ways. We can meditate on the victory of Christ's resurrection and its relevance for our lives. We can regularly remind ourselves that God is always with us. We can even keep a note of our past personal victories in difficult situations. As we do things like these, we deny our pessimistic hearts and build hope into our lives. If we don't, we limit ourselves and fall short of a vital, transforming spiritual life.

These days, admittedly, keeping hope alive asks much of us. But is there any other quality of life that offers so much in return?

DAILY MEDITATION TESTS FOR THE WEEK

Day 1   "To them God chose to make known how great among the Gentiles are the riches of the glory of this mystery, which is Christ in you, the hope of glory." (Col 1:27)

Day 2   "We have this hope, a sure and steadfast anchor of the soul, a hope that enters the inner shrine behind the curtain." (Heb 6:19)

Day 3   "Now faith is the assurance of things hoped for, the conviction of things not seen." (Heb 11:1)

Day 4   "Hope deferred makes the heart sick, but a desire fulfilled is a tree of life." (Prov 13:12)

Day 5   "Why are you cast down, O my soul, and why are you disquieted within me? Hope in God; for I shall again praise him." (Ps 42:5)

Day 6   "For surely I know the plans I have for you, says the Lord, plans for your welfare and not for harm, to give you a future with hope." (Jer 29:11)

Day 7   "Rejoice in hope, be patient in suffering, persevere in prayer." (Rom 12:12)

SUGGESTION FOR JOURNALING

Describe as fully as you can the hope that God gives you in your present life.

QUOTE

> *Hope sees what has not yet been and what will be,*
> *She loves what has not yet been and what will be,*
> *In the future of time and of eternity.*
>
> Charles Peguy

PRAYER

> *Lord, we believe that in knowing and serving you all men and women can rise to the full height of their humanity. But we do not see it happening. What we see is a world divided between the overfed and the hungry, between the comfortable and the homeless, between some entrenched in privilege and others clamorous for their rights. We see goodwill made ineffective by stupidity, and honest people failing to measure up to the demands of a crisis. We see the peacemakers and bridge-builders pushed aside because progress toward justice seems too slow. Yet also in this world, and identified with it, we see Jesus. We see his life of love: we see his cross. Not only as they were long ago, but as they are now, wherever his Spirit is allowed by men and women to govern human actions and purify human motives.*

And so we recover faith about the world, and through faith we find hope. You, Father, are the source of this faith and hope: and you are the source of the love which alone can make the hope come true. May those who believe this learn how to avoid obstructing your love. May all who revere you make haste to promote justice and to practice compassion and to overcome the terrible strength of evil with the power of good.

Caryl Micklem
More Contemporary Prayers

WEEK 25

Reducing Our
Levels of Fear

All of us, to some degree, know what it means to be frightened. Every day brings some kind of fear into our hearts and minds, whether it is fear of failure or success, fear of people or of death, fear of the past or the future, fear of ghosts or of God. Few of us can claim to have a life free of fear. I know this from personal experience and from relating to people on a daily basis. Just yesterday an outwardly confident corporate executive said to me, "These days there always seems to be something to fear."

These fears sabotage our lives. To begin with, they stifle spiritual growth. We find it difficult to trust God. Deep down we wonder if God really is with us. We feel alone. The emotional consequences are just as crippling, as fear often causes us to feel down, despairing and depressed, stealing the sparkle from our lives and relationships. Even at a physical level fear affects us negatively. When we are afraid, our breathing becomes heavier, our hearts begin to pound, our mouths become dry, and our bodies tense up. Only when our levels of fear are reduced can these reactions be brought under more conscious control.

The Bible knows what a paralyzing effect fear can have, so much so that the phrase "fear not" appears more than one hundred times in its pages. It may well be the most frequently given command. The biblical writers clearly believed that fear is one of our greatest obstacles on the spiritual journey. The challenge facing us is to find a practical way of putting this "fear not" command into practice. In other words, how can we go about dealing with fear in our daily lives?

There are three guidelines that we need to follow if we are to come to terms with our fears. The first is to quietly turn inward and identify what it is that we fear. Too often we resist this simple starting point. We prefer to fill our time with business. We think that if we stay busy enough, the ghosts will fade away and leave our souls in peace. This approach usually ends in disaster, because fears are really hints that something is wrong inside or around us and that we need to deal with this. So when we push our fears away and ignore them, the result can be catastrophic.

When we take stock of our fears, we usually find two types of fear. There are those that we can identify and there are those that are nameless and can bring fear on us like a dark cloud. The latter are the most difficult to tie down, and they bring on the worst kind of fear. They can get so out of proportion that a phone ringing or a knock on the door can set our nerves on edge.

The second guideline is to gather our courage and write down our fears on a piece of paper or in a journal. This technique is most helpful when fear appears to have the upper hand. When the burdens of life get too heavy, become quiet and listen to your worries or troubles. Name the fears that are threatening to swallow you, and write them down. Try also to identify the fears that you don't fully understand. This can take anything from a few minutes to an hour or two. Remember, we cannot heal a sickness if we do not first identify it, whether it is spiritual or physical.

Somehow, when we name our fears and write them down, they seem a little less scary. Then we can stop going over the same things, seeing fifty fearful things when there are really only five. And five of anything is easier to handle than fifty. So, although it takes time and courage to sit down and do this writing, it's well worth it. In the end the fears yield much of their power. As Anthony, one of the old saints, used to tell the other monks, the devil and his demons are really weak. They appear to be power-ful only because we are so afraid. This is a wonderful insight.

The third rule is to realize that these fears are not bigger than we can handle. This is the step of faith that we take as Christ-followers. Jesus hinted at this when he told us not to be anxious about tomorrow. Rather, we are to limit ourselves to take care of today. In other words, we must face the things that trouble us in the present and know that they will not overcome us. With God's help we are stronger than our greatest fear. We are not alone. As Paul writes in that moving eighth chapter in his letter to the Romans, there is nothing that can ever separate us from the love of God which is in Christ Jesus our Lord (Rom 8:39).

I like to give expression to this awareness in a time of simple prayer. After I have written out those things I am afraid of, I consciously turn towards God. In the Divine Presence I try to look at each fear as calmly as I can. Among them there may be things like fear of illness, fear of violence, fear of failure, fear of my children's choices, fear of another's opinion, fear of losing someone I love, fear of my own death. I name these fears in the presence of the risen Christ, realizing that not one of them can separate me from him. I ask him to help me to face them, to overcome them and to take whatever action I must. While my fears seldom go away completely, praying in this way usually makes them seem less ominous and more manageable.

Sometimes, however, we lose perspective because we cannot manage our fears by ourselves. Then we need a friend whom we can trust and with whom we can share our fears; someone who stands outside the circle of our fear and can point out some fac-tor we may have missed. A friend who is willing to listen takes away our burden of loneliness that often goes with our deepest fears. Somehow strength is given as this person's spirit mingles with our own and we commune. And did not Jesus himself say that he would be present when we got together in twos and threes (Matt 18:20)?

Perhaps this is the ministry you can offer someone else this week. Remember, your task is not to give advice or fix people up, and certainly not to tell them that their fears are foolish. Be there to listen and to share. Let the person know that you know what it means to be afraid. So often all they need is the quietness of mutual understanding, the simplicity of loving concern. We can all help one another if we will only listen and try to understand. When we do this, we step into the fellowship of God's kingdom where fear is diminished or even banished.

DAILY MEDITATION TEXTS FOR THE WEEK

Day 1   "God is our refuge and strength, a very present help in trouble. Therefore we will not fear…" (Ps 46:1–2)

Day 2   "Do not let your hearts be troubled. Believe in God, believe also in me." (John 14:1)

Day 3   "But immediately Jesus spoke to them and said, 'Take heart, it is I; do not be afraid.'" (Matt 14:27)

Day 4   "There is no fear in love, but perfect love casts out fear." (1 John 4:18)

Day 5   "You who live in the shelter of the Most High, who abide in the shadow of the Almighty, will say to the Lord, 'My refuge and my fortress; my God, in whom I trust.'" (Ps 91:1–2)

Day 6   "The Lord is my rock, my fortress, and my deliverer, my God, my rock in whom I take refuge, my shield, and the horn of my salvation, my stronghold." (Ps 18:2)

Day 7   "Do not worry about anything, but in everything by prayer and supplication with thanksgiving let your requests be made known to God. And the peace of God, which surpasses all understanding, will guard your hearts and your minds in Christ Jesus." (Phil 4:6–7)

SUGGESTION FOR JOURNALING

Describe the fear that most seeks to sabotage your life.

QUOTE

> *When we know we have a certain fear, we can face it, can*
> *tackle it, can try ways and means to minimise it and even*
> *make it disappear altogether from our life or at least learn to*
> *live with it. When we are unaware of our fears, when we deny*
> *them, refuse to see them, ignore them, they are free to exert*
> *their baneful influence undisturbed and we are the losers.*
>
> Carlos G. Valles
> *Let Go of Fear*

PRAYER

> *I call to you, O Lord, from my quiet darkness.*
> *Show me your mercy and love.*
> *Let me see your face, hear your voice,*
> *touch the hem of your cloak.*
> *I want to love you, be with you, speak*
> *to you and simply stand in your presence.*
> *But I cannot make it happen.*
> *Pressing my eyes against my hands*
> *is not praying, and reading about your*
> *presence is not living in it.*
> *But there is a moment in which you*
> *will come to me, as you did to your*
> *fearful disciples, and say, "Do not be afraid; it is I."*
> *Let that moment come soon, O Lord.*
> *And if you want to delay it, then make me patient.*
> *Amen.*
>
> Henri Nouwen
> *A Cry for Mercy*

———————

Using Our Single Talent

In my early twenties I took part in a three-month training program for community workers and youth leaders. One day we were asked, in small groups, to think about each other's lives and say what we valued about them. The exercise started well. Each person in the group took a turn to listen while the rest of us affirmed their giftedness. I was the last. For a while the group was quiet. I wondered what they were going to say. Finally, someone broke the silence and said, "Trevor, I think you listen quite well."

To be honest, I was a little disappointed. My friends had been affirmed in seemingly stronger ways. They had received accolades like "excellent people skills," "able to delegate well," "capacity for visionary leadership," "excellent managerial abilities," and the like. In comparison, being able to listen well sounded a bit tame. Nonetheless, two of the group still had to speak. Perhaps they would notice something more exciting. The next one said, "I agree. I think you are good at listening."

Far from feeling affirmed, I now felt quite deflated. When the third and last person said the same thing, I wanted to curl up in my corner and die. Listening just didn't seem that great a gift. However, to this day, I can still remember that night, kneeling at the side of my bed and praying, "Dear God, thank you for this listening gift. I offer it to you and commit myself to develop it as much as I can. Will you please use it to make a difference in the lives of others?" Looking back now, as I write these words, I am deeply moved by the opportunities that God has given me to put this talent to use. It has given my life tremendous meaning and purpose.

I begin with this personal story because I want us to consider a well-known parable of Jesus. Here is the gist of it. A wealthy landowner went on a long trip. Before he left, he took some extra profits that he didn't have time to invest and gave them to three of his servants to care for in his absence. To one he gave five talents (this amounts to about R30,000 or $5,000), to the second, two, and to the third, just one. The first servant took his five talents and bought a business. By the time his master returned, he had made another five talents, and so he was able to return ten in place of five. The second took his two talents and did the same. They had confidence in what they had been given and trusted their master. The last one, however, simply hid the money in the ground, which was the safe deposit box of the ancient world.

When the master returned he commended the first two and entrusted them with even greater responsibilities. But the third servant came with his coin, moldy from the ground, and said:

Master, I knew that you were a harsh man, reaping where you did not sow, and gathering where you did not scatter seed; so I was afraid, and I went and hid your talent in the ground. Here you have what is yours. (Matt 25:24–25)

When the master heard this, he was really upset.

You wicked and lazy slave! You knew, did you, that I reap where I did not sow, and gather where I did not scatter? Then you ought to have invested my money with the bankers, and on my return I would have received what was my own with interest. So take the talent from him, and give it to the one with the ten talents. For to all those who have, more will be given, and they will have an abundance; but from those who have nothing, even what they have will be taken away. (Matt 25:26–29)

What are we to make of all this? One thing is clear: although it uses money as a symbol, this parable doesn't refer in its essential meaning just to economic things. Those who quote this last verse as justification for keeping people in poverty or for not helping in cases of human need are actually being perverse. The master in the story refers to God. The talents represent the divine investment in our lives. Thus, the talents of gold represent all the abilities and opportunities that God has given to us. It is a simple fact that God has not distributed these talents equally. We could say that some people, such as Einstein, Lincoln, Joan of Arc, Mother Teresa, Schweitzer and Mandela, have five. Some, such as prominent business leaders, great literary figures, prominent national spokespersons, have two. Most of us, however, have just one. But it matters not so much how many talents we have; there is nothing we can do about that. What really matters is what we do with what we have been given. When it comes to using our talents, are we risk-takers or undertakers?

There is a great temptation for single-talented people, as most of us are, to become discouraged. Then, like the man in the story, we go and hide our talent. We say to ourselves, "What difference can I really make? I don't really have much ability. I can't make a big contribution. So what's the use of even trying? Besides, it's God's fault that I don't have better abilities." There is also another reason why we bury our abilities and don't make use of our opportunities. Like the third servant, we excuse ourselves by saying, "I was afraid. I didn't have the courage to use the one talent I was given. I thought that God would get angry if I failed." Perhaps you can identify with some of these excuses.

One of the most important tasks facing us average humans is that of accepting ourselves as we are and then trying to do the best we can with what we have. We can say to ourselves, "Even though I do not have many talents, I am still valuable and worth more to God than I will ever fully know. I can make something beautiful of this self of mine, without expecting so much that I am constantly discontent. I can develop my one talent to its full potential and use it in as many ways as possible." The talents faithfully used by one-talent people can change the face of the world. Their work is often vital to every creation and scheme dreamed up by "five-talent" people. A great architect may conceive a cathedral, but it takes the single talented, those who lay the bricks and paint the walls, to bring the dream into reality.

Most important, however, is what the single-talented person can do spiritually. It doesn't take extraordinary ability to dig deep into life and find God, letting his power flow through us like a mighty current. It requires nothing but courage, love, perseverance, and the willingness to risk. Greatness in the sphere of the spirit is not a built-in talent that we either have or lack; it lies within the grasp of everyone. Indeed, in spiritual things the single-talented person has perhaps the greatest opportunity to grow and develop because they are not constantly in danger of being diverted by a dozen abilities and interests. The whole point of the parable is to warn us not to fall into temptation like the one-talent servant and bury our gift. We don't need to become discouraged. In the greatest things of life, the things of the kingdom of God, the person with the single talent can live as fully as the one with five, sometimes even more fully.

The parable leaves us with one other thought: we cannot remain as we are. It is important that we keep growing and developing. There is no spiritual deep-freeze where we can stay the same without spoiling. We are either growing or dying. The human soul is never static. It either makes progress, seeks deeper spiritual levels, or else it shrivels up and dies. When we try to keep safe what we have, we stand in danger of losing everything. And the good news is that the single talented can grow as much as anyone else. They can soon outreach the significance of the five-talented who may not grow at all. So let's use what we have with courage and grow spiritually as much as we can, even if the only talent we have is being able to listen attentively.

DAILY MEDITATION TEXTS FOR THE WEEK

Day 1   "We have gifts that differ according to the grace given to us." (Rom 12:6)

Day 2   "But each has a particular gift from God, one having one kind and another a different kind." (1 Cor 7:7)

Day 3   "Now there are varieties of gifts, but the same Spirit." (1 Cor 12:4)

Day 4   "So then, each of us will be accountable to God." (Rom 14:12)

Day 5   "To each is given the manifestation of the Spirit for the common good." (1 Cor 12:7)

Day 6   "I praise you, for I am fearfully and wonderfully made. Wonderful are your works; that I know very well." (Ps 139:14)

Day 7   "All must test their own work; then that work, rather than their neighbor's work, will become a cause for pride." (Gal 6:4)

SUGGESTION FOR JOURNALING

Make a list of those things you can do well and give thanks to God for them.

QUOTE

We ask to know the will of God without guessing that his will is written into our very beings. We perceive that will when we discern our gifts. Our obedience and surrender to God are in large part our obedience and surrender to our gifts. This is the message wrapped up in the parable of the talents. Our gifts are on loan. We are responsible for spending them in the world, and we will be held accountable.

Elizabeth O'Connor
Eighth Day of Creation

PRAYER

*Dear God, thank you for the abilities
that you have placed in my life.
Help me to acknowledge them,
and give me the courage to develop
and use them in your service.
I pray for this so that your kingdom
may come more fully into my life
and the world around me.
Amen.*

Hanging on When
Life Is Difficult

Whenever I start reading a new book I always pay special attention to the first line. I have little doubt that the writer wants to get our attention and strike a responsive chord in those who are going to read the book. Over the years I have made notes of many good opening lines. One of the most memorable is the opening statement in M. Scott Peck's best-selling book titled *The Road Less Travelled.* He begins with the simple yet profound assertion: "Life is difficult."

He is right; life can get difficult. Think for a moment of some of the difficulties that we experience in our lives: loved ones get sick, children go off the rails, close friends betray us, marriages break up, business ventures fail, people are retrenched, and the list continues. At times like these it is not helpful to tell people to count their blessings or to look at how fortunate they are in comparison with others. When life's burdens pounce on us, the pain is great no matter what causes it.

Even people who seem to be sailing along smoothly can sometimes experience inner difficulties. Indeed, it is usually when the outer pains of life are removed that we have to face the more subtle and elusive struggles of our souls. Think of those of us who battle with a despairing feeling of worthlessness or depression; the stifling inner pain of shame, failure and guilt; or the anguish of immeasurable grief and loss. These inner difficulties are as real as the outward ones, and to tell someone to "snap out of it" is just as foolish as telling a hungry person to cheer up because they still have flesh on their bones!

If we are really honest with ourselves, we must admit that there are times when life can get very tough, situations where we find the pain and pressure too much to bear, and when we wonder whether we should even try to keep going. It is in these difficult and painful experiences of life that the Christian faith gives us something to hang on to. God does not have much to offer the self-satisfied and self-sufficient individual, but to those who are distressed and who wonder if they can carry on any longer, he as everything to offer.

What is God's word to us when we want to give up? The first thing our faith tells us is that we are not alone. When we experience difficulties, it does not mean that we have been singled out. The evil that is woven into the very fabric of our universe affects everyone. Even Jesus, the very best human being who has ever walked on this earth, was not exempt. Throughout time people of faith have suffered. Few books express this truth more clearly than the Psalms. How deeply comforting it can be to read the cries of the psalmists in the midst of their own pain. When we become aware of our bonds with these fellow sufferers, past and present, we are helped in our moments of extremity. I like to keep close to my heart Unamuno's statement that the chief sanctity of the sanctuary is that it is a place where we can come together and weep.

Second, our faith challenges us never, ever, to give up on life. We need to be very clear about this: God is always on the side of life. When we give up on life, either by giving up our will to live or by taking our own lives, we go against God's will. Both these actions are ways of committing suicide, and suicide is not an acceptable option for the Christ-follower. Nothing causes more damage in a family than when one of its members commits suicide. Nothing! One of the best reasons for hanging on, therefore, is that our failure to do so will scar our loved ones forever.

In saying this, I would never want to condemn anyone who has come to the point of giving up on life. We dare not stand in judgment of someone else. We can never have the full facts of what has gone on in that person's life; only God knows. But we can judge ourselves against the challenges and commandments that God has given us. This is what Paul makes clear in his letter to the Galatians (Gal 6:4–5). He says we should examine our own conduct. We must measure our faithfulness by comparing ourselves with ourselves and not with anyone else, because each one of us has our own burden to bear.

But what can we do when we are tempted to give up on life? The best medicine is to do something constructive, such as walking around the block, making oneself a cup of tea, taking a walk in the garden, building a puzzle, or phoning a friend. When I am discouraged, I sometimes visit someone who is struggling. This takes my mind off myself and my heaviness begins to lift a little. A purely passive diversion like reading or watching television is not enough to rouse us out of these dark and depressing moments. We need to act by summoning all our courage and doing something simple and constructive.

Finally, the greatest motivation for hanging on is the realization that Christ came for those who desperately needed rescuing. And he continues to do so today in the power of his Spirit and through those who care. So often, as we hang on in the midst of our difficulties, we are surprised by grace. This is one of the profound mysteries of our faith. Those of us who have never experienced dark moments seldom know God at a deeper level. But those who come to the end of their own resources, and call out to the risen Lord for guidance and strength, often find themselves lifted from their despondency. They discover that their difficulties have opened the door for them to experience the warmth and power of God's loving presence. If you are in a difficult place right now, I pray that you will open yourself to this experience. And, if necessary, also to someone who has passed through a similar experience and come out victorious. There is always hope.

DAILY MEDITATION TEXTS FOR THE WEEK

Day 1   "When you pass through the waters, I will be with you; and through the rivers, they shall not overwhelm you; when you walk through fire you shall not be burned, and the flame shall not consume you." (Isa 43:2)

Day 2   "I can do all things through him who strengthens me." (Phil 4:13)

Day 3   "So you have pain now; but I will see you again, and your hearts will rejoice, and no one will take your joy from you." (John 16:22)

Day 4   "I have said this to you, so that in me you may have peace. In the world you face persecution. But take courage; I have conquered the world!" (John 16:33)

Day 5   "My help comes from the Lord, who made heaven and earth." (Ps 121:2)

Day 6   "...but those who wait for the Lord shall renew their strength, they shall mount up with wings like eagles, they shall run and not be weary, they shall walk and not faint." (Isa 40:31)

Day 7   "May the God of hope fill you with all joy and peace in believing, so that you may abound in hope by the power of the Holy Spirit." (Rom 15:13)

SUGGESTION FOR JOURNALING

Describe one creative thing you enjoy doing that is worth keeping in mind for difficult times.

QUOTE

Life is difficult.

M. Scott Peck
The Road Less Travelled

PRAYER

Lord, sometimes it gets very dark in my life.
When this happens everything seems to be an effort,
everything is difficult, and I often want to give up.
Please give me the strength to hang on in these moments.
Help me not to give in to the difficulties I face.
Rather may I do something creative, reach out
to others and stay close to you.
Amen.

WEEK 28

Forgiving Those Who Have Hurt Us

In recent years we have witnessed some remarkable acts of forgiveness in South Africa. Many of these have taken place during the hearings of the Truth and Reconciliation Commission, a process designed to bring together the perpetrators and victims of apartheid. One of the most moving was the testimony of a sixteen-year-old teenager. Her father had been involved in the liberation struggle. In the mid-eighties he was detained, never to be seen alive again. She wanted to know who had killed him. As she put it, "I want to know the name of the person responsible for killing my father so that I can learn to forgive him."

Her words have challenged me deeply. Forgiveness must surely be one of the most difficult things any human being can be asked to do. But this is what we are called to as Christ-followers. If you have any doubts about this, read Matthew 18:21–22. When Peter asked Jesus how many times he had to forgive, he was told: "Not seven times, but, I tell you, seventy-seven times" (verse 22). In other words, "Stop counting, Peter. There can be no limit to your forgiveness, for there is no limit to God's forgiveness."

All this sounds well and good, but have you ever tried to forgive someone who has hurt you very badly? If you have, you will know how exceedingly difficult, how nearly impossible, it is. It almost seems as if those powerful feelings of resentment, anger, spite and revenge have a life all of their own. You know that God wants you to forgive, but you can't. So how, then, do we actually set about forgiving the hard-to-forgive? As I have struggled with this in my own relationships, I have found the following guidelines very helpful; I hope that you will too.

The first thing we have to realize is that forgiving is very difficult. This is partly because we feel it is our right to hold onto our resentment and hatred. Everything cries out from inside us that we have every reason to avenge our hurt. Furthermore, we live in a world that regards forgiveness as a rather peculiar weakness. Standing up for our rights, repaying grudges, getting our own back—these are the qualities that are highly valued by our society. When we set out on the road of forgiveness, we are going against the crowd and will come in for a lot of scorn, derision and ridicule. Staying close to God, the support of some of God's people, and lots of prayer and courage will be our only help.

But there's another reason why we find it difficult to forgive. When we look at ourselves honestly, we find that many of the world's attitudes are also deeply rooted within us. We usually only start facing the task of forgiveness because of one particular hurt in our lives. Then, as we become aware of our unforgiving nature, we look beneath the surface and find that our painful resentment is a symptom of a larger attitude toward life. If you are like me, you will find a whole tangled web of little resentments and unforgiving attitudes. Our lives are dominated by feelings of resentment and these feelings infect nearly every relationship, even those closest to us.

If you think I'm exaggerating, consider for a moment the following questions: Is there anyone at the moment with whom you are not on good speaking terms? Is there anyone who you usually try to avoid? Is there anyone against whom you feel resentful, angry and hateful? Is there anyone who you continually criticize when they are not present? I don't know about you, but there are quite a few people that come to mind when I consider these questions. They remind me of the enormous task ahead of me if I want to set out on the journey of forgiveness.

Next comes a major decision: Do we really want to forgive those who have wronged us? It is easy to answer yes, but it is an entirely different matter to put that "yes" into action, to plant the seed of forgiveness so firmly that we will pursue the goal against all the odds. Forgiveness may make great demands on us. For example, remember the man who had been sick for thirty-eight years. Jesus came to him and asked, "Do you want to be healed?" Well, do we really want to be healed of our unforgiving nature? Although we cannot become forgiving by an act of the will alone, we can make the decision to try to let forgiveness and mercy have control over our lives.

The next step is even harder. We need to open the cellar doors of our own lives and take a good look in. Do we have anything in our lives that we haven't forgiven in others? Is there anything deep within us or in our behavior and thinking that deserves censure by the same standards that we apply to others? Are there things that we have hidden so carefully that we have forgotten that they ever happened? If there is anything that helps us toward forgiving others, it is this kind of honest self-assessment. It is an interesting spiritual and psychological insight that the very things of which we are most critical and unforgiving in others are often the same things which we have buried in our own lives. Do you remember what Jesus said about first removing the log from our own eyes?

I feel very sad for someone who looks into his or her life and says sincerely, "There is nothing wrong with me. I have always done my best. I have been loving toward everyone. I have done no wrong and do not need anyone's forgiveness." Such a person simply doesn't know him- or herself. The mark of spiritual maturity lies not in seeing ourselves as perfect, but in realizing just how damaged and corrupt we are. When we realize what fragile glass houses we live in, the temptation to throw stones of resentment at others decreases considerably. On the other hand, when we know ourselves as people who need and have received forgiveness, we want to bring this pardon to others as well.

Even after we have done all this—realized the cost of forgiveness, made our decision to forgive, examined ourselves honestly—we still need the grace of God to help us. God alone can heal us of our unforgiving attitudes. All we can do is open the door and try to remove the main obstacles. It is only as the river of God's forgiving love and mercy floods through us that we will find ourselves able to forgive more completely. Absolute forgiveness does not lie within our power; it comes as the fruit of a living and real relationship with God. It is one of the richest treasures God gives to those who seek him persistently. And when this attitude of forgiveness flows through us, we are set free from the prisons of our resentment and given a foretaste of the freedom of the kingdom of heaven. I think this is what that sixteen-year-old teenager experienced.

DAILY MEDITATION TEXTS FOR THE WEEK

Day 1   "Do not judge, and you will not be judged; do not condemn, and you will not be condemned. Forgive, and you will be forgiven." (Luke 6:37)

Day 2   "Then Jesus said, 'Father, forgive them; for they do not know what they are doing.'" (Luke 23:34)

Day 3   "If you forgive the sins of any, they are forgiven them; if you retain the sins of any, they are retained." (John 20:23)

Day 4   "And if the same person sins against you seven times a day, and turns back to you seven times and says, 'I repent,' you must forgive." (Luke 17:4)

Day 5   "If you, O Lord, should mark iniquities, Lord, who could stand?" (Ps 130:3)

Day 6   "I therefore, the prisoner in the Lord, beg you to lead a life worthy of the calling to which you have been called, with all humility and gentleness, with patience, bearing with one another in love, making every effort to maintain the unity of the Spirit in the bond of peace." (Eph 4:1–3)

Day 7   "Above all, clothe yourselves with love, which binds everything together in perfect harmony." (Col 3:14)

SUGGESTION FOR JOURNALING

Write a brief letter to the Lord, sharing how you feel about his challenge to forgive.

QUOTE

> *Forgiveness...is letting go—letting go of the anger, letting go of the right to retaliate, and letting go of the right to savour any of the emotional consequences of the hurt.*
> David Benner
> *Healing Emotional Wounds*

PRAYER

> *You know, Lord, all the ways I have of treating people I don't like: I judge them, I avoid them, I gossip about them, I hector them. But I don't want to do it anymore. I want to learn to forgive, even as you have forgiven me, in Jesus Christ. Amen.*
> Eugene Peterson
> *Praying with Paul*

Understanding and Dealing with Our Anger

A few days ago I had an interesting conversation with a construction worker in his mid-thirties. He was telling me about his relationship with God. It turned out that his spiritual journey had begun after one of my sermons. I was intrigued and asked him if he could remember which one. To my surprise, he recalled it immediately. "It was a message on anger," he said. "For years I believed that my anger made me unacceptable to God. But when you said that anger itself was not a sin, I felt at last that I could have a relationship with God."

I wonder how many of us have had similar feelings? At times we may feel as if the Christian faith asks a lot more of us human beings than we can produce. It says, for instance, that we have to be loving, kind and gentle, yet this goal appears to be very far removed from the reality of our everyday lives, for when we look at ourselves honestly, we realize that we often carry around feelings like anger and hostility. Surely these emotions are contrary to the way of Christ? In moments like these, like the construction worker, we doubt whether God could ever accept or use us.

Whenever we feel this tension, it is helpful to turn to Paul's letter to the Ephesians, where we find these encouraging words:

Be angry but do not sin; do not let the sun go down on your anger, and do not make room for the devil. (Eph 4:26)

This instruction tells us that anger is not necessarily sinful. Indeed, human beings will always have feelings of anger. The important thing, though, is that we must make sure our anger does not cause us to harm and hurt others. When that happens, it does, indeed, become destructive and sinful.

When I first read Paul's advice it appeared to contradict some of Jesus' words in the Sermon on the Mount, where he says that anyone who commits murder will come before the judgment of God. He goes on to say:

> *Anyone who nurses anger against their brother or sister must be brought to judgment. If they abuse their brother or sister they must answer for it to the court; if they sneer at them they will have to answer for it in the fires of hell. (Matt 5:22, NEB)*

Strong language! Indeed, it makes those who want to take Jesus seriously stop and think carefully about what he is saying.

What are the differences between these two passages? First of all, there is a difference between anger and hate. Anger is a natural response to hurt; hate is nurtured anger directed toward another person. Allow me to explain this a bit more. Anger is a perfectly natural emotion, like fear. It is one of the warning signs God has built into us. We cannot live without it. When we are threatened or hurt, anger and fear mobilize our body and mind for the actions of flight or fight. For example, if I were to kick you on the shins, you would have an instinctive desire either to kick back or run away. Anger or fear would begin to rise in you. You would not be a living, responsive human being if you did not respond in this way. Indeed, if we deny having such feelings, we are kidding ourselves and not facing reality.

Hatred is altogether different. It is the nursing of the anger in us. It is heaping fuel on the little fire of anger so that the flames begin to burn with white-hot intensity. It is anger fired up with ill will and intention. When we hate, we start to mobilize our emotional feelings to bring harm and misery to another. It is this nursing of anger that Jesus condemns. It destroys both the hater and the hated one. It can come out in actions of carefully calculated cruelty, or it can be expressed in words that cut deeply to the heart.

The second difference is that Jesus spoke in times when it was considered honorable to nurture anger into hatred. The Christian faith had not yet begun to permeate the culture of the day. Those who had power often gave way to hate—an eye for an eye and a tooth for a tooth. Against this background, Jesus knew that human beings didn't have a chance of becoming loving until they put away hatred and learned to control their anger. If we seek to hurt another every time we are angry, we will simply never grow in love. Hence the strong words in his sermon.

The problem today is quite different. After two thousand years of Christian influence, a few things have rubbed off on us. Many of us who have been brought up in Christian homes were taught that it is wrong to be angry. We believe that we must suppress all our hostile feelings. But this is not healthy, as we have seen in the meditation of Week 23. And so, instead of getting rid of them, we bury them deep down. They become part of our subterranean depths where they take on a life of their own. The results can be devastating.

When we suppress feelings of anger and refuse to face them, the hostility in us begins to build up. It then bursts out unexpectedly, often aimed at the wrong person. Or we find ourselves doing or saying things we are not proud of, like making snide comments and ridiculing. To suppress feelings of anger can also have emotional and physiological consequences. When we put a lid on our anger, we cut ourselves off from some of our other feelings as well. We become emotionless or even cold and calculating. Physically, it can raise our blood pressure, decrease the clotting time of our blood and even make us more prone to a coronary attack. It can release the nervous energy into the muscles and give us a sore neck and shoulder, or gastric problems like ulcers or indigestion.

If it is destructive to let anger have its way and just as dangerous to bury it, how can we deal with it in a constructive way? First, we have to take time and look at it. We need to decide if the sore neck or the irritability is a result of anger we don't like to face, or of hatred we didn't think we had. Remember, there is no sin in being angry if we face the feeling and acknowledge it. If we find that we are angry about a situation that could be changed, we can rather channel our anger into doing something constructive. If we are angry about something we can do nothing about, then we can write out our anger on a piece of paper or in our journal, or maybe talk to a friend about it.

Morton says he has found it very helpful to bring his anger to God. He often does this in the middle of the night. He actually gets up and writes out his anger in prayer form. He has found that he can also listen to God more attentively during this time. Then he can go back to sleep, his inner turmoil under control. The next day is usually a much happier one, not only for him but also for those closest to him. Praying in this way helps him to see things in perspective. He can adjust himself to the reality around him and ask God's help in bearing and facing it. While we have to find our own best time, praying about our anger in this way can help us to deal with it more constructively.

Second, if you should decide to express your anger directly to the person you are angry with, please use what some people call "I language," rather than "you language." It is one thing to be called stupid and uncaring; it is quite another to have our loved one or friend say, "I am angry about what you have done and it makes me feel uncared for." This simple change from making negative, accusing statements into statements that express what we ourselves are feeling can go a long way in healing hostility, especially in our close relationships. This suggestion may sound very simple, but it can be incredibly effective, for it can help us to be angry without sinning!

Our anger does not have to stand in the way of our relationship with God. In fact, when it is understood and handled creatively, it can even help the holy flame of God's Spirit to burn more brightly in us. As a friend of mine often says, "We can get mad without going bad."

DAILY MEDITATION TEXTS FOR THE WEEK

Day 1   "Be angry but do not sin; do not let the sun go down on your anger." (Eph 4:26)

Day 2   "So when you are offering your gift at the altar, if you remember that your brother or sister has something against you, leave your gift there before the altar and go; first be reconciled to your brother or sister, and then come and offer your gift." (Matt 5:23–24)

Day 3   "A fool gives full vent to anger, but the wise quietly holds it back." (Prov 29:11)

Day 4   "The Lord is merciful and gracious, slow to anger and abounding in steadfast love." (Ps 103:8)

Day 5   "From the same mouth come blessing and cursing. My brothers and sisters, this ought not to be so. Does a spring pour forth from the same opening both fresh and brackish water?" (Jas 3:10–11)

Day 6   "Anyone who nurses anger against their brother or sister must be brought to judgement. If they abuse their brother or sister they must answer for it to the court; if they sneer at them they will have to answer for it in the fires of hell." (Matt 5:22, NEB)

Day 7   "One given to anger stirs up strife, and the hothead causes much transgression." (Prov 29:22)

Suggestion for Journaling

Who are you angry with at the moment? Write out these feelings and ask God to help you deal with them in a creative and constructive way.

Quote

> *Our chances of controlling anger and thus using it in constructive, creative ways for the building of community are greatly increased if we discern its clamouring voice and do not wait until a fever has grown in us to give it expression.*
>
> Elizabeth O'Connor
> *The New Community*

Prayer

> *Lord Jesus, as I follow your steps through the gospels, it becomes clear that you were able to direct your anger in positive ways. It seems you were so in touch with your passionate feelings that you had no need to fear them or hide them. You were always in control of them, and never at their mercy, so you could be angry without sinning. Lord, this hasn't always been true for me. Often in my anger I have hurt and harmed others. Forgive me and help me to be different. Show me how to express my anger at the right time and in an appropriate way. For the sake of your kingdom, I pray. Amen.*

WEEK 30

Watching Our Words

One of my favorite Jewish stories is about the use and abuse of words. It took place in a small East European town where a local inhabitant continually slandered the rabbi. One day, becoming aware of the error of his ways, he asked the rabbi for forgiveness and offered to do any penance required to make amends. The rabbi told him to fetch a feather pillow, cut it open, scatter the feathers in the wind, and then return. The man followed the rabbi's instructions, then he came back and asked, "Am I now forgiven?"

"You must do one more thing," answered the rabbi, "Go and collect all the feathers."

"But that's impossible," the man protested, "the wind has scattered them!"

"Exactly," explained the rabbi, "and although you truly want to correct the evil you have spoken, it is as impossible to repair the damage done by your words as it is to get back the feathers."

Like the feathers scattered in the wind, we cannot gather back all the unkind words we say. It would not be so bad if the painful results of a loose tongue came back on the talker only. Tragically, the poison and prejudice and cruelty and hurt that are spread in this world every day by the abused gift of speech are absolutely staggering. Harmful words destroy confidence, wreck reputations, spread rumors, split families and divide communities. James, the brother of Jesus, offers us a vivid word-picture of the destructive power of an uncontrolled tongue. He describes it as:

*...a small member, yet it boasts of great exploits. How great
a forest is set ablaze by a small fire! And the tongue is a fire.
(Jas 3:5–6)*

We need to watch our words. It is sad that Christ-followers constantly need to be reminded of this. We all know the commandment: "You shall not bear false witness against your neighbor" (Exod 20:16). It could be paraphrased, "You shall not gossip or speak badly about another." What is more, we have two basic gospel commands that would eliminate gossip forever if either of them were followed. At the very least, they would cause us to speak with care if we were to take them seriously.

Jesus' first command is: "Do not judge, so that you may not be judged" (Matt 7:1). Judging is God's business, not ours. Yet we still persist in talking maliciously or critically about people. I have often wondered who is more guilty in God's eyes—the one who commits adultery or the one who talks judgmentally about the adulterer. Going on what Jesus says in the gospels, it could very well be the latter. If we really want to let Jesus be our guide on the spiritual road, we must pay attention to his words about judging others. If we were to take this command more seriously, about 90 percent of our gossip and unkind words would cease.

How do we go about putting an end to our tendency to judge others? Anyone who has tried to do so knows how difficult this is. We make good resolutions and then, before we know it, out of the blue come the venomous words of criticism and condemnation. I have found that a good starting point is to face my own sins and shortcomings honestly. We are not always the virtuous people we like others to think we are. We fall very far short of God's command to live loving and holy lives. When we acknowledge this, we realize how hypocritical it is to sit in judgment of others. We also find ourselves becoming more compassionate and understanding towards those who have made a mess of their lives.

Jesus' second command is even better known: "Love your neighbor as you love yourself" (Matt 19:19). There are two main ways of expressing the opposite of love: one is to hurt or harm another person physically, the second is to say something bad about them. Most of us, however, are civilized enough not to strike out and hit someone. Yet that might even be kinder than starting a malicious rumor or passing an evil judgment. Remember the story about the feathers! We simply cannot say that we love those around us and continue speaking about them critically or judgmentally. G. K. Chesterton once wrote that Christianity has not failed; it has just never been seriously tried. In no area is this more evident than with the way we fail to watch our words.

"Yes, all this is fine," do I hear you objecting, "but there are some things that people do and say that have to be stopped or they might hurt someone." You are right. Some people need to be confronted, particularly if their words or actions are harming others and themselves. Jesus tells us exactly what we should do under these circumstances:

> *If a fellow believer hurts you, go and tell him—work it out between the two of you. If he listens, you've made a friend. If he won't listen, take one or two others along so that the presence of witnesses will keep things honest, and try again. If he still won't listen, tell the church. If he won't listen to the church, you'll have to start over from scratch, confront him with the need for repentance, and offer again God's forgiving love. (Matt 18:17, The Message)*

Morton tells how he learned a great lesson from a woman who told him that one rule she tried to follow was never to say an unkind word about anybody. Her statement struck a deep chord. He realized that this had not been one of his own values. Ever since that moment, he has tried to live by this command.

When he hears anyone speak badly about someone else, he deliberately tries to find something good to say about that person. Although he has broken this rule many times over the years, he believes that this commitment has deepened his experience of God considerably.

So, if we need to speak about others, let us learn to say complimentary and positive things. Perhaps we could call this "holy gossip." Not only will this habit bring a lot of inner joy and satisfaction; it will also bring us closer to God. And it is more fun!

DAILY MEDITATION TEXTS FOR THE WEEK

Day 1   "Death and life are in the power of the tongue, and those who love it will eat its fruits." (Prov 18:21)

Day 2   "I tell you, on the day of judgment you will have to give an account for every careless word you utter; for by your words you will be justified, and by your words you will be condemned." (Matt 12:36–37)

Day 3   "So also the tongue is a small member, yet it boasts of great exploits." (Jas 3:5)

Day 4.   "How great a forest is set ablaze by a small fire! And the tongue is a fire." (Jas 3:5–6)

Day 5   "Pleasant words are like a honeycomb, sweetness to the soul and health to the body." (Prov 16:24)

Day 6   "The words that I have spoken to you are spirit and life." (John 6:63)

Day 7   "The unfolding of your words gives light; it imparts understanding to the simple." (Ps 119:130)

SUGGESTION FOR JOURNALING

Write a paragraph beginning, "As I reflect on my use of words over the past twenty-four hours it becomes clear to me that…"

QUOTE

Words…can be weapons, and words can be healing. Words can unite in friendship or sever in enmity. Words can unlock who I am or mask me from others.

Walter J. Burghardt
Preaching—The Art and the Craft

PRAYER

Lord, teach me how to speak words
that bring light and life to those around me.
Amen.

SECTION FOUR

*Meeting Ourselves in
the Gospel Stories*

WEEK 31

Swinging Open the
Stable Door of Our Soul

Life can be messy. Sometimes we are ambushed by feelings that unsettle and disturb us, like fear, anxiety and jealousy. At other times, our relationships get snarled up and we find ourselves in conflict with our children, our partner, or a colleague at work. Then there are those moments when old compulsions and addictions reign again, turning our inner lives into a battlefield. These experiences don't make us feel very holy or close to God. In fact, deep down we wonder whether God would want anything to do with us. We feel so unworthy and unacceptable.

The good news of Christmas is that God really does want to enter our lives. "Love divine, all love excelling" came into this world in Bethlehem during the reign of Caesar Augustus and desires to be born again in every human heart right now, no matter how messy it may be. You may wonder about such a generous offer. Could it really happen in our messy lives? Let me share my reasons for making such a bold assertion by taking you back to the birth of Jesus over two thousand years ago.

Do you remember where the Christ child was born? Was it in a palace amid the splendor of servants and the glitz of affluence? Did he come into this world on silk sheets, adored by the elite and affluent? No, it was not in such a palace that he was born, and we need to celebrate this. Had he been born in such a place, there would be little hope that he could be born again in our souls. Our souls seldom look like palaces. Was he born in an inn, with a well-swept, tidy room and an attendant to help his mother in labor? No, the Bible tells us that there was no room in the inn. Again, we need to be thankful for this. Our hearts are seldom clean, comfortable and cosy. If the Christ child needed such a place in which to be born, there would be little chance that he could find a home in our lives.

Jesus was born in a stable. When he came among us as a help-less child, he wanted us to know that divinity was more accept-able in a stable than in an inn or a palace, or even in the comfortable home of one of Bethlehem's solid citizens. It is best not to think too imaginatively about what a Middle Eastern stable must have looked and smelled like in those days. It was probably dirty and foul-smelling. According to the Bible, this particular stable was built for an ox and a donkey, and it was not even comfortable for them.

There are many legends about this stable. Tradition has it that strangers often stopped there, coming in out of the cold, dark night to rest in the stable's shelter, and then slipping away the next day. A runaway slave came there one night after he had killed and robbed his master. On another night, a drunken sol-dier stayed there to sleep off his drunkenness. A prostitute came on another evening, weary from her work, and rested on the straw. An abandoned street child also once sought shelter there.

Such was the place where Christ was born. When God chose to enter the world, he entered through a stable. This should be a great comfort for us. Our souls more often resemble a stable than a palace or an inn. If Jesus could be born in a stable, then he can be born in any of our souls. None of us can say we are not good enough for Christ to be born in us. Indeed, Christ is seldom born in people who are complacent and satisfied and in whom everything is in good order. On the contrary, he is usually born in people who are filled with helplessness and frustration, people who cannot seem to make of themselves what they would like to be. This inability to make something of their lives gives them humility and a willingness to look beyond themselves for a

Savior. It is into such messy lives that Christ is most often born today.

This Christmas message offers us a new beatitude, similar to those that Jesus later shared with his followers in the Sermon on the Mount. It goes like this:

> *Blessed are those whose lives are like stables and who want it differently, for in them Christ can be born.*

Blessed indeed are those who take the message of Christmas seriously. Blessed are those who feel helpless and inadequate, those who are weighed down with guilt or addictions, those who are persecuted and heavy laden, and those in trouble, need, or adversity. These are the blessed, not because of their condition, but because it is into such stablelike lives that Christ wants to enter.

In this coming week may we swing open the stable doors of our souls and let Christ in, both newly born and risen from the dead. We are worthy enough to receive him. If we are quiet long enough, we may hear the gentle and persistent knocking of the Holy One who wants to come in and eat with us. From Genesis to the last book in the Bible, we find the same message: the Holy One seeks us far more than we seek him. This alone makes us worthy to receive what God's love offers us in the Christmas message. If you want to let the risen Lord in, here is part of a prayer that Morton shared with his congregation many years ago. You may want to pray it each day this week:

> *Oh, divine Creator, you who exist beyond our physical universe and within it. You created the heavens and stars and the infinite complexity of our material world. You are the source and foundation of all things. We are given courage to turn to you not because of our virtue but because you came to us many years ago in a stable.*
>
> *Were it not for your coming to us with such humility and grace, I doubt if I would be able to turn to you now. For some*

reason beyond my understanding, you cherish us human beings so much that you sent your Son, your own creative being, into the world. As I turn to you, Abba, I ask one thing only. Send the infant Christ to be born in my heart. Let him grow there to bring peace, joy, strength and courage, understanding and patience, love and gratitude. Once I experience these gifts, I can share them with all those around me.

Abba, I have tried to bring my confused life into order, and I find I cannot do it without your help. My life is torn and divided like the world into which the Christ child first came. There are parts of me like Herod who would destroy this divine child. There are parts of me like the Romans who would rule my life for their advantage. There are parts of me that are broken and sick, in bondage and in prison, just as there were in the world in which Jesus came.

I have tried again and again to bring harmony, peace and love into my soul but have failed to do so. Where joy might abide, there is often sorrow. Where I should find peace, I see conflict. Where I would like to find strength and courage, I discover cowardice and weakness. Where I would like to see love and gratitude, there is anger and selfishness. Where I look for humility and simplicity, I see pride and self-centeredness.

Lord, I do not like what I find in myself. It mirrors too much the world around me. As hard as I try, I cannot change myself without your help. Abba, send the Christ child into my heart and let his Spirit grow in me. May your Spirit knit the tattered, raveled edges of my soul. May the indwelling Christ reconcile the conflicting forces that war in the world and within me. May you make the lion lie down with the lamb.

Abba, send your Son into my heart, that he may not only be born there, but also grow and mature and take over the direction of my life. May your love make of me something of value and worth, someone in whom you can rejoice. May the stable of my soul be transformed and become a temple filled

*with your Spirit. May my soul become a beacon, shedding
light in the midst of a dark world. Oh, risen Jesus, I pray this
in your name, you who humbled yourself to be born of a virgin in a stable in order to show me the infinite mercy and love
of the divine Creator.*
Amen.

DAILY MEDITATION TEXTS FOR THE WEEK

Day 1   "All this took place to fulfil what had been spoken by
the Lord through the prophet: 'Look, the virgin shall
conceive and bear a son, and they shall name him
Emmanuel, which means, God is with us.'" (Matt
1:22–23)

Day 2   "While they were there, the time came for her to deliver
her child. And she gave birth to her firstborn son and
wrapped him in bands of cloth, and laid him in a
manger, because there was no place for them in the inn."
(Luke 2:6–7)

Day 3   "And the Word became flesh and lived among us, and
we have seen his glory, the glory as of a father's only
son, full of grace and truth." (John 1:14)

Day 4   "For God so loved the world that he gave his only Son,
so that everyone who believes in him may not perish
but may have eternal life." (John 3:16)

Day 5   "For I have come to call not the righteous but sinners."
(Matt 9:13)

Day 6   "For the Son of Man came to seek out and to save the
lost." (Luke 19:10)

Day 7   "They heard the sound of the Lord God walking in the
garden at the time of the evening breeze, and the man
and his wife hid themselves from the presence of the
Lord God among the trees of the garden. But the Lord
God called to the man, and said to him, 'Where are
you?'" (Gen 3:8–9)

SUGGESTION FOR JOURNALING

Write a letter to God expressing your desire to let Christ more
deeply into your life.

QUOTE

> *The obviously well-kept secret of the "ordinary" is that it is*
> *made to be a receptacle of the divine, a place where the life of*
> *God flows. But the divine is not pushy.*
>
> Dallas Willard
> *The Divine Conspiracy*

PRAYER

> *The prayer for this week is the one that appears at the end*
> *of the meditation.*

WEEK 32

Knowing Who We Are

I enjoy the story of a young boy who asked his mother, "Mom, where did I really come from?" She thought desperately for an answer. Then she remembered a verse from scripture and replied, "You came from dust, and one day you will return to dust." The child was fascinated by this explanation and went back to his room to play. While he was there he crawled under his bed. It hadn't been swept for a long time. He reversed in double-quick time and rushed back to his mother exclaiming, "Come quickly, Mom, there's someone either coming or going right under my bed."

This lighthearted moment points to the search for identity that goes on in all of us. It usually begins in our teenage years and remains with us throughout our lives, often surfacing in times of stress, crisis and change. At such times, like this questioning child, we wonder where we have come from or simply who we are. While we don't often pose the question in formal terms, it is always there, bubbling away under the surface of our lives. Perhaps it is a question you can personally identify with.

We usually search for answers in one of three areas. Some of us embark on a lengthy inward journey. We look inside ourselves and try to find the answer there. We believe that if we dig deep enough we will discover who we really are. When we move along this route we often end up defining ourselves solely in terms of temperament and personality or perhaps, more negatively, in terms of personal addictions and conflicts. While these psychological labels can be useful, they do not reveal the full story about who we are. As I said to a friend the other day, "I am far more than merely an introvert."

Sometimes we look to others for our source of identity. We believe that we are what people say about us. However, this can lead to living on an emotional seesaw: when they say good things about us we feel great, but when they criticize us or say bad things about us, we feel lousy. I'm sure you know what I'm talking about. Looking toward others to validate our own sense of worth can so easily turn our lives into a roller-coaster ride. One moment we are up, the next we are down, depending on what others are saying about us.

Looking toward our achievements is the third way in which we try to find our identity. We believe that we are what we achieve. However, this route is fraught with danger. There is nothing wrong with doing something well and celebrating our special achievements. But when they become the basis of who we are, our lives rest on very insecure foundations. What happens when we fail, or find ourselves in a position where we are no longer able to achieve? And what do we say to a person who experiences only inner emptiness in a moment of success?

In our quest for identity, Christ meets us right where we are. Like us, he also needed to know who he was. Even though he was the unique Son of God, he was not immune to the human quest for identity. He often needed to be reminded of who he was, especially in those transitional moments of his life. However, in contrast to the ways we go about trying to find our identity, he listened to his Father's voice, trusted that voice and claimed its truth for his life. Let me take you to one such moment in the gospels.

Do you remember the decisive moment when Jesus goes down to the river Jordan to be baptized by his cousin John? Thirty years of hidden preparation lay behind him. His public ministry was about to begin. In order to launch out into preaching and teaching, he needed to be affirmed in his identity. As he came out of the water, he heard a voice from heaven. Gospel writers Matthew, Mark and Luke all agree that God said: "This is my Son, the Beloved, with whom I am well pleased." Do you see what happened? Jesus' identity came from beyond himself. He is the Beloved of God. God delights in him. The Spirit of the Father rests on him. Now that he knows this, he is ready to begin his ministry.

You may be wondering what this has got to do with our search for identity. The wonderful news is that Jesus, the Beloved of God, also reveals that God loves us deeply. He did this throughout his ministry on earth. He kept reminding people, no matter who they were or how they had failed, that they were the beloved children of God. Remember how he shared meals with the outcasts, responded to the desperate cries of a roadside beggar, requested the company of a cheating tax collector, and refused to condemn a woman caught in the act of committing adultery? He came to say to each one of them and to us, "You don't have to earn God's love. It is not something that you have to achieve, but something to accept with open hearts and hands. You are already deeply loved and cherished by your heavenly Father."

I know that it may be extremely hard for some of us to believe that we are loved by God "warts and all." There are many things that prevent us from accepting the fact that God loves us. Childhood abuse, conditional acceptance by significant others, dehumanizing socioeconomic realities and tragedy can all mock the good news that each one of us is a cherished child of God. Nonetheless, I would like to invite you this week to try a simple meditation exercise based on the baptism of Jesus. It is one that has helped me to know myself more deeply as one of God's beloved. It goes like this:

Find yourself a place where you can spend some time alone with God. Ask the Holy Spirit to be with you and to assure you of your belovedness. Read the story of Jesus' baptism a few times until you are familiar with all its details (see Matt 3:13–17). Then put the Bible aside and, in the silence, imagine yourself walking down to the River Jordan in the company of Jesus. Talk with him about what is going to take place. Watch him as he wades into the water. Listen to that voice from heaven that affirms him as the Beloved of God. Watch how he turns toward you as you stand on the riverbank and calls you to be with him. As you join him in the water, he puts his arms around you and whispers to you the words, "You are God's beloved child. You are loved, accepted and forgiven. This is who you are." Hear these words as coming from a place deep within you.

You may not be able to receive this truth totally right away. In fact, you may experience strong feelings of resistance, ranging from boredom and dull familiarity to disbelief. Do not be surprised by this. It forms part of any growing, intimate relationship. Noticing these signs of resistance, befriending them without judgment and speaking about their possible sources with a trusted spiritual companion can often pave the way for the good news that God loves us to reach hitherto untouched depths of our inner being. When it does, it changes our lives forever.

Daily Meditation Texts for the Week

Day 1   "See what love the Father has given us, that we should be called children of God; and that is what we are." (1 John 3:1)

Day 2   "When we cry, 'Abba! Father!' it is that very Spirit bearing witness with our spirit that we are children of God." (Rom 8:15, 16)

Day 3   "…and if children, then heirs, heirs of God and joint heirs with Christ—if, in fact, we suffer with him so that we may also be glorified with him." (Rom 8:17)

Day 4   "And a voice from heaven said, 'This is my Son, the Beloved, with whom I am well pleased.'" (Matt 3:17)

Day 5   "As the Father has loved me, so I have loved you; abide in my love." (John 15:9)

Day 6   "You are my friends if you do what I command you." (John 15:14)

Day 7   "And because you are children, God has sent the Spirit of his Son into our hearts, crying, 'Abba! Father!'" (Gal 4:6)

SUGGESTION FOR JOURNALING

Describe your experience, or lack thereof, of being loved and accepted by God in Christ.

QUOTE

> *...we don't need to prove ourselves to God. We don't have to do anything at all, to be acceptable to Him. That is what Jesus came to say, and for that he got killed. He came to say, "Hey, you don't have to earn God's love. It is not a matter for human achievement. You exist because God loves you already. You are a child of divine love."*
>
> Desmond Tutu
> *Hope and Suffering*

PRAYER

> *Father, you love me not in some aloof, impersonal way, but with the cherishing love a mother pours on her child; with the adoring love a good father delights to give his first-born. With the disciplining love good parents give their children; with the protecting love shepherds shower on their lambs. Your love for me now is gift-love. Faithful, committed, unchanging, inextinguishable. Grant me the grace to experience that love here on earth even though on that glorious day when I see you face to face I shall experience it in even richer measure; and be eclipsed by it for all eternity.*
>
> Joyce Huggett
> *The Smile of Love*

WEEK 33

Facing Our Temptations

Let's be honest. We don't find it easy to talk about our temptations. I know this from personal experience, as well as from many years of ministering to people. Very few people know our deeper side as tempted human beings. From the outside, our lives often seem to be free from any kind of inner conflict. The reality is quite the opposite. All of us have evil thoughts, or dark passions and longings, or subtle forces that threaten to undermine our walk with God. These experiences are bound up with our spiritual journey; yet we struggle to speak openly about them.

How different it was with Jesus. Think for a moment about his wilderness experience where he was tempted by the evil one for forty days (Luke 3:1–2). We are able to read about this experience only because he shared it with his close friends. When he returned from the desert he must have called a few of the disciples together and said to them something like, "I've been through a time of tough temptation. Let me tell you about it...." As a result, we know today what took place in Jesus' heart two thousand years ago.

During those forty days Jesus did something we all have to do from time to time. He had to make a decision about how God wanted him to live. A crucial part of this discernment process involved him in facing up to his own particular temptations. It was an eye-opening moment for me when I first realized that Jesus actually listened to what the Tempter had to say. He heard the devil out. He knew that he could resist the evil one if he knew his tactics. Only then could he make sure that his life was not like the devil's, but lived according to God's way.

This is true for our lives as well. If we want to live according to God's way, we must face our temptations, whether they are our power motives, selfishness, pride, vain ambitions, cowardice, laziness, deceit or denial. We cannot get rid of things in ourselves that we do not first confront. We cannot renounce what we do not acknowledge. We cannot cast the log out from our eye until we see it. If this kind of confrontation was necessary for Jesus, it is all the more important for you and me.

However, this can be a disturbing process, and this is perhaps why we tend to steer clear of it. We would prefer to see ourselves as decent, respectable and well-meaning individuals, but this is not helpful in the long run. When we refuse to admit that we have evil tendencies inside us, these tendencies often take over in our lives. Then we find ourselves doing things that go against our deepest values. We hurt the people we love the most. And then, when we are asked why we behaved in this destructive way, we say, "I don't know what got into me." This is why it is far better to face up to the devil as Jesus did.

How do we go about doing this? Here again we need to take Jesus' example seriously. First, we need time alone, our own little "desert" experience. We can seldom square up to our temptations if we are always on the move. That's why the devil likes us to be busy! If we want to tackle our inner evil, we must stop and become silent. I believe this was the primary reason the Spirit of God led Jesus into the solitude of the wilderness. It was the arena where the evil one could be faced and overcome. In our struggle with evil, solitude is nearly always the place of greatest strength.

After we have found some quietness, we need to be specific about our temptations and name them just as Jesus did. His temptations were threefold: he was tempted to focus on material things at the expense of the spiritual, to become a religious superstar, and to exchange his God-allegiance for worldly power. We need to be just as clear about our temptations. One way of doing this is to write them down on paper. It isn't fun suddenly to see them for what they are. Sometimes we even realize that they may have already tricked us. However, if this has already happened, we can confess our sin to the Lord and express our desire to change.

Our temptations will probably not be as dramatic as those of Jesus. Instead, we may be tempted to be uncaring to our neighbors, or possessive of our children, or thoughtless toward our partners, or dishonest at work. Sometimes they may even come in religious dress, like the temptation to be out every night at church meetings rather than at home with family. Whatever they may be, the principle remains the same: what we do not face, we cannot deal with, and what we will not deal with, we will never control.

Once we have identified our temptations, we must realize that we cannot deal with the evil within us and around us on our own. We are not designed to run our lives by ourselves, with just our own wisdom and power. We need something or someone from beyond ourselves. We need the risen Lord, the resurrected Christ who has proven his superiority over this evil once and for all. As we turn to him, trust in him and ask for his help, he comes and stands by us, and we are protected and guided along our spiritual way.

Sometimes this struggle with inner evil gets too much for us to handle on our own. Then we need a spiritual companion, or a close-knit fellowship of recovering sinners, with whom we can share the battles that rage under the surface of our visible lives. Sharing our temptations in this way, as Jesus did, strengthens our spirit against the attacks of the devil. Allowing faithful friends to know how we are tempted not only reduces our sense of isolation, it also opens our lives to vital life-giving resources of the Spirit.

Before ending this meditation, let me point out that the last line of this story in Luke's Gospel also gives a clear warning. It says that after Jesus had come to the end of his temptations, the devil departed, biding his time. It will be so with us too. We need to be constantly vigilant against the devices of the evil one. Facing temptation is not something we do once and once only; it is something we have to keep doing throughout our lives. We need not fear, however, because Christ is our ever-present Companion. He will always come to our aid if and when we call out to him. He is far, far stronger than the devil. Indeed, we have an invincible friend. And with him at our side, we will overcome.

DAILY MEDITATION TEXTS FOR THE WEEK

Day 1   "Then Jesus was led up by the Spirit into the wilderness to be tempted by the devil." (Matt 4:1)

Day 2   "For we do not have a high priest who is unable to sympathize with our weaknesses, but we have one who in every respect has been tested as we are, yet without sin." (Heb 4:15)

Day 3   "Let us therefore approach the throne of grace with boldness, so that we may receive mercy and find grace to help in time of need." (Heb 4:16)

Day 4   "God is faithful, and he will not let you be tested beyond your strength, but with the testing he will also provide the way out so that you may be able to endure it." (1 Cor 10:13)

Day 5   "Because he himself was tested by what he suffered, he is able to help those who are being tested." (Heb 2:18)

Day 6   "...for the one who is in you is greater than the one who is in the world." (1 John 4:4)

Day 7   "But the tax collector, standing far off, would not even look up to heaven, but was beating his breast and saying, 'God, be merciful to me, a sinner!'" (Luke 18:13)

SUGGESTION FOR JOURNALING

Write down one way in which you see yourself as a tempted human being.

QUOTE

> *I have to face up to the choice between good and evil and admit my complicity in the evils of the world. I am convinced that such probing is part of the honest work of love. It is an experience of passion. It is that which drives me to my knees. The more we are able to face our own capacity for evil, the less likely we are to spread the disease.*
>
> Alan Jones
> *Passion for Pilgrimage*

PRAYER

> *Lord Jesus Christ, Son of God,*
> *have mercy on me, a sinner.*
>
> The Jesus Prayer

Week 34

Reaching Out to Touch

The other day I received a letter that, for me, underlined the healing effects of touch. It was written by a woman in her mid-seventies after an almost insignificant encounter between the two of us just a few days before. She had been standing in the doorway of one of our church halls, watching some children play. I went over to her, stood behind her, and placed my hand lightly on her shoulder. For a few moments we stood together without speaking. I then left her and went about whatever I was doing. I did not think of this fleeting episode again until I opened her letter and began to read. Let me quote a few of the lines.

"Do you remember standing behind me the other day and placing your hand on my shoulder? You will not know just how much it meant to me. My husband died seventeen years ago. Since his death I cannot recall anyone touching me. When I felt your hand, I felt like a human being again. It was a very special moment and I will not forget it."

This woman's experience puts into words the mystery and power of human touch. Touch can convey more than a thousand words. It can communicate a deeper level of feeling and sharing than words ever can. It can enable the giving of ourselves to each other in profoundly loving ways. Perhaps this is why the abuse of touch is such a terrible deed. Indeed, there are few things more harmful than abusing a partner or child physically, especially sexually.

Touch is such an important form of human contact in conveying our care and concern to each other. James Lynch tells of his experiments with patients in intensive care units. In his book, *The Broken Heart,* he describes how he noticed that monitoring devices showed an improvement in patients with heart ailments each time a nurse came in to take their pulse. Studies have also shown that a baby that is not touched may be affected psychologically or even die, and that patients who are touched heal faster than those who are not.

When we read about things like these, it comes as little surprise that Jesus often used touch in his ministry of healing. While his healing methods were as diverse as the kinds of diseases he healed, his most common means of healing was by speaking words and touching the sick person with his hand. He usually combined these two methods, although at times he also used them separately. Those who followed him used similar methods. In the later history of the church, this touching became known as the "laying on of hands." This healing ministry raises touch to the sacramental level, just as the Eucharist or holy communion is the sacramental use of eating and drinking. The use of touch in the healing ministry of Jesus and the early church reminds us that it is one of the most effective means of sharing God's love and power.

The one incident that shows most vividly the life-giving power of Jesus' touch was when he healed the leper. The story is told in the Gospels of Matthew, Mark and Luke (see Matt 8:2–4; Mark 1:40–42; Luke 5:12–14). Lepers were the outcasts of Jesus' day. No one was allowed to go too close to them. They would walk around, ringing a bell and calling out, "Unclean, unclean." God's love, however, cannot live at arm's length. So when Jesus was approached by a leper, he stretched out his hand and touched him. Can you imagine what effect this touch must have had on the leper? He must have felt accepted, valued and loved. His healing would also have been a source of indescribable joy and wonder. No wonder he couldn't keep quiet about what had happened!

Like Jesus' earliest followers, we also need to learn how to reach out and touch. We can begin by touching those closest to us with tenderness and care. Sadly, it is often the people closest to us who long to be touched in this way. When Morton lectured at the University of Notre Dame, some of his students complained to him about the lack of touch in their homes. Brilliant, capable young men in their early twenties would ask him, "Why did my father never touch me?" One very bright young man said that the only time he could remember being touched by his father was when he was given a spanking. This kind of touching is a prostitution of touch, as we have already noted. Unfortunately, we are very likely to perpetuate the patterns of our childhood with others when we are older. Old habits die hard, unless we become aware of them.

The next step is to remind ourselves that God wants us to learn how to become channels of healing and wholeness. Again, we can begin in our immediate family circle. When we take the time to open ourselves to God's love in prayer and ask for God's love to move through us, our touch can be healing for our children and partners. If we are a bit skeptical about this, it may be helpful to realize that even some medical professionals today acknowledge the healing possibilities of touch when empowered by faith and prayer. When we go about the laying on of hands in this way, we don't even have to mention that we are praying. It all depends on how open and responsive our family is to the idea of healing prayer.

Morton had a wonderful experience of this. One day, when he was fetching his car at a shop managed by a man in his congregation, he was given a book. It was on healing and was written by that remarkable woman, Agnes Sanford. He decided to put some of its principles into practice. There was an opportunity for this the very next day. He and his wife were on holiday in a motel in Berkeley, California. When they went to bed, Barbara complained of a headache. He decided to pray for her using the set prayer from the Episcopal prayer book. He didn't want suggestion to play any part in this experiment, and so he put his arms around her lovingly, and prayed silently. Barbara suddenly said, "Morton, what have you done? My headache is gone." What is more, it was as if the heavens had opened and Barbara was flooded with the Spirit of God. This significant experience lingered on for several days.

If we want to explore this ministry further, there are a number of things we can do. We can read the healing stories in the gospels and in the life of the early church. We can read books written by people like Agnes Sanford and Francis McNutt. We can ask God to bring across our path people who need healing prayer. We can begin to visit those in hospital or sick at home. We can start listening to those who are distressed and depressed. The important thing is that we go about this ministry with great care and respect. We don't rush into hospital wards saying, "Now I'm going to lay hands on you, and heal you." We simply reach out to those who are hurting and are in pain, and we begin to pray with them, either silently or aloud. In these situations, it is often the most natural thing to touch the other person on the arm or on the shoulder. The essential thing in this ministry is not our own giftedness, but keeping in communion with God so that God's power can flow through us.

For many years now, I have been seeking to reach out and touch in Jesus' name. It has been an adventure in faith, learning and mystery. There is so much I still don't understand. To my knowledge, I have not been unusually used by God in this ministry as some others have. Nonetheless, I have seen the life-giving power of new health come to some of those on whom I have laid hands and prayed. It has been my experience that even when mental or physical healing does not seem to take place, it often brings to others a deep sense of God's peace and presence. I hope you will also learn to share in this ministry.

DAILY MEDITATION TEXTS FOR THE WEEK

Day 1   "Moved with pity, Jesus stretched out his hand and touched him." (Mark 1:41)

Day 2   "Then suddenly a woman who had been suffering from hemorrhages for twelve years came up behind him and touched the fringe of his cloak, for she said to herself, 'If I only touch his cloak, I will be made well.'" (Matt 9:20–21)

Day 3   "People were bringing even infants to him that he might touch them; and when the disciples saw it, they sternly ordered them not to do it." (Luke 18:15)

Day 4   "Look at my hands and my feet; see that it is I myself. Touch me and see; for a ghost does not have flesh and bones as you see that I have." (Luke 24:39)

Day 5   "Do not lay hands on anyone hastily…" (1 Tim 5:22, NKJV)

Day 6   "She came up behind him and touched the fringe of his clothes, and immediately her hemorrhage stopped. Then Jesus asked, 'Who touched me?'" (Luke 8:44–45)

Day 7   "We declare to you what was from the beginning, what we have heard, what we have seen with our eyes, what we have looked at and touched with our hands, concerning the word of life…" (1 John 1:1)

SUGGESTION FOR JOURNALING

Describe one moment when you experienced human touch as an outward expression of an inward and divine love.

QUOTE

*Touch is essentially the sign and sense of love par excellence,
and in order to find the profound meaning of touch we must
see it from the point of view of love. When an outward and
human touch becomes transformed by an inward and divine
love, it is then, and then only, that we are able to bring solace
to the sad, strength to the weak and healing to the sick.*

Norman Autton
Touch—An Exploration

PRAYER

*Lord Jesus, teach me to see
all those who suffer and are sick
through your eyes, and may they feel
your touch through my hands.
Amen.*

WEEK 35

Taking Seriously the Reality of the Spiritual Realm

On August 6, 1945, the Western powers dropped the atomic bomb on Hiroshima. It must have been an agonizing decision for those involved. No doubt the debate surrounding the rightness of such an act will continue for the rest of human history. What seems to have escaped the notice of many historians, and certainly of those who made the decision, was that the day chosen for the bombing was also the day traditionally set aside by the church to commemorate the transfiguration of Our Lord. In the Eastern Orthodox Church this day is as important on the religious calendar as Christmas, Easter and Pentecost. If this is the case, how could the West have made this tragic oversight?

The answer is fairly obvious. Western Christians have failed to take the transfiguration seriously. We have failed to grasp its significance for our spiritual journey. Morton still remembers a discussion in seminary when his theology professor told him not to put too much emphasis on the transfiguration. Such things simply do not happen, he said. It was probably a story made up by Jesus' followers to show how important he was. However, people who follow this line of thought betray their own materialistic prejudices. They haven't understood what amazing experiences can happen when we open ourselves to God. They believe that we live in a completely rational world where nothing unusual happens. How blind we can be to the depth, wonder and mystery of God's universe.

People who apply this kind of logic to the experiences in Jesus' life also don't realize who they are dealing with. If God could break into this world in the person of Jesus, and if the kingdom of God was present in his life, then surely we could expect some unusual events to take place, even if these things are not the norm. How often do we really ponder the significance of Jesus, of what it means for him to be God in human flesh? Is it so surprising that around such a unique person unusual things might happen, especially when ordinary people like you and me also sometimes experience things that cannot be explained in rational terms?

I would like to suggest, therefore, that we take this story seriously. Anyone who truly wishes to be open to the mystery of life and explore its spiritual possibilities should do so. Start by reading Luke 9. Then compare it with the accounts in Matthew 17 and Mark 9. As you read you will begin to find a transcendence and a mystery, a power and an awe more profound and shattering than anything else you will come across in religious literature. In this gospel event we step onto the holy ground of Jesus' most profound experience as the beloved Son of the Father. It's well worth our time to look more closely at the details and meanings of this story.

The details are fairly straightforward. Jesus and three of his close friends went up a mountain to pray. As he prayed his appearance changed. He became visibly radiant. He glowed. It was as if the light of heaven was shining out of him. Then two figures appeared who talked with him. One was Moses, the other was Elijah—the two pillars of biblical faith and truly spiritual and powerful religion. Finally, a cloud covered them and the disciples became frightened. A voice came out of the cloud saying, "This is my beloved Son. Listen to him." Then, suddenly the two disciples found themselves alone with Jesus again.

Another important detail is that eight days earlier Jesus had been alone with his disciples. He had been praying when he stopped and asked them, "Who do people say that I am?" The disciples answered by telling him that some said he was John the Baptist come back to life, others that he was Elijah or one of the prophets. Then he said them, "And you, who do you say that I am?" It was then that impulsive Peter showed his spiritual perception. He cried out, "You are the Christ, the Son of the living God." The secret was out. Jesus told them to tell no one.

It is not by chance that the transfiguration followed this episode. The disciples at last understood who was in their midst. They were now ready to see more. Now Jesus could reveal his inner spiritual radiance, his overpowering reality as God's anointed one. If the disciples had not some glimmer of who he was, then the transfiguration experience would have been lost on them. Perhaps the reason why we don't have similar transforming experiences is because we have not fully realized the spiritual foundation upon which all of life is based. Perhaps we don't discover the depths of God's mysteries because we have not yet come to know who Jesus really is. This may well be a necessary preparation for experiencing God. If we have not found in our faith what we long for, it may be because we have not prepared for it.

Notice also that Jesus did not allow this transfiguration experience to happen in the marketplace in front of a crowd, or even with the twelve disciples. He took with him only those who were ready, those who could seal their lips until after the resurrection. He chose those who understood most and could be trusted. Spiritual experiences like these can often be misunderstood. People who have such experiences, and who talk too quickly about them, can misuse them. There must be a certain silence about such deep things or they can be lost. This could be why God often seems to break through into our lives more readily in secluded places, away from the rush, the noise and bustling crowds.

Another reason for going off alone with only the closest and most mature of his disciples was that Jesus knew that encountering

God could be quite dangerous. Those who think that meeting with God is like having tea with a beneficent old uncle or aunt are in for a big surprise. God is the central reality of the universe, the very core of power and dynamism in the heart of things. It is not easy to stand before a human sovereign unmoved, but to stand before divine power! Of course God is love, but God is also majesty, dominion, holy, glorious and powerful. I will never forget the time when one of my lecturers at university said to me, "Trevor, when you are in the presence of the real God, you either shut up or fall on your face."

The transfiguration event carries a number of meanings. It makes it very clear that there is an eternal realm that is not bound by time that can break through into our space-time existence. It tells us that Moses and Elijah are still real figures and that those who exist in the kingdom of heaven live on as distinguishable personalities. It reminds us that we can be so filled by divine reality that our lives can also glow with God's presence and power. It proclaims that the heavenly can become real in the earthly as it does in the mystery of holy communion. It underlines God's affirmation of Jesus of Nazareth as his unique Son, as the bearer of God's kingdom. In addition to all this, the transfiguration is a pre-glimpse of the resurrection. It prepares us to believe the greater and more earth-shattering event of Jesus' rising from the dead. If the transfiguration really happened, then we can expect anything on earth, even the resurrection.

This coming week, will you consider immersing yourself in these details and meanings? For when this mysterious gospel story becomes real for us, the Christian faith lights up with new possibilities. We realize that as Christ-followers we are connected to the eternal realm of God's kingdom. This is what Jesus showed us in his transfiguration. When we believe this, and start living as if it were so, we too will begin experiencing God in the most surprising ways.

DAILY MEDITATION TEXTS FOR THE WEEK

Day 1   "Now about eight days after these sayings Jesus took with him Peter and John and James, and went up on the mountain to pray. And while he was praying, the appearance of his face changed, and his clothes became dazzling white." (Luke 9:28–29)

Day 2   "For we did not follow cleverly devised myths when we made known to you the power and coming of our Lord Jesus Christ, but we had been eyewitnesses of his majesty." (2 Pet 1:16)

Day 3   "When I saw him, I fell at his feet as though dead. But he placed his right hand on me, saying, 'Do not be afraid; I am the first and the last, and the living one…'" (Rev 1:17, 18)

Day 4   "The Lord is king, he is robed in majesty; the Lord is robed, he is girded with strength. He has established the world; it shall never be moved; your throne is established from of old; you are from everlasting." (Ps 93:1–2)

Day 5   "Now to him who is able to keep you from falling, and to make you stand without blemish in the presence of his glory with rejoicing, to the only God our Savior, through Jesus Christ our Lord, be glory, majesty, power and authority, before all time and now and forever. Amen." (Jude 1:24–25)

Day 6   "For the eyes of the Lord range throughout the entire earth, to strengthen those whose heart is true to him." (2 Chr 16:9)

Day 7   "I will give thanks to the Lord with my whole heart; I will tell of all your wonderful deeds. I will be glad and exult in you; I will sing praise to your name, O Most High." (Ps 9:1–2)

SUGGESTION FOR JOURNALING

Describe one of your deeper experiences of God.

QUOTE

> On the whole, I do not find Christians, outside of the cata-
> combs, sufficiently sensible of conditions. Does anyone have
> the foggiest idea what sort of power we so blithely invoke? The
> churches are children playing on the floor with their chem-
> istry sets, mixing up a batch of TNT to kill a Sunday morn-
> ing. It is madness to wear ladies' straw hats and velvet hats to
> church; we should all be wearing crash helmets. Ushers should
> issue life preservers and signal flares; they should lash us to
> our pews.
>
> Annie Dillard
> *Teaching a Stone to Talk*

PRAYER

> Father of light, in you is found no shadow of change but only
> the fullness of life and limitless truth. Open our hearts to the
> voice of your Word and free us from the original darkness that
> shadows our vision. Restore our sight that we may look upon
> your Son who calls us to repentance and a change of heart,
> for he lives and reigns with you for ever and ever.
>
> *Glenstal Bible Missal*

WEEK 36

Coming Down the Mountain

Have you noticed that the significance of what we do is often determined by what precedes and follows it? An act of bravery, for example, is a heroic thing in the midst of darkness and calamity, yet not as courageous when everything is going well. Or think about a particular deed of caring. Its impact is often much greater when we receive nothing in return than when it is reciprocated. The sequences of life sometimes influence the importance of what we do as much as the actions themselves.

This is especially true of the stories about Jesus in the gospels. His temptations would have lost half their significance had they not followed immediately after his baptism. The events of Palm Sunday would not have been worth relating were it not for the tragedies that followed. The Last Supper has a more powerful impact because of the betrayal that took place later that same night. So it is with many of the gospel events. We do not understand them fully unless we look at them in their context.

This week we continue to examine Jesus' transfiguration experience. Did you ever stop to think about what the other disciples were doing the morning that Jesus, Peter, James and John went up the mountain? Do you know what Jesus did as soon as he descended from the mount of exaltation? The gospel tells us, and what it shares is a truth of the most tremendous importance about Jesus and our spiritual journey.

Let me remind you what the disciples were doing while Jesus was being transfigured by God's glory. They were doing their best to heal an epileptic boy who had been brought to the Master by his desperate father. They tried everything but to no avail. There was gloom in their hearts, in the father's heart, and in the heart of the young boy. They had failed. I can imagine the father thinking to himself, "There is no hope for my son at all."

Then Jesus returned, from divine brightness into the darkness of human hearts, from the glory of the mountaintop experience into the valley of the shadow of sickness, doubt and failure. He brought joy to a father who had cried out in his unbelief. He brought healing and wholeness to a child suffering from epilepsy. He taught his disciples so that their failure was transformed into new understanding. In a nutshell, he brought the radiance of the transfiguration experience into the gloom of the valley. He refused to stay on the mountain as Peter had wanted him to. Rather, he translated spiritual experience into action.

This is the truth we need to grasp. We are not followers of God unless we also translate our spiritual experiences into action, unless we bring the light, as much or little as we have experienced, into the gathering darkness of our pain-filled world. Sometimes we don't want to look at the suffering and misery around us. We prefer to forget that there is a sinful world out there needing what we can bring. Granted, thinking about the sick and ugly side of life is upsetting, but our task as Christ-followers is to face what is there and then to bring the healing beam of God's presence into it.

Let's look a little closer at what Jesus did, so that we can do the same. First of all, he took aside the boy's father, a man whose heart was nearly breaking for the love of his son. "All things are possible for someone who believes," he told him. With tears in his eyes, the man burst out, "I believe, help my unbelief." And Jesus did. He was able to give him something of what had happened just an hour before on the mountain. The nearly hysterical father calmed down as the confidence of Jesus possessed him. Healing was now possible, for no healing can take place in a atmosphere of despair, doubt and unbelief.

This is what you and I also need to do. We must bring the same confidence into the despairing darkness around us. But we can't bring light that we don't have, no matter how outwardly brave and reassuring we may act. If we are to bring some relief to the unbelief that strangles our world, we must bring the radiance of God's splendor in us, that we ourselves have found from spending time with God on the mountain. If we are to minister in the darkness of our world, we must first seek the light!

The next thing Jesus did was to turn to the child. His experience on the mountain wasn't complete until the boy had been healed. No Christ-follower can be at peace while any child or adult suffers. With our prayers and actions we should bring hope and life to those who are sick. God can use ordinary people like you and me as instruments to bring healing. One way or another, the light our God gives us demands expression in bringing wholeness to the spirits, minds and bodies of our suffering neighbors. This is what Jesus meant when he said, "Let your light so shine before others that they will see your good works and give glory to your Father in Heaven."

After Jesus had healed the child, he was finally left alone with his disciples. They could hardly wait to ask, "Why could we not heal this boy? Why did we fail?" Jesus answered that it needed a greater dedication, a brighter concentration of God's light in the lives of those who heal. Healing the sickness of the world isn't done by some magic formula; it happens when we open our hearts to God so that we can bring the healing and light we receive back into the world that longs for it. Exposing ourselves to the light of God doesn't happen by chance; it happens when we turn in prayer and adoration, in fasting and self-control, to the Source of all being and life. Then our lives begin to shine as transmitters of God's life and power.

Take time to explore this week's truth as deeply as you can. Remember, the way we can tell whether our "spiritual highs" are genuine is to observe what flows from them. Do they result in kindness and mercy, love and healing, sharing and concrete acts of good? To be more specific, do they lead us to visit the sick, befriend the lonely, comfort the sorrowing, encourage the depressed and reach out to those in material need? A real relationship with God expresses itself in actions like these. This is the lesson Jesus tried to teach us that day when he climbed the mountain to be transfigured and then came down to the valley to heal. Let us learn to shine with the love of God that has touched our lives.

DAILY MEDITATION TEXTS FOR THE WEEK

Day 1   "What good is it, my brothers and sisters, if you say you have faith but do not have works? Can faith save you?" (Jas 2:14)

Day 2   "If a brother or sister is naked and lacks daily food, and one of you says to them, 'go in peace; keep warm and eat your fill,' and yet you do not supply their bodily needs, what is the good of that?" (Jas 2:15–16)

Day 3   "But someone will say, 'You have faith and I have works.' Show me your faith apart from your works, and I by my works will show you my faith." (Jas 2:18)

Day 4   "The commandment we have from him is this: those who love God must love their brothers and sisters also." (1 John 4:21)

Day 5   "For the love of God is this, that we obey his commandments." (1 John 5:3)

Day 6   "Everyone then who hears these words of mine and acts on them will be like a wise man who built his house on rock." (Matt 7:24)

Day 7   "Not everyone who says to me, 'Lord, Lord,' will enter the kingdom of heaven, but only the one who does the will of my Father in heaven." (Matt 7:21)

SUGGESTION FOR JOURNALING

Write down one practical step you intend to take during the next few days that will express your faith in action.

QUOTE

I was hungry and you formed a humanity's club and
*   discussed my hunger, thank you.*
I was imprisoned and you crept off quietly to your chapel
*   and prayed for my release.*
I was naked and in your mind you debated the morality of
*   my appearance.*
I was sick and you knelt and thanked God for your health.
I was homeless and you preached to me of the love of God.
I was lonely and you left me alone to pray for me.
You seem so holy, so very close to God, but I am still very
*   hungry and lonely and cold—thank you.*

Robert Roland
Listen Christian

PRAYER

O Lord,
so many sick
so many starving
so many deprived
so many sad
so many bitter
so many fearful.
When I look at them my heart fails.
When I look at You I hope again.
Help me to help You to reduce the world's pain.
O God of infinite compassion
O ceaseless Energy of love.
Amen.

George Appleton

WEEK 37

Righting Wrongs with Christ

In our church there is an accountant who seeks to follow Christ in his daily work. For eight years he has managed the finances of a medium-sized engineering concern. One day he was told by his directors to submit false figures to the firm's bank. He refused, knowing that this refusal would place his job on the line. When asked for his reasons, he shared with his superiors his commitment to live as a Christ-follower. In spite of ongoing pressure, including manipulative threats, he stuck to his decision. Although his stand may have sidelined possible promotion, he continues to work in his managerial position. Outwardly, his words and actions seem to have had little effect, but who will ever know the eternal consequences of his brave witness?

My friend stands in the long line of those who have sought to right wrongs with Christ. Like the Holy One he follows, he wants to bring light where there is darkness, truth where there is falsehood, healing where there is sickness. He knows that the Jesus we meet in the gospels was not always gentle, kind and self-effacing. Sometimes he got really angry, especially when he was face to face with evil. Unfortunately, we are not always aware of these dimensions of decisiveness and firmness in his life. And as a result we fail to take action against the wrongs we come across in our daily lives.

There is a story in Mark's Gospel that tells of Jesus acting firmly against evil. It concerns the leper who knelt before Jesus and said, "If only you will, you can cleanse me." The New English Bible gives Jesus' reply in these words: "In warm indignation Jesus stretched out his hand, touched him, and said,

'Indeed I will. Be clean again.'" The leprosy disappeared immediately. Then Jesus sent the man away with a "strong warning"
not to tell anyone about it except the priest who, according to
the law of Moses, had to certify that he was cured. But the man
disobeyed and spread the news far and wide.

If we look closely at the story, we get quite a different picture
of Jesus, not the meek and mild Jesus we all know. Here is the
Son of Man in an angry mood. The Greek version of these
words indicates that he was really stirred up. Why? He was unal-
terably opposed to illness and disease. These things were the
work of evil in the universe, and he was against evil in all its
forms. And so, when faced with any expression of evil, he always
got involved in doing something about it. Because he cared
about people, he let his concern show in dramatic and personal
ways. It was almost as if he couldn't stop himself. When confronted with evil he needed to defeat it.

There are other examples of this in his life. When injustice
was taking place in the temple courts, he took a whip and drove
out the buyers and sellers with their cattle. He was so incensed
by the hypocrisy of the scribes and pharisees that he denounced
them in language that made his death certain. He was so upset
with people who refused to make a clear decision between God's
way and the world's way that he declared in no uncertain terms
that those who followed the broad way would come to destruction. Clearly, Jesus was opposed to evil in all its forms. Whether
it was leprosy, injustice, or religious abuse, Jesus came to conquer evil, whatever shape it took.

The idea that we as Christ-followers should merely be passive
and look with detachment upon the world's wrongs is an utter
distortion of Christian discipleship. Any kind of spirituality that
does not lead us into some form of positive and definite action
against evil cannot be called a gospel spirituality. It fails to reflect
the heart of Jesus who was so indignant about every kind of evil
that he stretched out his hand to heal, restore and make new. We

may not have the power to heal with a word as he did, but each one of us can do something to add to the balance of hope and health in the world. If some of the evil around us doesn't make us angry enough to fight it, then I wonder how seriously we are taking our relationship with Jesus. True disciples resemble their master. But what can we, as individuals, do to right the wrongs of our world?

+ We can begin by getting tough with ourselves and dealing with those personal vices we have grown to accept.
+ We can quit gossiping, rumor-mongering and criticizing people behind their backs.
+ We can be young people who resist pressure from peers to do drugs or abuse alcohol.
+ We can be business persons who take a stand against dishonesty and corruption because these evils enrage us.
+ We can be nurses, teachers and social workers who treat people as individuals and not as numbers and cases.
+ We can be managers and administrators who refuse to stand for abuse of power and position.
+ We can be workers who put in an honest day's labor because wasted time galls our conscience.
+ We can be politicians fighting for better laws because we hate injustice.
+ We can be doctors combating sickness because suffering makes us indignant.
+ We can support relief agencies in their good work both financially and through volunteer efforts because poverty and homelessness makes us burn with indignation.
+ We can write letters to our local newspapers and sign petitions when there are community practices that hurt and oppress our neighbors.

The list of possible ways in which we can right wrongs with Christ goes on and on. Of course, we cannot respond to every manifestation of evil we come across. But we can look around our communities and places of work and ask God to guide us and show us where we must take action. Our light, the light of Christ in us, must shine before the world in word and in deed. Only then will people everywhere see that God is their ally against every form of evil. Only then will they believe that Jesus came so that we may have fullness of life.

Daily Meditation Texts for the Week

Day 1   "The Spirit of the Lord is upon me, because he has anointed me to bring good news to the poor. He has sent me to proclaim release to the captives and recovery of sight to the blind, to let the oppressed go free, to proclaim the year of the Lord's favor." (Luke 4:18–19)

Day 2   "Seek good and not evil, that you may live; and so the Lord, the God of hosts, will be with you, just as you have said." (Amos 5:14)

Day 3   "And he answered them, 'Go and tell John what you have seen and heard: the blind receive their sight, the lame walk, the lepers are cleansed, the deaf hear, the dead are raised, the poor have good news brought to them.'" (Luke 7:22)

Day 4   "Cease to do evil, learn to do good; seek justice, rescue the oppressed, defend the orphan, plead for the widow." (Isa 1:17)

Day 5   "I came that they may have life, and have it abundantly." (John 10:10)

Day 6   "Do not be overcome by evil, but overcome evil with good." (Rom 12:21)

Day 7   "But let justice roll down like waters, and righteousness like an ever-flowing stream." (Amos 5:24)

Suggestion for Journaling

Describe the "wrong" in your community that stirs you up the most.

Quote

> *Christ has no body now on earth but yours, no hands but yours and no feet but yours. Yours are the eyes through which Christ looks out with compassion on the world. Yours are the feet with which he is to go about doing good. Yours are the hands with which he is to bless people now.*
>
> Teresa of Avila

Prayer

> *Dear God, bless me with anger at injustice, oppression, exploitation of people and the earth, so that I may strive for justice, equity and peace. Bless me with tears to shed for those who suffer, so that I will reach out my hands to comfort them and to change their pain into joy. And, Lord bless me with foolishness to think that I can make a difference in the world, so that I will begin to do the things that others say cannot be done. Amen.*

WEEK 38

Taking a Stand

I was standing in the foyer of a neighboring church when I saw the poster for the first time. It caught my attention immediately. It was a starkly drawn portrait of Jesus with a crown of thorns pressed into his head. Underneath were the words, "If you were tried in court for being a Christian, would you be found guilty?" The question disturbed me. As I write these words I still struggle to give a clear answer. How would you respond?

The question got me thinking about the importance of taking a stand for the gospel. There are times when every Christ-follower is called to do so. Usually we begin by committing ourselves to being faithful in our personal relationships, being honest in our business dealings and acting with integrity in matters of morality. Then we move outward into the public arena. We start wrestling with issues of wealth and poverty, race and gender, violence and nonviolence, crime and justice. In these areas and countless others we try to discern what position will be most life-giving and most expressive of the great commandment. And then, when the time comes, we nail our colors to the mast.

This is what Jesus did that first Palm Sunday. He had made his decision. He would go into Jerusalem. He would witness to God's purposes and will right there in the Holy City. Not only would he go there, but he would go in such a way that no one could ignore him. He would take on the messianic role, the role foretold by the prophet Zechariah in the Old Testament. He would go humbly and vulnerably, riding on a donkey. This was how he would take his stand.

The story tells us that there were thousands of pilgrims camped outside Jerusalem. As Jesus rode towards the city, they lined the roads, palm branches in hand. Seldom before had there been such a demonstration. The whole city was emotionally on fire. There was no one in Jerusalem who did not understand the meaning of the moment. Jesus was throwing down the gauntlet to the religious leadership of the day. He was saying in effect, "It is you or me, your way or God's."

Why did Jesus take this stand? For one who ordinarily did not seek the spotlight, this entrance certainly seemed out of character. Until now Jesus had been working quietly, trying not to draw too much attention to himself. He had avoided seeking public approval. He had told those whom he had healed to go home and tell no one. Yet now he walked straight into the Holy City. Why? In a nutshell, the time had come for a showdown. He had to face the corrupt religious establishment of his people and bear witness before them of what he knew and believed. The time had come for him to declare who and what he was. He had to declare himself as the long-awaited Messiah, the Anointed One of God. The powers of God had to face the powers of this world. And this conflict could not be fought privately. It had to take place in public view, in the bright sunlight.

There are times when you and I, like Jesus, have to take a stand. And we need to take care that we do this at the right time and not prematurely. Some people are foolhardy and reckless, taking a stand on every count. This is silly and more often than not achieves very little. On the other hand, there are those who are too cowardly ever to stand up for what they believe in. It is not easy to know which is the right action and when is the right time. We need to pick our battles carefully. This means that we need to pray and work hard at having discernment and courage. If we don't put careful thought and prayer into knowing when to act, we might not stand up at the right moment. How hard it is to discern when it is our Palm Sunday.

Let's return to the meaning of that first Palm Sunday. When Jesus mounted the donkey and rode into the city amid wild acclaim, he was saying in effect, "My life counts. It stands for something. What I do matters. Even if I am destroyed I will be faithful to myself and to God." The time had come for him to be true to his deepest convictions. He could no longer condone the massive structure of evil that surrounded him. He knew he must confront the evil in the temple and face the evil in the world, no matter what happened to him personally. His conscience, his inner truth, his very soul demanded that he face these enemies. If he did not, he would not be the Son of Man and he would not be true to his humanity at all.

This action of Jesus was a combination of courage and faith. Courage is the capacity to live constantly with our deepest beliefs, no matter what confronts us. It is steadfastly holding on to what we put first and standing by it in every circumstance. Faith is the hope that what we believe and stand for will be ultimately vindicated by God. It provides the foundation for courage. On Palm Sunday Jesus prepared the stage for a great showdown between the forces of good and evil. He did that which his human side cried out against, but which represented the deepest convictions of his soul. His action that day set the stage for the cleansing of the temple, for his death and resurrection. It was the essential first step in his final action to save all humankind.

If we are followers of Christ, we will seek to live our lives as he would if he were in our place. We will identify those things in the depths of our being that we cannot deny, except at our soul's peril. Indeed, Jesus' example on that Palm Sunday poses the question:

What is so important to you and me that we are willing to witness for it before the whole world? What do we stand for so deeply and strongly that no matter who opposes us, we would carry it through?

Jesus decided on Palm Sunday to take a stand for his deepest convictions. Will you and I do the same? Perhaps then the jury will find us guilty for being a faithful Christ-follower!

DAILY MEDITATION TEXTS FOR THE WEEK

Day 1   "Rejoice greatly, O daughter Zion! Shout aloud, O daughter Jerusalem! Lo, your king comes to you; triumphant and victorious is he, humble and riding on a donkey, on a colt, the foal of a donkey." (Zech 9:9)

Day 2   "A voice cries out: 'In the wilderness prepare the way of the Lord, make straight in the desert a highway for our God.'" (Isa 40:3)

Day 3   "I know your works; you are neither cold nor hot. I wish that you were either cold or hot." (Rev 3:15)

Day 4   "Everyone therefore who acknowledges me before others, I also will acknowledge before my Father in heaven." (Matt 10:32)

Day 5   "For whoever does the will of my Father in heaven is my brother and sister and mother." (Matt 12:50)

Day 6   "Salt is good; but if salt has lost its saltiness, how can you season it? Have salt in yourselves, and be at peace with one another." (Mark 9:50)

Day 7   "See, I am sending you out like sheep into the midst of wolves; so be wise as serpents and innocent as doves." (Matt 10:16)

SUGGESTION FOR JOURNALING

What do you stand for so deeply and strongly that no matter who opposes you, you will carry it through?

QUOTE

If you were to be put on trial for being a Christian, would you be found guilty?

Church poster

PRAYER

Dear Lord, renew in me the courage to live my life as Jesus would if he were in my place. Help me especially to stand for those values that he taught, and give me the wisdom to discern how best to do this. When opposition comes my way may I not give way to fear and cowardice. I ask this for Jesus' sake. Amen.

———

Finding Forgiveness
at the Cross

Personal stories sometimes convey far more than abstract theories and logical discussions. This is especially so when it comes to talking about the meaning of the cross. Theological language often leaves us untouched, whereas stories and meditations reach beyond our rational minds and move into the heart and emotions. So let me share with you a modern-day parable about a woman who was touched by the cross of Jesus and found victory on the other side of defeat.

Alice Maywell (not her real name) found herself one Good Friday attending the three-hour service at a local church. She wasn't sure exactly why she had come. She had only been in church a few times in her life. Going to church was for occasions like baptisms, weddings and funerals. As for God or Jesus, she really only used these words when she swore. She was definitely not the religious type, but something happened in church that afternoon that changed her forever.

Her life had been filled with every luxury money could buy. Her father had started with a small grocery store and through hard work had built it up into the biggest store in town. Then he opened another store in a city a few miles away. He ended up with a chain of over fifty stores and a fortune that made him a household name for miles around. At first his wife had been interested in the business, but things started going wrong in their marriage and they went their separate ways—he in his business and she in her club work and social activities.

For their oldest child, a son, nothing was too good and the whirl of parties staged at their country estate was the talk of the town. Alice was born to them late in life. She was sickly at birth and remained so throughout her life. She received little love or attention from her parents. They gave her many things materially but not those things her heart longed for, such as time, attention and love. Alice grew up to be the envy of town and yet a most unhappy and lonely little child.

When her father died, burned out at fifty, he had left enough money in trust to give her a generous income each year. At twenty she was totally independent. She decided to live her life exactly as she pleased. She found an apartment in an up-market suburb and began to travel wherever her heart took her. A few years later her mother died in an accident, and Alice found that her income had doubled.

She tried all the popular remedies for unhappiness—large cars, servants, beautiful homes, overseas trips, even marriage. Each of these was a miserable failure. She found that most of her friends were looking to her for favors rather than wanting to give any real care or concern. Even her husband had his eye on her money. He tried to swindle her out of part of her fortune, but fortunately she caught him at it and they were divorced. Now she was alone. She trusted no one. She had no reason to. In desperation, she turned to that well-known remedy for unhappiness, the bottle. In the last ten years or so she had not been sober very often. Her money protected her from the shocks of reality. She became bitter and resentful. She blamed her family for what they had done to her, the world because it did not accept her, herself whom she could not tolerate. Indeed, at the heart of everything, she could not live with herself. She could not forgive herself for making so little of her life.

Alice Maywell fled from one failure to another. If she could not find some release or happiness, she decided, she would end

her life. And so, half drunk, she drove past the church on Good
Friday and read the words on the bulletin board:

*Is it nothing to you, all you that pass by? Is there any sorrow,
like unto my sorrow?*

These words struck her deeply and convinced her to go in. She
took a seat at the back of the church, hardly knowing where she
was or what to do. She knew so little about the Christian gospel
that she had no idea why so many people had come together on
a Friday afternoon.

Then the story of Good Friday unfolded dramatically before
her. Her imagination was vivid and somehow she could see Jesus
—a strong, virile young man, courageous and outspoken, the
joy and admiration of those who knew him. Then she could see
him abandoned by his friends and followers, turned upon by the
religious leaders of his own people, betrayed by one friend and
denied by another, the laughing stock of the religious leaders
and Herod, the pawn of Pilate, the sport of the soldiers, and
now hanging upon a cross. She felt a deep connection. She herself had been on a cross for fifty years, and it had taken much
wine to help her forget in the last decade and a half.

Then a deeper realization struck home. This man was on a
cross because he had lived his life in faithfulness. His integrity
had provoked the anger of the religious authorities and now they
wanted him dead. She, on the other hand, had come to where
she was by her own choice. She had had many opportunities to
change. Several real friends had tried to help her, but those who
disagreed with her were soon rejected. Stubbornly and persistently she had refused to look for any good in the world or see
any in herself. She had not allowed herself to care for anyone,
because she thought no one would care for her. She understood
what he felt, this pain of crucifixion, but he was without blame.

Then during the meditation she heard the unforgettable
words. "Father, forgive them for they know not what they do."

Jesus spoke them to all who were there that day. He spoke them to the religious authorities and to Pilate, to the indifferent spectators and to the soldiers, to the disciples and to his friends. Instinctively she knew that he spoke them even to her, to Alice Maywell, who had had so many chances to discover hope and new life and who had, instead, gone her own way into self-hate and self-pity. She understood all too clearly that there was a Father who was offering forgiveness. She could be forgiven, her parents could be forgiven for what had happened between them and for their indifference to her. Slowly it dawned on her that she had worth and value and that she, too, could forgive those who had used and abused her.

It was amazing how quickly she sobered up and how clearly she began to see things. She realized she was a child of infinite preciousness and meaning. She heard few of the other words that were spoken. She was remembering, feeling through the past, receiving forgiveness and giving it. It was not too late. She was still alive, and with this fresh solid ground on which she now stood, she could make a new beginning. She did not have to end it all. She could make a new life, and she would. She wept honestly for the first time in years. She had a chance to start all over again. So do you and I!

Daily Meditation Texts for the Week

Day 1   "Then Jesus said, 'Father, forgive them; for they do not know what they are doing.'" (Luke 23:34)

Day 2   "Who can forgive sins but God alone?" (Mark 2:7)

Day 3   "…if my people who are called by my name humble themselves, pray, seek my face, and turn from their wicked ways, then I will hear from heaven, and will forgive their sin and heal their land." (2 Chr 7:14)

Day 4   "For Christ also suffered for sins once for all, the righteous for the unrighteous, in order to bring you to God." (1 Pet 3:18)

Day 5   "And when you were dead in trespasses and the uncir-
cumcision of your flesh, God made you alive together
with him, when he forgave us all our trespasses, erasing
the record that stood against us with its legal demands.
He set this aside, nailing it to the cross." (Col 2:13–14)

Day 6   "Have mercy on me, O God, according to your steadfast love; according to your abundant mercy blot out
my transgressions." (Ps 51:1)

Day 7   "Create in me a clean heart, O God, and put a new and
right spirit within me." (Ps 51:10)

SUGGESTION FOR JOURNALING

What do you need God's forgiveness for at this moment?

QUOTE

*God forgives me, for he takes my head between his hands and
turns my face to his to make me smile at him. And though I
struggle and hurt those hands—for they are human, though
divine, human and scarred with nails—though I hurt them,
they do not let go until he has smiled me into smiling; and
that is the forgiveness of God.*

Austin Farrer

PRAYER

*Father, over and over again I have fallen into the same temp-
tations. It does seem as if I am slow to learn Thy ways and
Thy laws. I blush to recall my vows to Thee: never again to
do what I have just come from doing, not again to stain
myself in the same mudholes. Yet O Lord, stained as I am,
and conscious of my own weakness, I have no choice but to
pick myself up again, to ask Thee to forgive me once more
and make me clean again. I thank thee, O Lord Jesus, for the
glory of the Gospel of the Second Chance.*

I would claim from Thee that chance to begin all over again. Thou hast heard my prayer of confession. Now I claim Thy promise to forgive me and to cleanse me. From this moment I accept that forgiveness and that cleansing by faith, because I believe that thy promise is the "word of a Gentleman of the most strict and sacred honour."

And now I ask for Thy spirit to come into me like cool fresh air to revitalise me, to shock me into a new discipleship, to invigorate me for a new life in Christ Jesus, my Lord. Amen.

The Prayers of Peter Marshall

WEEK 40

Exploring a Resurrection Faith

This past Easter Sunday I started my sermon with a true story. During communist rule in Russia there were tremendous efforts on behalf of the governing party to do away with the Christian faith. On one occasion, a university lecturer, addressing a packed auditorium, was seeking to squash all evidence of the resurrection of Jesus. For over an hour he put forward his arguments. Eventually the time came for questions from the floor. An elderly man sitting in the back row asked if he could say something. He was told that he could have only one minute. He answered that he would only need a second. Then he walked to the front of the lecture hall, turned to the audience and shouted, "Christ is risen." With a mighty roar the crowd responded, "He is risen indeed."

This story stirs me deeply. It is a powerful reminder that the resurrection of Jesus lies at the heart of our faith. On the third day after his crucifixion his disciples and women friends found the tomb empty. The love that Jesus had proclaimed, the love that he had lived, the love that he was had not been defeated by the dark powers of evil. This is incredibly good news. No faith could be more tragic, no belief more futile, than Christianity without its risen Lord. It would be foolish and sad to base our lives on a dead hero. Why struggle for God's values if there's only the agony of the cross at the end of our best efforts? Perhaps Paul was also thinking thoughts like these when he wrote:

If for this life only we have hoped in Christ, we are of all people most to be pitied. (1 Cor 15:19)

But this is not the case. Christ has risen! This one supreme fact of history overturns once and for all every stronghold of doubt and despair, every fortress of distress and pessimism. Those who say that evil is stronger than good, hatred stronger than love, and lies stronger than truth must show convincingly that he did not rise again. For if he has risen, our confidence and faith in the ultimate triumph of the kingdom of God can stand secure. We have something to cling to, something on which to base our lives. How else does one explain how his frightened and grieving disciples were transformed into bold witnesses who were willing to die for their faith? Something most extraordinary must have taken place after the crucifixion. Something like the resurrection.

However, Easter means more than this. If Jesus died and rose again, we can hope for the same thing to happen to us. We can dare believe that there is a life beyond the bounds of our mortal bodies. We may pretend that such matters do not bother us, but a sneaking fear lurks in our hearts when we hear someone deride any possibility of life beyond death. After all, life on earth lacks so much. Many people live unfulfilled lives. They have suffered torture, oppression, natural disaster, poverty and pain. They have been crippled physically or mentally, as well as having been injured by prejudice, discrimination and rejection. For these people, this life is a bad joke unless there is something more. Only a new and eternal dimension of life such as Jesus described can compensate for what many suffer on this earth, both psychologically and physically.

This is also true for those of us who have led reasonably comfortable lives. If there is no life beyond this one, even the best of lives remain empty, the very finest careers are in vain, our deepest loves only mock us, and the most noble actions are a waste of time. If our lives end at the grave they are robbed of all meaning and significance. Furthermore, when life's value consists only of what life on earth has to offer, material things become central. The struggle for possession of these objects then becomes intense, and the very worst of human nature is brought out. These material things, once obtained, eventually turn to dust and ashes. No wonder that those who view the grave as final often lose themselves in compulsive business or in the oblivion of alcohol, drugs or crude pleasures.

Thankfully, we need not fear: Christ is risen! Life holds something greater in store for us. He was not just resuscitated, brought back to experience more of this earthly life. On that first Easter Sunday morning the disciples did not just see a revived body, but a new creation, something entirely original and unique. Here in the risen Christ was all the reality of the earth and all the glory and power of God and heaven. And so it will be for those who, through faith, share in his life and being. We, too, will be given new bodies. Because of Easter we will also enter a new dimension filled with God's goodness, love and mercy. As Jesus himself promised his disciples:

Very truly, I tell you, whoever keeps my word will never see death. (John 8:51)

Easter offers us another great mystery to celebrate. On the cross evil unleashed its very worst against God's very best. Jesus responded by absorbing it all with the vulnerability of self-giving love. When he died it seemed as if evil had won. But God acted and raised him to life. In rising from the dead, Jesus exposed the ultimate weakness of the evil powers in this world. No matter how powerful evil may be, we know that it does not need to reign supreme in our lives. We can call out to the risen Christ and ask him to help us overcome.

This is wonderful news for you and me. Few of us continuously show the Spirit of Christ in our day-to-day lives. Often we are swept over by dark feelings of anger, fear, anxiety, selfishness, lust, cowardice and even outright cruelty. Sometimes we even put these attitudes into action. Furthermore, we often experience the powers of darkness around us. We live in a world characterized by poverty, crime, war, child abuse, and the like. These things naturally contribute to feelings of hopelessness, despair and doubt in our hearts. As powerful as this evil is within and around us, Christ is able to deliver us from it. This is what resurrection faith is all about.

Finally, a resurrection faith enables us to experience "little Easters" in the midst of the things that make us "die" each day, such as the lack of appreciation by our children or our partners, the betrayal of a friend, the cruelty of a colleague, the shameful things we do, or even the failure of a dream. All these things involve us in miniature crucifixions. They happen to each of us and there is no avoiding them if we live our lives at any depth. But Easter reminds us that the risen Christ is able to bring light and life where there seems to be only darkness and death. When this happens, even in a small way, we experience a "little Easter."

Can you see why Easter is the day of days? It is the foundation of our faith. It strengthens our hope for a fuller life beyond this one. It sets us free from the powers of evil that seek to dominate our lives. It enables us each day to rise into newness of life. What good news this is! No wonder that communist lecturer could not deceive his believing audience. They had a resurrection faith. May we, too, explore a similar relationship with our risen Lord.

DAILY MEDITATION TEXTS FOR THE WEEK

Day 1   "But he said to them, 'Do not be alarmed; you are looking for Jesus of Nazareth, who was crucified. He has been raised; he is not here.'" (Mark 16:6)

Day 2   "For I handed on to you as of first importance what I in turn had received: that Christ died for our sins in accordance with the scriptures, and that he was buried, and that he was raised on the third day in accordance with the scriptures, and that he appeared to Cephas, then to the twelve." (1 Cor 15:3–5)

Day 3   "Blessed be the God and Father of our Lord Jesus Christ! By his great mercy he has given us a new birth into a living hope through the resurrection of Jesus Christ from the dead..." (1 Pet 1:3)

Day 4   "Jesus said to her, 'I am the resurrection and the life. Those who believe in me, even though they die, will live, and everyone who lives and believes in me will never die.'" (John 11:25)

Day 5   "Now he is God not of the dead, but of the living; for to him all of them are alive." (Luke 20:38)

Day 6   "Very truly, I tell you, whoever keeps my word will never see death." (John 8:51)

Day 7   "But God raised him up, having freed him from death, because it was impossible for him to be held in its power." (Acts 2:24)

SUGGESTION FOR JOURNALING

Describe one moment in your life when it seemed that God brought life out of death.

QUOTE

> *Legal proofs of the resurrection have their place as useful books—but they remain books. The real "proofs" of Jesus' resurrection are resurrected lives, transformed by the living Christ in their hearts.*

> James Houston
> *The Heart's Desire*

PRAYER

Lord Jesus Christ, alive and at large in the world, help me to follow and find you there today, in the places where I work, meet people, spend money, and make plans. Take me as a disciple of your kingdom, to see through your eyes, and hear the questions you are asking, to welcome all others with your trust and truth, and to change the things that contradict God's love, by the power of the cross and the freedom of your Spirit.

John V. Taylor
A Matter of Life and Death

SECTION FIVE

Going Deeper

WEEK 41

Nurturing Silence in a Noisy World

We live in a noisy world. A buzzing alarm clock wakes us up. The television goes on and the news and music bombardment begins. We drink our first cup of coffee while a constant flow of words tell us about what is going on in our world. If both parents are going to work and there are children, there is a mad rush to get everyone on their way. As we drive to work, we tune in on our local radio station. Daily work happens in the midst of ringing telephones, blaring background music and the hubbub of human chatter. On the way home, we turn the car radio on again. Then, in the evening, we watch television or a violent video before falling into bed too tired even to dream. And the next day the same diet of noise starts all over again.

Sound familiar? Much of modern life looks like a concerted attempt to avoid ever being alone and quiet. This kind of living reveals far more about what we actually believe than anything we may say. It exposes our trust in those things that are material. It expresses our doubts about the value of taking time to listen to God. It reveals our reluctance to follow Jesus in his practice of silent solitude. Given such noisy lives the Spirit of God has little chance of breaking through, except in sickness or old age, and then who heeds its call? Until we cease our all-consuming business and nurture times of silence, it is highly unlikely that we will ever embark upon a significant spiritual journey.

This is what happened to a minister who came to the psychologist Carl Jung suffering from a nervous breakdown. The story he shared was a familiar one. He had been working four-teen hours a day and his nerves were shot. Jung's instructions were quite simple. He was to work only eight hours and then go home and spend the evening quietly in his study, all alone. Since the man was in real agony, he made up his mind to follow the prescription exactly. After he had worked his eight hours, he returned home, had his supper, told his wife about the plan and went into his study and closed the door. He played some Chopin and read a Hermann Hesse novel. The next day was the same, except this time he read Thomas Mann and played a Mozart sonata. The following morning he went back to see Dr. Jung, who asked him how he felt.

When he complained that he was no better, Jung enquired just what he had done. The minister recited his many activities. "But you didn't understand," Jung told him, "I didn't want you with Hermann Hesse or Thomas Mann, or even Mozart or Chopin. I wanted you to be alone and silent with yourself." When he heard this, a look of terror crossed the man's face and he exclaimed, "Oh, but I can't think of any worse company than myself." To which Jung gave his classic reply, "But the self you cannot stand, is the one you are inflicting on other people four-teen hours a day."

Silence is an important ingredient of the spiritual journey. We see this clearly in the life of Jesus. Many of the major events of his life took place when he went off by himself. After his bap-tism, he went alone into the desert for forty days to wrestle with his calling. It was in the silence of a lonely mountain that the transfiguration took place. After the Last Supper, Jesus prepared for the ordeal ahead by taking his followers into the Garden of Gethsemane, where he prayed alone and in quiet while his dis-ciples slept. Again and again, he went away to some quiet place, away from activity and people. Even though he was the divine incarnate, Jesus tried to keep his relationship with Abba in good working order through the regular practice of silence.

If Jesus needed silence, so do we. It has the potential to enrich our spiritual lives profoundly. Its benefits are enormous. Sometimes we receive special gifts of peace and quiet confidence that help us live more creatively amid our stress-filled circumstances. At other times, we may experience stirrings that we did not know were within us. We discover hidden things about ourselves—some wonderful, others quite shocking. These self-discoveries usually take our relationship with God to new levels of depth and maturity. Perhaps most importantly, silence teaches us that prayer is a two-way experience. Not only should we speak to God, but we must also listen. The discipline of silently waiting on God opens the lines for us to hear "the still small voice."

How do we go about making space for silence in our hectic lives? First of all, we need to deliberately make time for it. When we claim that we are too busy to be silent, then usually we are too busy! For many, the best time is in the early morning, for some it is in the middle of the day, others like a period of quiet just before going to bed, and then there are those who wake up during the night and find their silence then. These times may change in different phases of our lives. Personally, I like to get to my office half an hour before my working day begins. No one else is around and I'm able to spend some twenty minutes quietly with God and myself.

Second, we need to find a practical way of actually getting quiet and still within. If you are like me, as soon as you want to be silent, all kinds of thoughts and images come rushing into your mind. Don't give up if this happens. Experiment with different ways of stilling your mind. Some people find it helpful to focus on a simple word or phrase which expresses their longing for God, such as, "Abba," "Jesus," "Maranatha," the well-known Jesus Prayer: "Lord Jesus Christ, Son of God, have mercy on me, a sinner," or the Rosary. Repeating our prayer word or phrase for ten minutes or so, and gently returning to it when our attention starts to wander, leads us into a restful place where we can immerse ourselves more deeply in God. Others prefer to look at a picture or a symbol—a lighted candle, crucifix, or flower—while focusing their heart and mind on God. Whatever method you choose, the important challenge is to create a little pool of inner stillness in which to learn to "...know that I am God" (Psalm 46:10).

Third, we can build moments of silence into our fellowship groups and prayer meetings. Many people find that being quiet with others helps them to still their minds and become silent. An atmosphere of quiet engenders quiet. This is the great secret of the Quaker movement. Underpinning their vibrant social witness of peacemaking and nonviolence is a highly effective and careful ritual for the communal practice of silence. If you really struggle to become silent on your own, find a group where others like you pray silently together.

In closing, may I add that becoming aware of the rewards of silence is rather like eating. Few of us would argue about our need to keep on eating. In much the same way, the life of the soul needs to be nourished by the regular practice of silence, day after day, month after month, and year after year. Otherwise the soul becomes starved of those nutrients that give life, vitality and depth. One loses the capacity to have a sustained relationship with the world of the Holy Spirit and with Abba. Silence allows the soul to grow and develop spiritually. In fact, the more we discover the reality of silence, the more significant it becomes. I hope this will be your experience in the coming weeks.

DAILY MEDITATION TEXTS FOR THE WEEK

Day 1   "Be still, and know that I am God!" (Ps 46:10)
Day 2   "Be still before the Lord, and wait patiently for him..."
           (Ps 37:7)
Day 3   "...a time to keep silence, and a time to speak." (Eccl
           3:7)

Day 4   "But the Lord is in his holy temple; let all the earth keep silence before him!" (Hab 2:20)

Day 5   "For thus said the Lord God, the Holy One of Israel: in returning and rest you shall be saved; in quietness and in trust shall be your strength." (Isa 30:15)

Day 6   "But whenever you pray, go into your room and shut the door and pray to your Father who is in secret; and your Father who sees in secret will reward you." (Matt 6:6)

Day 7   "He makes me lie down in green pastures; he leads me beside still waters; he restores my soul." (Ps 23:2)

SUGGESTION FOR JOURNALING

How do you experience silence and stillness in your life?

QUOTE

> *Deep within us all there is an amazing inner sanctuary of the soul, a holy place, a Divine Centre, a speaking Voice, to which we may continuously return.*
>
> *Eternity is at our hearts, pressing upon our time-torn lives, warming us with intimations of an astounding destiny, calling us home unto Itself.*
>
> Thomas Kelly
> *Testament of Devotion*

PRAYER

> *My Lord and my God, listening is hard for me. I do not mean exactly hard for I understand that this is a matter of receiving rather than trying. What I mean is that I am so action-orientated, so product driven, that doing is easier for me than being. I need your help if I am to be still and listen. I would like to try. I would like to learn how to sink down into the light of your presence until I can become comfortable in that posture. Help me to try now. Thank you. Amen.*
>
> Richard Foster
> *Prayer*

WEEK 42

Giving Generously of Our Material Possessions

A while ago there was a delightful cartoon in a Christian leadership magazine. It showed two men walking out of church naked. The one said to the other, "That was the best sermon on giving I've ever heard!" I trust that this week's meditation will not leave you without clothes, but I do hope it will underline the special place that generous giving has in our spiritual journey.

Money is a touchy subject. Even though it plays such a huge part in our personal and social lives, we find still it difficult to express our feelings on the subject. We live in an age of increasing emotional honesty and openness; yet many of us remain stuck in secret and hidden financial obsessions. It's just not something we find easy to talk about.

This hit home for me at the last executive meeting of our church. Before we started on the business agenda for the evening, each of us shared our response to the question, "What have been your happiest and saddest experiences with money?" We discovered that this simple question arouses deep feelings, evokes much resistance and helps to identify where present attitudes about money may have originated. In fact, you may find it helpful this coming week to reflect on your own response to this question. Writing out your memories about money and sharing them with a trusted friend can be very enlightening.

In contrast to our reticence and reserve, Jesus talked openly about money and possessions. Numerous biblical scholars have pointed out that he spoke more about this topic than any other, except for the kingdom of God. His message had two sides. On the one hand, he strongly warned against the spiritual dangers of wealth and greed. And on the other, he made it clear that the wise use of our financial resources can enhance our relationship with God as well as contribute to the common good. Two gospel stories shed light on this dilemma.

The first is about a rich young ruler who approached Jesus, keen to discover how to live the best possible life (Mark 10:17–22). "Good teacher," he asked, "what must I do to inherit eternal life?"(verse 17). In the conversation that followed, Jesus discerned a serious problem in the young man's life. He was addicted to his wealth. Money had become his god. Instead of controlling his possessions, his possessions controlled him. Knowing that one cannot serve two masters at the same time, Jesus told him to sell everything he owned, give the proceeds to the poor and come and follow him as his disciple. The young man turned away sorrowfully. Jesus had hit a deep nerve.

Some Christ-followers have taken Jesus' words in this story to be a universal requirement for all disciples. However, this was not what he was saying. Jesus does not require poverty of everyone any more than he demands that all his followers be celibate. In this case, Jesus was laying down a specific challenge to a specific person within a specific context. Possessions had become the single major focus of this wealthy young man's life. The god of money had gained his total allegiance, hence the challenge by Jesus for him to break with his possessions if he wanted to experience the abundant life that God alone could give him.

The second story concerns Jesus and Zaccheus (see Luke 19:1—10). Even though the gospel record tells us that Zaccheus was very rich, Jesus did not tell him to give away all his money. It was enough to give half his possessions to charity and repay fourfold those whom he had defrauded. This act of generous giving deepened his participation in the new life that God wanted to bring him, for immediately after he had announced his intentions to share his wealth, Jesus said to him: "Today salvation has come to this house" (verse 9).

Clearly, it is nearly impossible to make progress on our spiritual journey in the company of Jesus unless we give away some of our material substance for spiritual and charitable purposes. It doesn't make any sense to say that we want to deepen our relationship with God while we spend most of our energy and financial resources on ourselves, our desires and our interests. This attitude smacks of hypocrisy, and Jesus made it clear what he felt about hypocrites. When we live totally for ourselves, the spiritual path usually goes dead on us. In contrast, as the story of Zaccheus reminds us, when we learn to give generously, our experience of God takes on new meaning, depth and significance.

Morton discovered the truth of this for himself. One of the factors responsible for his deep interest in the spiritual life was his own experience of giving. Many years ago, when he had been a minister for only a few years, he heard a speaker at a clergy conference say that it is wicked to tithe. At first this seemed to be just what he wanted to hear. He had been feeling uneasy about the small amount that he was giving to the church and had been looking for a good excuse not to give more of his small income. But the speaker went on to say that the reason why it is wicked to tithe is that this practice gives the idea that we can pay God off with a straight 10 percent tip. He said real commitment requires that we give of our time and energy as well as our money, and this means more than just a 10 percent tip.

Right there and then Morton decided that he had better get into the "wicked" category to begin with. As he and his wife began to give a larger portion of their income for spiritual purposes, the following thought came to him: "This matter of spirituality and faith really is important. I had better get deeper into the real business of it." And so he began to give a lot more time to reading the Bible, meditating and praying. In the process, he found out, as so many others have, that giving is a sacramental action that reminds us of our commitment to God and of our need to relate to our Holy Creator.

I hope that, like Morton, you will discover how learning to give generously can turn your life into a spiritual adventure. Not only is it a measure of our love for God, but it also opens our lives to divine encounters, it returns money to its rightful place and it blesses those less fortunate than ourselves. Let us therefore take some time this coming week to reflect on some basic money questions. How much do we have? How much do we really need? How much do we need to give? What people or projects or organizations most need our help? Wrestling with questions like these guides us toward discovering what it means to follow Jesus into the kingdom of God.

DAILY MEDITATION TEXTS FOR THE WEEK

Day 1   "No one can serve two masters; for a slave will either hate the one and love the other, or be devoted to the one and despise the other. You cannot serve God and wealth." (Matt 6:24)

Day 2   "The earth is the Lord's and all that is in it, the world, and those who live in it." (Ps 24:1)

Day 3   "But strive first for the kingdom of God and his righteousness, and all these things will be given to you as well." (Matt 6:33)

Day 4   "Each of you must give as you have made up your mind, not reluctantly or under compulsion, for God loves a cheerful giver." (2 Cor 9:7)

Day 5   "But those who want to be rich fall into temptation and are trapped by many senseless and harmful desires that plunge people into ruin and destruction." (1 Tim 6:9)

Day 6   "For the love of money is a root of all kinds of evil, and in their eagerness to be rich some have wandered away from the faith and pierced themselves with many pains." (1 Tim 6:10)

Day 7   "And whoever does not provide for relatives, and especially for family members, has denied the faith and is worse than an unbeliever." (1 Tim 5:8)

SUGGESTION FOR JOURNALING

Describe your most painful and most pleasant memories concerning money before the age of thirteen. What do these memories tell you about your present attitude toward money?

QUOTE

> *Money is not evil in itself. Money is essential for life in this world. Money can do a great deal of good. But absolutely nothing, including money and the power it represents, must be allowed to come between ourselves and God. God, and not our material wealth, is the source of light and life.*
>
> Edward Bauman
> *Where Your Treasure Is*

PRAYER

> *Eternal and almighty God, it is so easy for me to worship money and power.*
>
> *If I do Lord, forgive me. If my trust is in possessions and things rather than you, forgive me. Heal the fear, doubt and insecurity that may generate faith in the wrong things.*
>
> *Restore a wholesome perspective that puts you at the center. I know you will help me structure my life around lasting values. My hope is in you, the one true God.*
>
> Edward Bauman
> *Where Your Treasure Is*

WEEK 43

Passing the Acid Test

It goes without saying that compassion lies at the heart of our Christian faith. Any spiritual experience, no matter how holy or deep, which does not flow out into a deeper concern for others can hardly be called Christian. The acid test of our relationship with God is always the quality of our love for those around us. If our communion with God isolates us from the painful realities of our society, anaesthetizes us against feeling the pain of our suffering neighbor, and leads us into an excessive preoccupation with our own inner well-being, it does not stand the test. If, on the other hand, it finds expression in great compassion and a willingness to show care, then it passes the gospel criteria for genuineness.

This acid test is clearly illustrated in Jesus' well-known parable of the sheep and the goats in Matthew chapter 25. It was a familiar scene in the villages of Galilee. During the day sheep and goats grazed on the hillside. The sheep normally stayed close together near the shepherd, while the daring and energetic goats came and went, searching for food in more adventurous places. When the sun went down, the shepherds returned home again with the entire flock of sheep and goats. When they got within sight of the sheepfold, the shepherd would stop to separate the sheep from the goats. Since the goats could better protect themselves and were not as valuable as the sheep, they were left outside, while the sheep were brought in.

In the same way, Jesus said, the time will come when people will be separated from one another like the goats from the sheep. The righteous will be gathered into the safety of the sheepfold, while the rest, like the goats, will be left to fend for themselves. And then the king who does the separating will say to the righteous:

> *Come, you that are blessed by my Father, inherit the kingdom prepared for you from the foundation of the world; for I was hungry and you gave me food, I was thirsty and you gave me something to drink, I was a stranger and you welcomed me, I was naked and you gave me clothing, I was sick and you took care of me, I was in prison and you visited me. (Matt 25:34–36)*

When the righteous inquire about these encounters, they will be told by the king:

> *Truly, I tell you, just as you did it to one of the least of these who are members of my family, you did it to me. (Matt 25:40)*

The message of this parable is crystal clear: true and false believers are as distinguishable as sheep and goats. What is more, God can see this difference. The Holy One, this parable explains, can see into our souls by looking at our deeds. Of course, it is not our business to judge who is a sheep or who is a goat. We cannot see into people's hearts, even if we try. When we do, our judgments of people are often horribly wrong. As this jingle puts it:

> *There is so much good in the worst of us,*
> *And so much bad in the best of us,*
> *That it hardly behoves any of us*
> *To talk about the rest of us.*

Rather than sit in judgment of others, our responsibility is to ensure that the fundamental direction of our lives is pointed toward the good. The choice of the basic goal of our lives is ours, and ours alone to make. In fact, it is probably the most important decision we will ever have to make, for it has eternal significance. But how does God decide if we really mean what we say? According to Jesus, God's acid test consists of simple, straightforward actions: feeding the hungry, quenching thirst, welcoming strangers, clothing the naked, caring for the sick and visiting those in prison. These are the good deeds that manifest the loving spirit. They reveal that the basic set of our souls is not a concern for ourselves, but for others. They show that the fundamental tendency of our lives is characterised by love. If love is the bottom layer of our being, then caring actions begin to flow naturally from us, as water flows from a mountain spring.

Our calling as human beings and Christ-followers is to pour love on all other human beings—on those who are happy and healthy as well as those in need. But the reason that we need to pay special attention to those who suffer is because they usually receive so little love and caring from the world. I wonder if we realize how much a friendly conversation with a stranger or a sympathetic call to someone who is sick really means to them. I wonder how many minds have been saved from utter despair and how many suicides prevented because of a caring word or action at the right moment. This is something every one of us with a warm heart can do, something that is probably more needed today than anything else.

You may be wondering why God places such importance on these acts of mercy. It is simply because when we do these things, we do them also to Christ. This is one of the profound mysteries of our faith. Like two people who are so close that what hurts the one hurts the other, so too is the risen Lord close to every person. Perhaps he is closer to the hungry and thirsty, the naked and the lonely, and the sick and the imprisoned because they need him so much more. Every act of mercy done to them is therefore also a direct kindness to Christ who dwells with them. This we must never ever forget.

Perhaps the person who has made us most aware of this was Mother Teresa. Her ministry on the streets of Calcutta bore witness to the compassion that comes with recognizing Christ in the least of his family. Having taken these words from the parable of sheep and goats to heart, she went about serving the poor and destitute as if she were serving Christ. When questioned in a television documentary by Malcolm Muggeridge about her motivation for doing what she did, this humble Christ-follower drew a distinction between her vocation and that of a secular social worker. When ministering to those who suffered, she told him, she and her team of nuns "do it to a Person." She truly believed that in caring for the most needy, she was alleviating the pain of Christ himself.

While this story in Matthew 25 may not be all there is to the Christian faith, it is such a large plank in the hull of discipleship that none of us can float in the sea of life without it. Unless our spirituality results in this kind of human care and concern, we have missed the boat. Caring for others is not a responsibility we can delegate to the priest, or the pastor, or the Red Cross, or some social welfare program. The king will just ask you and me, "Did you do these deeds?" Let us therefore take a few moments to review our responses to those who suffer in our midst. Here are some questions that I ask myself on a regular basis:

- When last did I do something practical on behalf of the hungry, the thirsty, the homeless?
- How often have I gone out of my way to welcome strangers, particularly those who were not too interesting or attractive?
- When was the last time I visited a sick person, someone who was bereaved, or one of the many depressed and despairing people I know?
- Have I ever reached out to someone in prison or a prisoner who has been released recently?

♦ How do I show my care and concern on a daily basis to those around me, especially those who are suffering, broken or hurt?

I know that these are tough questions. I frequently struggle with them myself. But I raise them because they are the acid test of our faith. Compassionate caring is not an optional extra for the serious disciple; it lies at the very heart of a life dedicated to following Christ. Are you and I really following Jesus? Would the king see us as sheep or goats? And perhaps most importantly, if we think we are goats, what are we going to do this week to be among those who God would regard as sheep?

DAILY MEDITATION TEXTS FOR THE WEEK

Day 1   "When the Son of Man comes in his glory, and all the angels with him, then he will sit on the throne of his glory. All the nations will be gathered before him, and he will separate people one from another as a shepherd separates the sheep from the goats, and he will put the sheep at his right hand and the goats at the left." (Matt 25:31–33)

Day 2   "Then the king will say to those at his right hand, 'Come, you that are blessed by my Father, inherit the kingdom prepared for you from the foundation of the world; for I was hungry and you gave me food, I was thirsty and you gave me something to drink, I was a stranger and you welcomed me, I was naked and you gave me clothing, I was sick and you took care of me, I was in prison and you visited me.'" (Matt 25:34–36)

Day 3   "Love does no wrong to a neighbor; therefore, love is the fulfilling of the law." (Rom 13:10)

Day 4   "As he went ashore, he saw a great crowd, and he had compassion for them, because they were like sheep without a shepherd." (Mark 6:34)

Day 5   "Thus says the Lord of hosts: Render true judgments, show kindness and mercy to one another, do not oppress the widow, the orphan, the alien, or the poor; and do not devise evil in your hearts against one another." (Zech 7:9–10)

Day 6   "You shall not wrong or oppress a resident alien, for you were aliens in the land of Egypt. You shall not abuse any widow or orphan." (Exod 22:21–22)

Day 7   "For the whole law is summed up in a single commandment, 'You shall love your neighbor as yourself.'" (Gal 5:14)

SUGGESTION FOR JOURNALING

What did you discover about your life from going through the questions in the meditation?

QUOTE

It is possible to have spiritual experiences which are not authentic. A warm heart is not enough. The presence of Christ must be carefully discerned. The Christ is always the One for others. His whole life was spent in service to the most undesirable people. He sought out the least acceptable, the most needy, the rejected. Any spiritual experience that does not lead us to share Christ's passion for others is misunderstood or imaginary.

Howard Rice
Resurrection: Radical Love and Justice

PRAYER

Lord of all life, I remember with gratitude the times others have been sensitive to my needs. Thank you for those friends and neighbors who have reached out to me when I have needed them. I also remember thankfully the times I have been able to be helpful to others. Increase my understanding and awareness of what is happening around me so that I may respond compassionately and effectively. Whatever the need, let me notice it and respond with imagination, good judgment and love. May no one who knocks on the door of my life go weeping away. In Jesus' name, I ask this. Amen.

WEEK 44

Stepping Imaginatively
into the Gospel Stories

Over the years I have found that using pictures in my imagination helps me to build my relationship with God. I discovered this early on in my spiritual journey when I was learning to pray. Before going to sleep I would picture the risen Jesus sitting at the side of my bed, the blazing light of his love shining through the darkness. Then I would share aloud with him my deepest secrets, my joys, my struggles, and my hopes. In the silence afterward I would wait for his whisper in my thoughts and feelings. For many years this was the picture I used to help me relate to Christ. Gradually his presence became more real and tangible throughout my daily life.

Reflecting on these childlike beginnings, I see now that I was learning in those early days of discipleship how to place my imagination at the service of my faith. My Bible told me that Jesus was always with me. My imagination helped me to enter more deeply into this reality. Of course, the picture was not the reality. Nonetheless, the image helped to deepen my experience of the reality it sought to describe. It came as no surprise when, later on in my pilgrimage, I learned that some of the great Christ-followers in the past had encouraged a similar use of the imagination, especially with regard to our devotional reading of the scriptures. This is the practice I want to explore with you this week.

The reason I do this is because it is so easy to turn Bible reading into a mere intellectual exercise. This happens when we read without being touched and transformed by what we read. Jesus himself warned us against this kind of reading (see John 5:39–40). One way of avoiding this danger is to learn how to read the scriptures more imaginatively. As we have seen, our imagination helps us to "see" and enter into what we believe in a deeper way. The Old and New Testaments describe a breakthrough of God's eternal kingdom into our world, and so these events are not limited by time. By stepping into them with our imagination, we can be brought into living contact with the glorious reality that came into our world in Jesus Christ two thousand years ago and is still available to us today.

The best place to begin is with the gospel stories. They have a wonderful way of introducing us to God's transforming love and to our own hidden depths. In my work as a pastor I frequently meet people who yearn for a firsthand, living relationship with God. Reflecting on my conversations with these God-seekers, I've detected a remarkable similarity in the yearnings they express. How do I get to know God? How can I deepen my relationship with Christ? How can I open myself more to the inner work of the Spirit? Usually I answer with one simple bit of spiritual guidance: keep company with Jesus in the gospels. We do this best by stepping imaginatively into those stories told about him and by him. Let me describe what I mean.

We can begin with the birth narratives of Jesus, imagining what it was like to be Mary, pregnant by the Holy Spirit. How did she face the village gossip, the fear of being rejected by Joseph, and then the long, hard trip to Bethlehem? What would it be like to be in the shoes of Joseph as he tried to come to terms with God's unorthodox way of doing things? We don't need to wait for Christmas to meditate on these things. Our purpose is to reflect on how Christ can be born in our lives, and this is certainly not seasonal. In fact, when we live with Mary and Joseph in this way, we add tremendous depth and meaning to our experience of Christmas when it does come along.

We can move on to the hidden years of Jesus' life. Those years before the start of his ministry which culminated in him leaving home to be baptized in the River Jordan by his cousin, John the Baptist. We can start home with Mary and Joseph after the Passover celebration in Jerusalem, turning back frightened when we find that Jesus has gone missing. Or perhaps we can picture ourselves standing in the temple with Jesus, sharing the amazement of the learned religious leaders at his answers to their questions. What was going on in the hearts of Mary and Joseph at this time, and how did Jesus come across as he gave his answers? Or later on, what were Jesus' days like in the carpenter's shop after Joseph died? Did Mary secretly worry when he decided to leave home? We can follow Jesus to the Jordan and stand with him in the water as the heavens opened around him and he heard a voice saying, "You are my Son, my Beloved." This kind of imaginative entering into the life of Christ fills in the story and helps us to grow as we understand its depth.

Next, we can accompany the disciples when they first heard the call to become disciples of Jesus. It could mean talking with Matthew at the customs table, or standing beside Peter at the lake, or sitting with Nathaniel under the fig tree. What exactly came to their minds as they answered the call? And what comes to ours as we hear the call given to us? How did their situation differ from that of the rich young ruler who decided that the price was too high for what could be gained? When it comes to responding to the call of the gospel we can ask, "How am I like Matthew or Peter or Nathaniel or the rich young ruler?"

From here we can go to some of the healing stories. We can pick out one with which we identify, live with it for a few weeks and try to feel its meaning for our own lives. For instance, in our real lives we may find ourselves "stuck" in some way or another and be drawn to the story of the paralytic who was carried to Jesus by his four friends. We can imagine ourselves being lowered down through the roof, lying at Jesus' feet and hearing him tell us to get up and walk again. As we imagine ourselves in a scene like this, our meditations may trigger thoughts like, "Who are the friends that I can rely on at this moment? How am I 'paralyzed'? What does Christ want me to do next to break out of my 'paralysis'?"

If we are going through grief and anxiety we may find it helpful to spend time meditating on the events that surround the crucifixion of Jesus. We could be alone with Jesus in the Gethsemane garden when his soul was torn apart and he wondered if he could go on. Sometimes we need to see the bloody sweat dropping off his face in order to feel that we are not alone in our struggles. Or we may stand with Mary and John at the foot of the cross and listen to the words that the crucified Jesus speaks to them. When we do this we begin to realize that there is someone who shares our agony and pain when all our hopes are crushed.

But it's also crucial, when we are in a dark place, to imagine one of the resurrection stories of Jesus. We can go with Mary as she walks into the garden only to find the tomb empty, or accompany the downhearted pilgrims on the Emmaus road when they are surprised by the stranger, or wait with the disciples huddled together in such fear that Jesus had to appear to them to show them who he really was. When we imagine the events of the resurrection again and again, we begin to experience for ourselves the inner power of the Christian message to overcome darkness with light, sorrow with joy, and defeat with victory. If we only focus on Christ's suffering, we can get bogged down there. But when we expose ourselves to the victory of Christ over death and evil, the powerful message of his resurrection can touch our lives and bring about transformation. Remember, after the darkness comes a new day.

I would like to end this meditation with a brief testimony. Faith has not come easily to me. But as I have exposed myself to the gospel stories imaginatively, the risen Jesus has gradually become more real to me. He has become someone to whom I can turn at any moment, but especially when life gets difficult and dark. Furthermore, I now carry in my heart and mind a treasure store of gospel images, ranging from Mary's bewilderment when she finds herself to be the Christ-bearer, to the risen Jesus standing before Peter by the Sea of Galilee asking him, "Peter, do you love me?" Such images help me to relate in a meaningful way to the living God who came into this world in Jesus Christ so that we might live our lives to the full. May this be your experience too as you learn to use your imagination in your relationship with God.

DAILY MEDITATION TEXTS FOR THE WEEK

Day 1   "You search the scriptures because you think that in them you have eternal life; and it is they that testify on my behalf. Yet you refuse to come to me to have life." (John 5:39–40)

Day 2   "Come to me, all you that are weary and are carrying heavy burdens, and I will give you rest." (Matt 11:28)

Day 3   "Take my yoke upon you, and learn from me; for I am gentle and humble in heart, and you will find rest for your souls." (Matt 11:29)

Day 4   "But Mary treasured all these words and pondered them in her heart." (Luke 2:19)

Day 5   "Jesus said to him, 'Have you believed because you have seen me? Blessed are those who have not seen and yet have come to believe.'" (John 20:29)

Day 6   "But there are also many other things that Jesus did; if every one of them were written down, I suppose that the world itself could not contain the books that would be written." (John 21:25)

Day 7   "Now to him who by the power at work within us is able to accomplish abundantly far more than all we can

ask or imagine, to him be glory in the church and in
Christ Jesus to all generations, forever and ever. Amen."
(Eph 3:20–21)

SUGGESTION FOR JOURNALING

Think about your favorite gospel story. Why does it mean so
much to you?

QUOTE

*Imagination is the capacity to make connections between the
visible and the invisible, between heaven and earth, between
present and past, between present and future. For Christians,
whose largest investment is in the invisible, the imagination
is indispensable, for it is only by means of the imagination
that we can see reality whole, in context.*

Eugene Peterson
Subversive Spirituality

PRAYER

*Lord, help me to see the invisible with
the eyes of my heart.
Amen.*

Becoming Channels
of God's Healing

Early one winter's morning in the late seventies I was awakened by the phone ringing. The caller was a woman in severe pain who wanted someone to pray with her. She had found our church's phone number in the local directory. I asked if she had made contact with her own pastor. "Oh," she said, "he doesn't believe in this kind of thing." I did not want to say that I also had reservations about praying for healing. Nothing in my seminary training had prepared me for this kind of ministry. However, even though I had little idea of what I was going to do, I told her I would come around and pray.

When I arrived I saw immediately that she knew more about the healing ministry than I did. On the small table in the middle of her lounge, she had placed a Bible and a small container of olive oil. I opened the Bible at the one passage on healing that I knew well, James 5:13–16, and read it aloud. It speaks plainly about the need to call for the elders when we are sick, confess our sins to each other, and anoint those who are ill in the name of the Lord. I decided to take these words literally and act on them.

When I asked whether there was anything she needed to confess, she became quiet. Then, in a soft voice, she started to share some things that weighed heavily upon her conscience. I listened, asked a few questions to better grasp what she was saying, and then asked whether I could anoint her and pray with her. The problem was that I had little idea what to do next. Even though I had been a regular worshiper for over ten years, I had never seen anyone praying for healing. I wasn't sure if you should pour the oil over the person's head or into one's own hand first, or put a thumb into the bottle and then make a cross or use one's fingers. Clumsily, I managed to get some oil onto her forehead, muttered a hasty prayer, pronounced the forgiveness of Christ and beat an embarrassed retreat. I secretly hoped that our paths would never cross again.

But early that evening I received another call from this woman. I immediately sensed a lightness and joy in her voice. During the day there had been a remarkable improvement and she was not having as much pain as before. She wanted to say thank you. I couldn't believe it. In spite of my bumbling efforts and very small faith, I had been used as an instrument of God's healing love and power. Inwardly I resolved to do two things. One, I would learn all that I could about the Christian healing ministry. Two, I would begin to pray with any person who asked for healing prayer.

It has been almost twenty years since I made that commitment. One of the first books I read was Morton's *Psychology, Medicine and Christian Healing*. When it was first published in 1973 under the title *Healing and Christianity*, this book was hailed as the only serious history of Christian healing available. It opened my eyes to the unique healing ministry of Jesus of Nazareth and made me aware of how this ministry has persisted throughout the centuries. It offered me a trusted method for engaging in this ministry myself. After praying for healing now with literally hundreds of people, including members of my own family, certain essential elements have become clearer. I share them very briefly and hope they will encourage you to step out and become a channel of God's healing love and power:

+ The ministry of Jesus makes it clear that God is on the side of healing and wholeness. If Jesus had any one mission, it was to bring God's healing love to bear on the moral, mental and physical illnesses of the people around him. His healing ministry was a natural outflow of his love and compassion for all human beings.

♦ The disciples were expected to continue this ministry. When we read the books and letters that contain the record of the first Christian churches, it is clear that these early followers did exactly this. Like Jesus, they practised a ministry of healing because they wanted to express God's love to those around them.

♦ As we stay in communion with God, we can also become channels of God's healing through the Holy Spirit. The same healing power that operated through Jesus and raised him from the dead can operate in and through anyone who has a deep spiritual relationship with him.

♦ With compassion and sensitivity we can begin praying with others for healing. What we do is always a better indication of what we believe than what we say. If we really believe in God's healing love and power, we need to remain in close communion with the Holy One through prayer, Bible reading and worship, and then we need to reach out to others with prayer, the laying on of hands and anointing. True belief requires obedience, response and action.

♦ Healing prayer often results in sick people getting better rather than being totally healed. It could be that we need to continue praying with the person or that we don't have enough spiritual resources to deal completely with the illness. Whatever the reason, it is helpful to see healing as a mysterious process that involves our emotions, minds, bodies and relationships.

♦ We never promise anyone that they will be healed. Nor do we, if the person for whom we are praying does not get well, ever blame them for not having enough faith. It is far better for us to conclude that we may have been inadequate channels of God's healing love and power. We need to build our confidence in God's loving will, no matter what answers we may receive. God knows best and sees the picture in a way we can never fully see.

 ♦ In addition to the genuine caring that flows through healing touch and anointing, it can be very helpful to use our imagination. Personally, when I am praying with a sick person, I like to picture the light and love of the risen Jesus flowing into the diseased parts of the person, bringing wholeness and healing. I have found that this way of praying involves me deeply in the process, and often wonderful things happen.

 ♦ God works through the medical profession and all those involved in it. It is always a good thing to cooperate with other health care practitioners. I will always remember the words of the head of the local Medical School of Psychiatry when he said to me, "Trevor, there are things I can do which you cannot do, but there are things that can happen in your church when people pray for each other, that I can never do."

 ♦ When we become agents of God's healing love and power, it won't be long before we will find ourselves plunged into the deep mysteries of suffering and evil. In these dark moments we are sometimes tempted to give up. I am learning, however, that it is far better to hold onto the faith that God's purposes will ultimately triumph. Certainly, if there was no eternal kingdom beyond this life where we will become all that we are meant to be, the healing ministry would be meaningless. The final and total healing that we can receive is living eternally in that kingdom with God.

There is so much more that I could say. But I do hope these few thoughts will encourage you to become a channel of God's healing love and power. While this is a ministry for which some people have a special gift, it is also one in which all of us can participate through prayer. It is God who heals. The power is not ours. We are simply prayer channels. All that God requires is that we keep close to Christ, learn from him and risk ourselves in praying for healing. Join me in this healing adventure.

DAILY MEDITATION TEXTS FOR THE WEEK

Day 1   "Are any among you sick? They should call for the elders of the church and have them pray over them, anointing them with oil in the name of the Lord." (Jas 5:14)

Day 2   "Moved with compassion, Jesus touched their eyes. Immediately they regained their sight and followed him." (Matt 20:34)

Day 3   "And now, Lord, look at their threats, and grant to your servants to speak your word with all boldness, while you stretch out your hand to heal, and signs and wonders are performed through the name of your holy servant Jesus." (Acts 4:29–30)

Day 4   "...for I am the Lord who heals you." (Exod 15:26)

Day 5   "But for you who revere my name the sun of righteousness shall rise, with healing in its wings. You shall go out leaping like calves from the stall." (Mal 4:2)

Day 6   "He heals the brokenhearted, and binds up their wounds." (Ps 147:3)

Day 7   "Then Jesus called the twelve together and gave them power and authority over all demons and to cure diseases, and he sent them out to proclaim the kingdom of God and to heal." (Luke 9:1–2)

SUGGESTION FOR JOURNALING

Describe one healing moment in your life.

QUOTE

Christian healing is Jesus Christ meeting you at your deepest point of need.

Morris Maddocks
Twenty Questions About Healing

PRAYER

Lord, deepen my confidence in the healing power of your Spirit to work in me and through me. Above all, help me to become an open channel through which your healing love can flow to others. For Jesus' sake. Amen.

———

Making Sure We Have
the Right Ticket

There is a delightful story that is told about that great scientist Dr. Albert Einstein, who once was on a train out of New York City. As the conductor was doing his rounds, Einstein began to look through his pockets for his ticket. He couldn't find it. By the time the conductor arrived at Einstein's seat, he had emptied all his pockets, searched through his briefcase and was proceeding on all fours to look around on the floor of the coach. When the conductor recognized Einstein he said, "Don't worry about finding the ticket, Dr. Einstein, I trust you." In response, Einstein turned his head upward from his position on the floor and said, "Young man, this is not about trust. I need to find that ticket, otherwise I have no idea where I'm going."

This story provides a helpful parable for our lives. In a sense, all of us are riding the train of life. In order to find our destination we need to have our ticket. If we don't, like Einstein, we may not know where we are heading. In this week's meditation I want to suggest that that ticket is a real and vital faith. Without it life is empty, futile and without direction. On the other hand, when we do possess it, we find that our lives take on new meaning and purpose. Two questions, therefore, are important for us to consider. What does it mean to have such a faith? How does one get it?

One of the problems with the word *faith* is that it means different things to different people. So let me clarify first how I am *not* going to use the word. I am not using it to describe some kind of intellectual ascent to certain doctrinal propositions. Nor am I describing a form of wishful thinking or "whistling in the dark" type of disposition. Neither am I trying to interpret faith merely in terms of positive thinking and an optimistic outlook. While all these meanings have some merit, they are not the ones I want to associate with the word *faith*. New Testament faith is very different.

Faith is a kind of inner knowledge. It is the blessed assurance that, in spite of all the evidence to the contrary, the loving God is the ultimate heart of our universe and that healing of body, mind and soul will ultimately come to all those who are open to it. Paul expresses this heart-faith beautifully in his letter to the Romans when he says:

> *For I am convinced that neither death, nor life, nor angels, nor rulers, nor things present, nor things to come, nor powers, nor height, nor depth, nor anything else in all creation, will be able to separate us from the love of God in Christ Jesus our Lord. (Rom 8:38–39)*

When the New Testament speaks about faith, it is referring to this kind of inner confidence, the conviction that the power of good and love are infinitely more powerful than the power of destruction and negativity.

Faith as an inner knowledge grows most naturally out of a childhood where we have been valued, cared for and loved, even if we were difficult, angry or disobedient. This kind of unconditional love fosters an attitude that the world is supporting and caring at the core and that not only those close to us, but also our body, our community, the physical and even spiritual reality can be relied upon. But if we suspect and doubt the caring concern of those around us, or, on the other hand, when we expect concern and care from them, then it will have a negative impact on our spiritual journey. When we learn from our childhood experiences that life is uncaring, it could take either the concerned love of a good friend or relative or a deep spiritual experience to turn around our basic attitude toward life. Sometimes it takes both.

As we grow up and our horizons expand, those attitudes we acquire in childhood are widened to take in the whole world. Those with faith see the universe as essentially friendly and caring, accepting the evidence to the contrary as one of the puzzling problems of living in an imperfect world. Those who lack confidence and who find it hard to trust see the difficulties and pains as normative and moments of caring as chance occurrences. To such people the universe is either meaningless or hostile, and God is to be feared as some kind of police person who is always on the prowl. Fortunately, an alternative view can be learned. Here are three simple clues as to how this may happen.

First, we must open our hearts and minds to the simple message that Jesus brought. We do this best by immersing ourselves in the gospels of the New Testament. There we will discover that God is our loving Abba who never gives up on us, no matter how much we mess up! There we learn that this is God's world and that our heavenly Father treasures every part of it and every human being in it. There we find that, although we live in the midst of incredible pain, suffering and unfairness, God's loving purpose will have the final word. These are just some of the truths that Jesus brings to our hearts. As we begin to take them seriously, we will find that our faith begins to grow. Paul puts it so well:

So faith comes from what is heard, and what is heard comes through the word of Christ. (Rom 10:17)

Second, we can get together on a regular basis with other God-seekers and Christ-followers. When we do this, we will discover that faith engenders faith. This has happened for me so many times over the past thirty years or so. I doubt whether I would be writing these pages if it were not for those friends in the faith who have stood by me in dark and difficult moments and cared for me. When we try to go it alone along the spiritual path, it is very easy for the flame of faith to begin to flicker and sometimes even go out. Perhaps this is why when we open our lives to the risen Christ he always brings his brothers and sisters with him to share our lives.

Third, our faith will grow as we use the little we have. We can do this in a number of different ways. We can start praying on a daily basis about those things that are worrying us and causing anxiety. We can ask God for power, strength and wisdom to go the way of love. We can use our words to bring blessing and consolation to those around us. We can see the goodness of God in all the things that we enjoy. We can refuse to give in to the forces of negativity, despair and darkness. We can take a stand against those things that break God's heart. We can connect with a suffering person in our midst and seek to be an instrument of peace. When we put our faith into practice in these various ways, our faith will begin to grow. This is why the New Testament tells us that faith without action is not alive (Jas 2:17).

One final word as I close this meditation. Living with faith does not mean that we will never get angry or scared, neither does it mean that we are carried about in an eternal womb. However, the fear and anger will be in proportion to each situation in which we find ourselves. Our faith will help us to face reality and to know that the difficulties we are experiencing can be overcome. In addition, we will know that the loving God we have known on this side will provide for our ongoing growth and healing in the eternal future that lies before us. When death leads to such a kingdom as Jesus portrays, it loses its sense of horror. We begin to believe that even tragedies can be redeemed on the other side. Do you see why we need the ticket of faith for our journey through life?

Daily Meditation Texts for the Week

Day 1 "For I am convinced that neither death, nor life, nor angels, nor rulers, nor things present, nor things to come, nor powers, nor height, nor depth, nor anything else in all creation, will be able to separate us from the love of God in Christ Jesus our Lord." (Rom 8:38–39)

Day 2 "For just as the body without the spirit is dead, so faith without works is also dead." (Jas 2:26)

Day 3 "Although you have not seen him, you love him; and even though you do not see him now, you believe in him and rejoice with an indescribable and glorious joy, for you are receiving the outcome of your faith, the salvation of your souls." (1 Pet 1:8–9)

Day 4 "For truly I tell you, if you have faith the size of a mustard seed, you will say to this mountain, 'Move from here to there,' and it will move; and nothing will be impossible for you." (Matt 17:20)

Day 5 "Then he touched their eyes and said, 'According to your faith let it be done to you.'" (Matt 9:29)

Day 6 "Jesus answered them, 'Have faith in God.'" (Mark 11:22)

Day 7 "For this very reason, you must make every effort to support your faith with goodness, and goodness with knowledge, and knowledge with self-control, and self-control with endurance, and endurance with godliness, and godliness with mutual affection, and mutual affection with love." (2 Pet 1:5–7)

Suggestion for Journaling

Make a note of the things that deepen your faith in God and help it to grow.

QUOTE

Faith, then, is fragile, something that needs tending.
Kathleen Norris
Amazing Grace

PRAYER

[Lord], I do believe; help me overcome my unbelief!
Mark 9:24, NIV

Letting Down the Walls
of Our Inner Fortresses

If you have ever visited Europe you will have noticed the many ancient castles and fortresses. They are everywhere. On almost every hilltop and in nearly every village people have built ramparts and walls for defense. Most of them now stand in ruins. Yet, they still exercise a strange fascination in many hearts and minds. They seem to stir something in the human spirit. What is it that they touch deep within us? Could it be that they are symbolic of the way we as human beings relate to one another?

These fortifications, citadels, moats and drawbridges are concrete reminders of the way we act inwardly. Just as the bread and wine are sacraments of Christ's love for us, so these fortresses are negative sacraments of our fear, our hatred, our greed for power, and our alienation from our loved ones and our neighbors. No wonder these fortresses exert such a power on our imaginations. They represent our deep-seated tendency to build walls around our lives and to protect ourselves against one another.

Many of us believe that others approach us only to overwhelm and destroy us. We feel that we can only survive in this world if we build towers to watch for invaders and inner walls to keep them out. We have become convinced that we stand alone in this world, with no one to help or support us. Granted, there is some basis for this fear. Perhaps one of the reasons why we build walls around ourselves is because we have been badly hurt in the past and we are not going to let it happen again. Also, the people who build no walls, who have no place to call their own, seldom achieve much. They can easily be blown around by every wind, every desire. Part of growing up is learning where to draw lines, knowing who we are and discovering our strengths and gifts. These processes of maturing require that some walls be built inside our lives.

However, if we are to develop into true children of God and open ourselves to the transforming love of Christ, we are going to have to abandon some parts of the fortress we have so carefully constructed. We have to throw open the gate, let down the drawbridge, even demolish a portion of the wall. Yes, this sounds scary, perhaps even foolish, but is this not what God did in coming to us in Jesus Christ? The Holy One chose to put aside all power, to forego the citadel of divinity and to become like us. This vulnerable and self-giving way was the only way God could meet us as one of us.

Certainly, letting down the walls of our inner fortresses can be painful and dangerous. We could be overwhelmed by those around us. People hunger desperately for fellowship, understanding and concern. When our walls are down and they know we care, they can crowd in, perhaps in such a stream that we have no time or space to ourselves. But this is better than the dangers of a securely locked castle that separates us from those around us and makes them want to conquer and destroy.

There is also the danger of being hurt. When we truly care for others, people come in, take what is offered and often give little in return. Sometimes those to whom we have given the most repay us with the most spite. We let them into the most secret chamber of our soul, and they turn and trample us. If we keep the walls down, we can be trampled on again and again. Only one in ten people (if we are lucky) will thank us for the shelter of our fortress, for listening and for the food and love they received. Sometimes our hearts will come close to breaking. There is a real danger that we could become bitter and build up the walls and become more isolated than ever. Yet, as followers of Christ we must go on.

It takes real discernment to know when it is constructive to allow people to misuse us or when it is better for us to keep certain people out. However, one thing is certain: most of us are too quick to close the doors of our fortresses and retire within. We need to listen to the inner voice of love, the voice of Christ, if we are to know which way to go. He will tell us to go his way, and the gospels tell us quite clearly what that way is. It is the way of openness and giving and giving and giving some more. As Paul the apostle teaches us:

> *Let the same mind be in you that was in Christ Jesus, who, though he was in the form of God...emptied himself...(Phil 2:5–7)*

How do we go about letting down the walls of our inner fortress? First of all, we need to be sick and tired of our sterile, isolated and cut-off existence. We must decide that we cannot continue living like this any longer because it hurts too much and sours our life. We also need to believe that pulling down our defenses will do some good. We must deepen our confidence that the nature of the universe leans more toward union, love and connection than toward separation and death. This is our act of faith that the God of love lies at the heart of all things.

I have to remind myself constantly of this truth, especially when it comes to my relationships with those closest to me. There is a part of me that really wants to discover what it's like to love with no strings attached, to give and not to count the cost. On the other hand, there is another part of me that repeatedly mocks this intention and wants to remain firmly self-centered. It is often this part that wins, particularly when things don't go my way. When this happens, the temptation to withdraw into my fortress becomes very strong. I have learned that in order not to give in I need to get help from beyond myself. Usually my prayer goes something like this:

> *O God, I turn again to you in my need. The temptation to withdraw from those closest to me is again very strong. I hear that mocking voice trying to tell me that I'm hopeless when it comes to loving deeply, and it would be far better just to give up. Just look after yourself, it seems to be saying, and don't worry about the needs of others. I really need your strength and wisdom, Lord. Please help me. Empower my will to choose life, strengthen my capacity to love, and show me how best I can let down the walls of my inner fortress.*

Next, we must begin to meet those who stop by our fortress and let them in. God will bring visitors (sometimes too many!) as soon as we are genuinely ready to give of ourselves in ministry. We are ready only when our understanding, consoling and loving have no strings attached. As long as we expect something in return for opening our fortress, we are not truly opening it. We are merely retiring to a more subtle kind of citadel. We all know how difficult it is to give and expect nothing in return, to be genuinely surprised when something does come back as gift and grace. The teachings of Jesus, as well as his example, give clear instructions on how to overcome this. God will empower us as we risk becoming vulnerable and open.

Lastly, there is the question of approaching someone else's fortress. One thing is sure: if we attack, either the walls will be raised higher and built thicker, or else we will conquer and thereby be shut out from that person's innermost center forever. Most of us err on the side of too much aggression, too many demands, too much power and too little openness and self-giving love. Here again, Jesus is our example. Remember how he approaches the fortress of our soul? Quietly he stands at the doorway of our lives, knocks gently and waits, listening for our response, hopeful for our yes, ready to give his all. Is this not the only way to reach another in his or her fortress? Of course, we cannot do this until we have risked stepping out of our own.

Are we ready for this kind of serious Christ-following? Fortresses don't work; the many ruins lying around Europe remind us of this. But the way of Christ will work, if only we will try it.

DAILY MEDITATION TEXTS FOR THE WEEK

Day 1 "And may the Lord make you increase and abound in love for one another and for all, just as we abound in love for you." (1 Thess 3:12)

Day 2 "I pray that, according to the riches of his glory, he may grant that you may be strengthened in your inner being with power through his Spirit, and that Christ may dwell in your hearts through faith, as you are being rooted and grounded in love." (Eph 3:16–17)

Day 3 "For the love of Christ urges us on, because we are convinced that one has died for all…" (2 Cor 5:14)

Day 4 "Freely you have received, freely give." (Matt 10:8, NIV)

Day 5 "For those who want to save their life will lose it, and those who lose their life for my sake will find it." (Matt 16:25)

Day 6 "And this is his commandment, that we should believe in the name of his Son Jesus Christ and love one another, just as he has commanded us." (1 John 3:23)

Day 7 "Since there will never cease to be some in need on the earth, I therefore command you, 'Open your hand to the poor and needy neighbor in your land.'" (Deut 15:11)

SUGGESTION FOR JOURNALING

How does the image of a fortress remind you of the condition of your life and relationships?

QUOTE

> *For the most part, we are terribly isolated from people and we remain in a defensive stance toward those with whom we come in contact. To be alienated from people is to be alienated from God.*
>
> Gordon Cosby
> *By Grace Transformed*

PRAYER

> *Lord, remind me that when I allow others to enter my life, especially those who are needy, you often slip in among them. Amen.*

WEEK 48

Listening to Our Dreams

Once there was a captain of a slave-trading ship who had a dream that changed his life. He dreamed he was on a sailing boat in Venice. Suddenly, a stranger approached him and gave him a ring. He was told that the ring had wonderful properties and, if treasured, would bring much happiness and well-being. Later in the dream another person started mocking him for his superstition and so he removed the ring from his finger and threw it into the sea. Just then he looked up and saw a huge fire in the Alps. Fearfully he stood gazing at the raging fire and regretted his stupidity for throwing the ring away. The stranger appeared again, recovered the ring from under the water and promised to hold it in trust until the captain would need it again.

The dreamer was John Newton, an eighteenth-century slave-trader who became one of the great Christ-followers of his time. As he reflected on his dream, he realized that God had spoken to him through his dream and he was dramatically converted. He gave up slave trading, left the sea, trained for the Anglican priesthood and subsequently wrote some wonderful hymns, among them *Amazing Grace*. Today, his testimony bears powerful witness to the way the Holy One often uses our dreams to communicate with us.

However, this is not the way many of us regard our dreams. We seem to have been convinced by our materialistic culture that dreams are nothing but the subconscious rehash of recent experiences or anticipated happenings. More vivid dreams, according to this point of view, result from some immediate stimulus, like eating too much pizza or overdoing the apple pie. Or they may be brought on by something that happens while we are asleep, like hearing the siren of a passing fire engine or the creaking of a door, or letting in too much night air. To be concerned about our dreams is really silly and a waste of time, we think. It is simply indicative of a superstitious or overactive mind.

Morton strongly believes that this is not the view represented in the scriptures or in the Christian tradition. Some years ago he read through the entire Bible, noting specifically all the references to dreams and visions. He found hundreds and only one or two that were negative. As he studied these passages in the original Hebrew and Greek, he found that in both languages the words for dreams and visions were used so interchangeably that it was difficult to tell them apart. Then, when he studied the history of the early church during the first three centuries, he discovered that all of its leading theologians had believed in the importance of dreams. But from that time onward, opinions about their place in the spiritual life seesawed back and forth, eventually culminating in a deathly silence during most of the nineteenth and twentieth centuries. When Morton's book *God, Dreams and Revelation* was published in 1968 it was the first serious study on the subject since 1791!

His interest in dreams was not just academic. It was prompted by a dream that he had during a time of spiritual crisis. He had just started working at a new parish and was trying to do everything in his power to revive an unhappy and disinterested congregation. His own faith at this time was very intellectual, with little experiential knowledge of the Holy One. He was working long hours, relying on his own resources, and was motivated by strongly self-centered desires. However, almost as soon as he achieved the goal of being "successful," the skies caved in. When he got up to preach one morning a voice on his shoulder kept whispering into his ear that he didn't really believe in everything that he was saying. Then one night he had a dream.

He had entered the church to conduct a service. First, he could not find his vestments. Then he could not find his sermon notes. In his third experience of fear and despair, he could not find his place in the prayer book. When he turned around to face the congregation, he saw that a dead tree had fallen through the nave of the church. Finally, in panic, he wondered how the ushers would take up the collection through the branches of the dead tree.

The dream made Morton realize that he was at war within. One part of him was clinging to faith; the other side doubted. He needed a real experience of God if he was going to continue with his ministry. He sought out someone to talk to, a German Jew who had survived a Nazi concentration camp and who believed that God really operated in the present world. This psychologist showed Morton that, through his dream, God was trying to lead him out of the deep hole into which he had been sinking. Gradually, Morton's life began to mend, his faith became more real, and people started to knock on his door and talk about spiritual issues. And the voice on his shoulder ceased its whispering.

But how can we interpret our dreams as people of faith? Space does not allow for a full response to this important question, but let me suggest some basic guidelines. (For those who would like to explore this question more fully, I recommend Morton's book *Dreams, A Way to Listen to God.*)

First, welcome the dream as a possible gift from God. Consider it a possibility that God has given you this dream for your benefit and growth and to reveal something to you.

Second, write the dream down. Most dreams are lost forever if we do not record them within five minutes of awakening. Dreams have to be remembered before they can be interpreted, as the book of Daniel tells us.

Third, pray and ask God to help you as you reflect upon the dream. Recognize that with the help of God, it is you and no one else who is in the best position to understand what the dream may mean for your life. When Joseph was asked in Egypt who could interpret dreams, he replied:

> *Do not interpretations belong to God? Please tell them to me.*
> *(Gen 40:8)*

Fourth, allow the dream to raise such questions as: What feelings did I have during the dream? Is the dream about pain and guilt of the past or the present? Could it be telling me that I have lost my way? Could it be suggesting how to go forward? Is the dream warning or encouraging me about my present path?

Next, think about the people and objects in the dreams as parts of yourself. So, if you dream about someone else, think about the essential quality of that person and ponder what it represents about yourself. In this way, physical objects in dreams can also point to a certain part of you. Most dreams are telling you about yourself, rather than someone else, and how you can be brought to wholeness and healing.

Finally, write down some conclusions. When you have finished praying and thinking about a dream, it can be quite helpful if you write down in a paragraph or two what you think the meaning of the dream was.

I hope your appetite to listen to your dreams has been whetted. As Christ-followers, we must not hand over the subject of dreams to the New Ager or to the secular psychologist. We Christ-followers have a long and vital tradition concerning the way God touches our lives through dreams and visions. Let's embrace this heritage and again begin to consider whether God may be using our dreams to say something to us.

Pleasant dreams!

DAILY MEDITATION TEXTS FOR THE WEEK

Day 1 "I bless the Lord who gives me counsel; in the night also my heart instructs me." (Ps 16:7)

Day 2 "In the last days it will be, God declares, that I will pour out my Spirit upon all flesh, and your sons and your daughters shall prophesy, and your young men shall see visions, and your old men shall dream dreams." (Acts 2:17)

Day 3 "But just when he had resolved to do this, an angel of the Lord appeared to him in a dream and said, 'Joseph, son of David, do not be afraid to take Mary as your wife, for the child conceived in her is from the Holy Spirit.'" (Matt 1:20)

Day 4 "And he said, 'Hear my words: When there are prophets among you, I the Lord make myself known to them in visions; I speak to them in dreams.'" (Num 12:6)

Day 5 "My soul is satisfied as with a rich feast, and my mouth praises you with joyful lips when I think of you on my bed, and meditate on you in the watches of the night." (Ps 63:5–6)

Day 6 "I slept, but my heart was awake." (Song 5:2)

Day 7 "They said to him, 'We have had dreams, and there is no one to interpret them.' And Joseph said to them, 'Do not interpretations belong to God? Please tell them to me.'" (Gen 40:8)

SUGGESTION FOR JOURNALING

Make a note of one dream you have during the week. Reflect on this dream using the suggested questions in the meditation and write out your thoughts.

QUOTE

A dream that is not interpreted is like a letter that is not read.
Joel Covitz
Visions of the Night

PRAYER

Lord, help me to hear your whisper in my dreams. Amen.

Experiencing the Power
of Pentecost

There's a great story about a rather timid pastor who visited an elderly woman who was at death's door. She was lying in her bed, her mouth hung open and she was struggling to breathe. He said to her, "Mrs. Jones, before I leave, is there anything you would like me to say or do?" She told him she wanted him to pray. He asked if there was something specific she wanted him to pray for. "I'd like you to pray for my healing, of course," she answered. "Oh God!" he thought to himself. So he prayed cautiously that, if it was God's will, God would heal her and, if it was not, then to help everyone to adjust to the situation.

As the prayer ended, the woman sat up and said, "Wow!" She threw her feet over the side of the bed, stood up, flexed her muscles and said, "This is unbelievable! I feel wonderful!" Then she walked down the hallway and called out to the nurses' station, "I think I'm well! I think I'm well!" The pastor left the hospital, got into his car and said to God, "Don't you ever do that to me again!"

This is a funny story, but it illustrates a sad truth. Sometimes we fail to grasp what Christianity is all about. We think it is a matter of telling people what rules and regulations to follow. Nothing, however, can be further from the truth. Christianity is about becoming more like we want to be through God's power. It is not primarily about laws and regulations, but about spiritual power and fire. The basic point of the Christian faith is the granting of spiritual power so that we can deal with those problems of life which we cannot deal with by ourselves, and so live more fully and abundantly.

Most people know what they ought to do. I'm sure that you have discovered this in your conversation with others. Very few people complain that they went wrong because they did not know any better. But again and again we hear them say, "I don't know why I did what I did. I know what the right thing is, but I don't seem able to do it." Perhaps this is something we hear ourselves say as well. Deep down we know what is right and wrong, but we cannot seem to follow through with it. Even the great apostle Paul once cried out:

> *For I do not do the good I want, but the evil I do not want is what I do...Wretched man that I am! Who will rescue me from this body of death? (Rom 7:19, 24)*

What we need is not judgment or more laws and regulations but the power to become what God wants us to be. This is what the message of Pentecost is about. You can read about it in the second chapter of Acts. On that day the disciples received power from above. It was a power than enabled them to go out and outlive, outthink and outlove the ancient world. They received something extra, something new, something they did not have before. They received a new spirit of power in their hearts. The flames of fire and sounds of the wind were only the outward signs that the Holy Spirit had been given to them. What they received, all of us desperately need, which is for the Spirit of God to fill us and enable us to overcome the evil within and around us.

Many Christians are binitarians. They do not believe in the Trinity. They believe in God the Father and God the Son, but they don't really believe in God the Holy Spirit. They believe in the God who created the universe and in the man by the name of Jesus who came to save them. But they do not take seriously the work of the Spirit of God that has been sent to enable us to live life at its best. They do not believe that God is actively present among them and that the Holy Spirit is available to strengthen their minds, deepen their love, heal their bodies and give them more than human understanding of things human and divine. Really believing in the Trinity means believing in God the creator, Jesus the redeemer and in the Holy Spirit, the present power of God waiting to come into our lives.

From a practical point of view it seems that to try to follow Jesus without the pentecostal power of the Holy Spirit, without some inner strength greater than our own is an impossible ideal. We just cannot do it. From a biblical point of view, it appears that everything that happened before Pentecost was a preparation for this gift of spiritual fire and power. The world was created so that we might have fellowship with God and be given the Holy Spirit. Jesus, God made flesh, lived, died and rose so that our eyes would be opened to the nature of the divine love and we would be made ready to receive his gift of power. This indeed is the central thrust of the New Testament. It tells us of a new power that is available, the very power of the kingdom of heaven. It describes a living faith that built a community, healed the sick, opened up new vistas of life, released material resources and empowered ordinary men and women to love in extraordinary ways.

For the first three hundred years of its existence, before it became the political tool of the Roman Empire, the early church did the same things. As we read the writings of that time, we learn about the power of men and women to withstand martyrdom, and even to go with joy into the arena to meet their death. We learn about their power to understand the deeper things of life, their power to free others of evil, their power to bring healing and wholeness into the lives of those around them. Today we don't speak much of these things or of this power. It is not easy to speak of things that we have not experienced. Nonetheless, we must ask ourselves if we are not missing out on something that God wants for each one of us.

So let us this week think deeply about the place of the Holy Spirit in our lives. Is the Spirit of God really at work in us? Are we being transformed inwardly into a more radiant Christlikeness? Are we growing in love and exercising some of the spiritual gifts listed for us in 1 Corinthians 12 and Romans 12? I know that before we can experience the Holy Spirit, we need to know something of the God who created the world. I realize that before we can manifest this fire and power we must have yielded ourselves to the risen Christ. But this is not enough; we must become men and women in whom the Holy Spirit of God is known and manifested; people on fire. This is the New Testament expectation for every one of Jesus' disciples.

Do you need to experience this pentecostal power more deeply? If you do, perhaps you are wondering how we can better foster the activity of the Spirit within our daily lives. Here are some suggestions. We can take Jesus' word seriously and ask the Father to give us the Holy Spirit (see Luke 11:13). We can ask a trusted friend in whom we see evidence of God at work to lay hands on us and pray for us. We can step out in faith and risk following what we sense may be an inner prompting of the Spirit. We can follow Paul's spiritual direction and begin to strive for those spiritual gifts that build up the church (see 1 Cor 14:12). We can rid ourselves of those attitudes and actions that may be blocking the power of God from flowing freely through our lives. Whatever it is that we are led to do, few things are more crucial in the life of faith than remaining open and yielded to the Spirit of God.

Daily Meditation Texts for the Week

Day 1   "But you will receive power when the Holy Spirit has come upon you; and you will be my witnesses in Jerusalem, in all Judea and Samaria, and to the ends of the earth." (Acts 1:8)

Day 2   "If you then, who are evil, know how to give good gifts to your children, how much more will the heavenly Father give the Holy Spirit to those who ask him!" (Luke 11:13)

Day 3   "He said to me, 'This is the word of the Lord to Zerubbabel: Not by might, nor by power, but by my spirit, says the Lord of hosts.'" (Zech 4:6)

Day 4   "If you love me, you will keep my commandments. And I will ask the Father, and he will give you another Advocate to be with you forever. This is the Spirit of truth…" (John 14:15–17)

Day 5   "Now the Lord is the Spirit, and where the Spirit of the Lord is, there is freedom." (2 Cor 3:17)

Day 6   "But the Advocate, the Holy Spirit, whom the Father will send in my name, will teach you everything, and remind you of all that I have said to you." (John 14:26)

Day 7   "If the Spirit of him who raised Jesus from the dead dwells in you, he who raised Christ from the dead will give life to your mortal bodies also through his Spirit that dwells in you." (Rom 8:11)

Suggestion for Journaling

How would you describe your relationship with the Holy Spirit?

QUOTE

The Holy Spirit is that power which opens eyes that are closed, hearts that are unaware and minds that shrink from too much reality.

John V. Taylor
The Go-Between God

PRAYER

O God, our Father, give us your Holy Spirit in our hearts and in our minds that we may ever choose aright.

Give us your Holy Spirit that we may know which way to choose, and which way to refuse; which choice to make, and which choice to reject; which course of action to take, and which course of action to avoid.

Give us your Holy Spirit to enlighten our minds, to see what we ought to do; to strengthen our wills, to choose the right course of action, and to abide by it; to empower our lives, to follow the right way to the end.

Give us your Holy Spirit, to cleanse our minds of all evil and impure thoughts; to fill our hearts with all lovely and noble desires; to make our lives wise with knowledge, beautiful with love, useful with service.

Give us your Holy Spirit, to light up the pages of your Book for us; to teach us for what we ought to pray; to enrich our lives with the fruit which only he can give.

Grant us all this for your love's sake. Amen.

William Barclay
Prayers for the Christian Year

Exploring the Mystery
of the Trinity

"In the name of the Father and of the Son and of the Holy Spirit." These familiar words, taken from Jesus' Great Commission at the end of Matthew's Gospel, have been a stumbling block for many God-seekers and Christ-followers. After all, how on earth can God be one-in-three and three-in-one? Perhaps you wonder about this yourself. If you do, this meditation has been written especially with you in mind. May it help you to explore the mystery of the Trinity and its meaning in your life.

Belief in the three-in-one God arose from the early church's experience of God. It puts into words the kind of contact the disciples had with the Holy One. This doctrine simply states that we can experience the one God in three different ways. We can know God as the mighty Creator and Shaper of history. We can also experience God as we come to share in a personal relationship with Jesus. And then, we can encounter God within us in the transformation and new life that comes when we yield ourselves to the Holy Spirit. This is the way Christ-followers throughout the centuries have known God in their lives.

Let me tease out these three ways of experiencing God. First of all, we know God as the one who made the universe and everything in it. This world is either the product of a cosmic accident, or it is the unfolding of some personal meaning and plan. As we commune with nature, look into the starry heavens, examine the miracle of matter, marvel about the cycle of the seasons, and meditate on the development of life, we experience behind all these mysteries a Creator and Shaper, someone who has directed it all and given it purpose. Looking at the physical universe and history with open hearts and minds, we can sense the hand of God at work, not always, but often enough for us to be certain in spite of our doubts and disappointments. We find ourselves able to sing with recognition and amazement the words of this popular hymn:

> *O Lord my God! When I in awesome wonder*
> *Consider all the works thy hand hath made*
> *I see the stars, I hear the mighty thunder*
> *Thy power throughout the universe displayed.*
> *Then sings my soul, my Savior God to thee*
> *How great thou art! How great thou art!*
> *Then sings my soul, my Savior God to thee*
> *How great thou art! How great thou art!*

Second, we can know God in the person of Jesus Christ. Those who knew Jesus firsthand and experienced his rising from the dead were so astounded that they discovered they had met the Holy One in him. Here was one who mastered life and conquered death, one whose wisdom and depth brought them into touch with the same reality that they knew as they experienced the Creator of the universe and the God of history. They heard this man call himself the Son of God, and in holy awe in his presence they knew themselves to be in the presence of God. They also realized something new about the nature of God, that the Holy One was essentially love and compassion, with a special concern and love for those who suffer.

These disciples wrote about what they knew of Jesus of Nazareth. They put down as best as they could what they had experienced. A strange and wonderful document it was, abounding in supernatural and miraculous experiences, in healing of body and mind, in power over the very forces of nature, in moral wisdom and understanding, and in love and insight into the human soul. Indeed, no other book is quite like it. Those who have taken the trouble to read it with thoughtfulness and care and who have put aside their prejudices find that a strange thing happens. By just reading this book and looking into its very depths, we experience the living reality of the one of whom they wrote. His presence still lives on through his words and actions and we can actually come to know him. This is why reading the Bible is so incredibly important. It helps us to experience the risen Christ, not as a dead hero, but as the living Lord.

Certainly this is part of my testimony. As I have sought to keep company with Jesus in the gospels, I have come to see him as the most alive, aware and responsive human being who ever lived. I have come to recognize his dying as a revelation of love in the face of evil. I have come to realize that something most extraordinary must have taken place after the crucifixion in order to transform those frightened and grieving disciples into bold witnesses willing to die for their beliefs. I have come to accept the biblical explanation for this transformation, that this man Jesus was both fully human and God come in the flesh, was tortured and killed, was resurrected from death and still comes to us today as a living presence, especially in those words written about him.

Third, these disciples knew God in yet another way. They experienced God in the depths of their inner beings as a power from beyond themselves. Their first experience of this was at Pentecost some fifty days after Easter. Ordinary people suddenly felt that they were filled with the power and presence of God and the most astounding things began to happen again. It was as if Jesus himself were continuing to live in and through the lives of his followers. They found that the very power of healing and understanding, which had been present in their Master, was also present in them in a lesser way. They learnt that God could touch their inner lives, speak to them personally and give them so much.

Morton first came to experience this reality when he discovered the wisdom of God leading him in his dreams. As he reflected on his dreams he came to know God as one who touched his life directly. He found out more as he studied the subject of speaking in tongues and the interpretation thereof. Then as he began to listen to the spiritual experiences of people from all over the world, he became convinced that God leaves no man or woman who truly seeks God without some direct touch of the Divine Presence. His involvement in the healing ministry further strengthened his belief in the here and now of God through the Holy Spirit.

Have you gained some insight into how the early church experienced God? They knew God as a mysterious hand undergirding the universe and directing the course of history. They knew God in Jesus of Nazareth as they walked and talked with him. They knew God as the Holy Spirit who came to them in the secret chambers of their own souls and transformed them. This is the reality of God that the church in its wisdom calls the blessed Holy Trinity. What a glorious mystery!

Daily Meditation Texts for the Week

Day 1   "Go therefore and make disciples of all nations, baptizing them in the name of the Father and of the Son and of the Holy Spirit." (Matt 28:19)

Day 2   "Then God said, 'Let us make humankind in our image...'" (Gen 1:26)

Day 3   "And when Jesus had been baptized, just as he came up from the water, suddenly the heavens were opened to him and he saw the Spirit of God descending like a dove and alighting on him." (Matt 3:16)

Day 4   "At that same hour Jesus rejoiced in the Holy Spirit and said, 'I thank you, Father, Lord of heaven and earth, because you have hidden these things from the wise and the intelligent and have revealed them to infants; yes, Father, for such was your gracious will.'" (Luke 10:21)

Day 5   "The grace of the Lord Jesus Christ, the love of God, and the communion of the Holy Spirit be with all of you." (2 Cor 13:13)

Day 6   "But when the goodness and loving kindness of God our Savior appeared, he saved us, not because of any works of righteousness that we had done, but according to his mercy, through the water of rebirth and renewal by the Holy Spirit. This Spirit he poured out on us richly through Jesus Christ our Savior, so that, having been justified by his grace, we might become heirs according to the hope of eternal life." (Titus 3:4–7)

Day 7   "Peter, an apostle of Jesus Christ, to the exiles of the Dispersion...who have been chosen and destined by God the Father and sanctified by the Spirit to be obedient to Jesus Christ and to be sprinkled with his blood." (1 Pet 1:1–2)

SUGGESTION FOR JOURNALING

How do you respond to the mystery of the Trinity?

QUOTE

> *O eternal Trinity! O Godhead! You are a deep sea, into which the deeper I enter the more I find, and the more I find the more I seek.*
>
> Catherine of Siena

PRAYER

> *Father, Son and Holy Spirit,*
> *Lord of majesty,*
> *Trinity of love and power:*
> *accept and make holy all that we are,*
> *all that we have, and all that we offer you.*
> *Keep us firm in our faith and strong in your service;*
> *create in us a new heart, that we may respond to your*
> *great mercy: one God, our savior, now and for ever.*
> *Amen.*
>
> *Prayers for the People*

The Pilgrim's Goal

Picturing What Heaven
Is Like

Many people today dismiss any talk about heaven as a waste of time. They say that, since we are trying to describe a reality that we have not experienced, we are in no position to speculate about the nature of life in heaven.

There is a delightful story that challenges this attitude and invites us to think again about the afterlife in a way that is more in harmony with our gospel faith as Christ-followers. It is about a conversation between twins in their mother's womb. As they snuggle up against each other, the sister suddenly turns to her brother and says, "I believe there is life after birth."

"Nonsense," answers her brother, "this dark and cozy place is all there is."

"There must be something more than this confined space," insists the baby girl, "there must be somewhere where there is light and vision and freedom to move."

Her twin brother is still not convinced. After a few moments of silence, she goes on hesitantly, "There is something else, and I'm afraid you won't believe that either, but I think there is a mother!"

"A mother! A mother!" shouts her brother furiously. "What are you talking about! I have never seen a mother and neither have you. Who put that crazy idea in your head? This place is all we have. Why do you want more? It's good to be here. We have all we need, so let's be content."

The sister is quite taken aback by her brother's anger and doesn't say any more. However, she cannot ignore her instincts and, since there is no one to speak to except her twin brother, she finally plucks up the courage to ask him, "Do you sometimes feel those unpleasant and painful squeezes that come every once in a while?"

"Yes," he answers. "What's so special about that?"

"Well," explains his sister, "I think those squeezes are getting us ready for that other place, which is much more beautiful and spacious than this, where we will see our mother face to face."

It is not hard to see the parallel between this story and the life beyond. Heaven was central to the message of Jesus. To the people who heard him it was an amazing teaching. It was different in two ways from anything they had heard before. They knew about hoping for heaven in the future and trying their best to earn it and avoid punishment. But Jesus spoke about finding heaven within and around and among us, as well as in a future that is hidden from us. Heaven, he said, has drawn very close (see Matt 4:17). And then he also made it very clear that this heaven is a kingdom of a loving, caring God. It is a spiritual realm where God rules with tender love and amazing grace. In fact, he said to them that they could call God *Abba Father.*

One of the best descriptions of the nature of heaven is given in the beatitudes. They are found in Matthew 5:3–12 and Luke 6:20–26. If we look at Matthew's version we can see how all the references to heaven fit together. Here is the simple yet comprehensive description he gives us:

Blessed are the poor in spirit, for theirs is the kingdom of heaven. Blessed are those who mourn, for they will be comforted. Blessed are the meek, for they will inherit the earth. Blessed are those who hunger and thirst for righteousness, for they will be filled. Blessed are the merciful, for they will receive mercy. Blessed are the pure in heart, for they will see God. Blessed are the peacemakers, for they will be called children of God. Blessed are those who are persecuted for righteousness' sake, for theirs is the kingdom of heaven. (Matt 5:3–10)

Notice that the first and last beatitudes carry the same blessing or reward, "For theirs is the kingdom of heaven." This promise encloses the other six like brackets. It follows that the six intervening statements are also descriptions of what God's eternal kingdom, the fellowship of heaven, is like.

Now, while it is wonderful when we experience these blessings in this life, they don't always, or even very frequently, occur on earth. Those who mourn and are sorrowful are not always comforted and consoled in this life. Some go on finding life a painful struggle. Those that are gentle in spirit do not noticeably inherit the earth in this world. Those who hunger and thirst for food and drink often die of starvation, and those who seek righteousness sometimes end up on crosses or in jails. The merciful often lose their shirts and come out with the short end of the stick in business deals. The next two descriptions tell us that the pure in heart and the peacemakers behold God and will be called the children of God. The total fulfillment of these promises makes sense only in an eternal heaven; they do not occur in this life.

So what was Jesus trying to say with these beatitudes? Quite simply, he was describing the nature of heaven. It is that eternal state of being where we are comforted and strengthened, where we are made heirs of all earth's real treasures, and where we have our deepest longings filled and transformed into even deeper longings. In heaven we will receive pardon, mercy and love. We will know the utter joy of being an intimate part of the family of the loving God. We will do heavenly work and play heavenly games. Here we will find clearness of vision, and fulfillment and consummation. Finally, we will have come home. This is heaven.

Elsewhere in the gospels Jesus used more concrete pictures to describe heaven. He said it is like a treasure that exceeds our wildest imagination, like a pearl so magnificent that we would sell everything we owned to possess it, and like a king's banquet where every known delight is served. But as the beatitudes show, the best part of heaven goes beyond such physical images. It is a state in which we will no longer be frustrated by the pettiness, failure, guilt, alienation and loneliness that is so much a part of our lives. During our lifetimes we are never able to shake off these frustrations completely, no matter how hard we try. In heaven, however, we will at last become the people we long to be. We will be given new visions and ways of reaching out to that wholeness which is our God-given destiny.

I invite you this week to spend some time imagining what heaven is like. Find a quiet place where you can be alone and uninterrupted. Ask God to meet with you and speak to you personally. Read Jesus' beatitudes again and again, until you have these qualities of heavenly life fixed firmly in your mind. Meditate on them. Imagine what your future in the company of Christ will be like—seeing God for the first time, delighting in meeting with your brothers and sisters in the faith, experiencing complete wholeness and creatively going about God's work in his vast universe. As you share in this meditation, you will discover how a perspective of the eternal can guide and strengthen our present lives.

DAILY MEDITATION TEXTS FOR THE WEEK

Day 1   "Then he began to speak, and taught them, saying: Blessed are the poor in spirit, for theirs is the kingdom of heaven." (Matt 5:2–3)

Day 2   "Blessed are those who mourn, for they will be comforted." (Matt 5:4)

Day 3   "Blessed are the meek, for they will inherit the earth." (Matt 5:5)

Day 4   "Blessed are those who hunger and thirst for righteousness, for they will be filled." (Matt 5:6)

Day 5   "Blessed are the merciful, for they will receive mercy." (Matt 5:7)

Day 6   "Blessed are the pure in heart, for they will see God." (Matt 5:8)

Day 7   "Blessed are the peacemakers, for they will be called children of God. Blessed are those who are persecuted for righteousness' sake, for theirs is the kingdom of heaven." (Matt 5:9–10)

SUGGESTION FOR JOURNALING

Write down, as honestly as you can, your feelings about dying.

QUOTE

The development of spirituality, the growth of our life in God, flows naturally into a life with God after death, the kind of life in which we will see God and know Him in the same way He knows and loves us, a life in which we share with Jesus the eternal ecstasy of God's presence and the joyful and endless companionship of God's family and own loved ones whom God has called home.

Joseph Girzone
Never Alone

PRAYER

God be in my head,
And in my understanding.
God be in my eyes,
And in my looking.
God be in my mouth,
And in my speaking.
God be at my end,
And in my departing.

Celtic Prayer

Balancing Heaven
and Earth

When it comes to matters of heaven and earth there are two mistakes we can make. On the one hand, we can focus entirely on the life beyond death. In fact, there was a time in history when the church did this. It avoided dealing with the anguish of this world by saying that everything would be set right on the other side. This, however, was not the teaching or the practice of Jesus of Nazareth. He taught and showed us how to live life fully as God intended us to. He urged us to reach out to the poor, the forgotten, the sick, the lonely, and did so himself. As Christ-followers we need to do everything we can to change the structures of society that crush and destroy human beings and create injustice.

On the other hand, we can focus so much on this world that we neglect the issues of the life beyond. This seems to be our modern predicament. Over the past twenty-five years I cannot remember hearing too many sermons on the subject of the afterlife. Usually the topic is only mentioned at funerals, and then often in a half-hearted and fleeting way. We seem intent on avoiding any real discussion about heaven or hell, or what may happen to human beings after they die. This is a very different attitude from that of the early Christ-followers who seemed to talk as much about the next life as they did about the present one.

In this last meditation I want to explore how we can balance heaven and earth more creatively in our daily lives.

Here are three suggestions:

First of all, we need to open ourselves to experiences of the kingdom in the here and now. Remember that Jesus spoke of the immediate availability of the kingdom of heaven to all who turned to him. This was an invitation for us to begin living an eternal life today. We do not have to wait until we die before we can experience heaven. Participation in the eternal life begins in this world. Jesus' life, death and resurrected presence throughout the universe opens the door for us to enter the kingdom of heaven at this very moment. If we as Christ-followers don't experience the kingdom's closeness, our faith becomes dull and intellectual.

Throughout this book I have suggested several ways in which we can open ourselves to this eternal realm. We can pray the Lord's Prayer slowly and meditatively. We can step into the scriptures imaginatively. We can listen to those strange intimations that break in upon us, such as our dreams and our visionary experiences. All of these efforts, however, assume one thing. We need to end our total preoccupation with the physical world. We must turn away from our obsession with material things, success and power. We have to stop and reflect, and be silent and listen. In this way we

> *look not at what can be seen but at what cannot be seen; for what can be seen is temporary, but what cannot be seen is eternal. (2 Cor 4:18)*

Second, once we have made a decision that we are going to be emigrants to the kingdom Jesus spoke of, we will want to find out everything we can about the place and prepare ourselves so that we can fit in. Isn't this what we do on our earthly travels? Few of us set off on an extended visit to a strange land without first learning as much as we can about the place to which we are going. What kind of clothes do we need? What's the weather like? What are the customs of the people? Some of us will even try to learn a little of the language. And, if we are emigrating to a new country, we will do this even more thoroughly. It is no different when we begin to prepare ourselves for the life beyond this one.

So what do we know about heaven in practical terms? There is one thing I'm absolutely sure of. Heaven is that sphere of reality where love reigns, where we will find the kind, humble, understanding, forgiving, caring, compassionate spirits whom we have known on earth. The language of the kingdom is the language of self-giving love. Participation in this kingdom demands one central commitment from our side. It requires sharing with others the same kind of compassion, mercy and caring that we have received from God. This is the essential distinguishable characteristic, the "acid test" as I called it earlier, of being a follower of Jesus. Think about those startling words that he spoke to his disciples:

> *I give you a new commandment, that you love one another.*
> *Just as I have loved you, you also should love one another. By*
> *this everyone will know that you are my disciples, if you have*
> *love for one another. (John 13:34–35)*

Finally, we can share the gospel's vision of heaven with those around us. Jesus wants us to pass on the hope, joy and consolation of his message to the world. Sometimes we don't do this very well. Nevertheless, this is the good news we have to offer our broken and hurt world. The kingdom of heaven is open to all. Empowered by the victory of Jesus on the cross and with a vision of coming home to the kingdom of heaven when this life is over, we can go out and help men and women who are battling in the storms of this life. Only the perverse among us will fail to offer this message to our hurting world; this message of infinite hope that opens up for everyone through the resurrection of Jesus.

Morton had the privilege of sharing this vision with his own son. When John, his younger son, fell ill with an untreatable form of encephalitis, he and Barbara immediately canceled all their engagements and went to be with him. Together they were his principal caregivers until he died on December 3, 1988. Sitting by his son's bed while he slept, Morton finished writing a book entitled *Reaching: The Journey to Fulfillment.* John had specially asked him to complete it. One day as he sat there in silent communion with his son, some words came vividly into his mind. He wrote them down in the form of a poem. When he shared the poem with John, he asked for a copy. Later Morton overheard his son reading the poem to a mutual friend and at the end John said, "My father understands how I feel." Here is the poem:

Fear not for me. I'm not afraid.
A new adventure awaits me,
A new, more brilliant being
Is about to birth
Into a different place and time.
The garden of heaven and those abiding there
Are calling me insistently. They want me soon.
They sing of my courage and frustration,
Of years of seeking, restless searching...
So many roads that petered out
In scorching desert and burning sand
And still I kept on, was guided.
Those voices promise
To answer all my questions
With love abounded, limitless.
They offer intimacy, closeness, far richer
Than I had dared to hope for, and wisdom, too,
And living water drawn from the deepest well
That holds the secret mysteries safe
From vain and curious wanderers,

The voices also sing of love and loving,
Of giving all I had and only at this moment
Knowing that my arrow struck its mark.
Do not hold me back. I'll be with you still
In fuller measure than I've ever been before.
The sun is rising from the sea
As one by one the stars are lost in light.
The broken has been mended.
I can be loved and love.
It is time to go.
Pushed beyond the limits
Of death and pain and hope.
I find the real, Eternal Love.

Our high calling is to balance heaven and earth, in our lives and in our society. This goal of the Christ-following life coincides with the desperate plight of our suffering and broken world. Our times cry out for men and women who will live out the words of the Lord's Prayer, "Your kingdom come, on earth, as it is in heaven." Only then will human life be kept sacred. It is my deep hope and prayer that these fifty-two meditations will help you to experience the kingdom of heaven so that you can bring it to those friends and neighbors with whom you live on this earth. May God guide and keep you in this adventure.

DAILY MEDITATION TEXTS FOR THE WEEK

Day 1 "And going a little farther, he threw himself on the ground and prayed, 'My Father, if it is possible, let this cup pass from me; yet not what I want but what you want.'" (Matt 26:39)

Day 2 "I delight to do your will, O my God; your law is within my heart." (Ps 40:8)

Day 3 "For I have come down from heaven, not to do my own will, but the will of him who sent me." (John 6:38)

Day 4   "I appeal to you therefore, brothers and sisters, by the mercies of God, to present your bodies as a living sacrifice, holy and acceptable to God, which is your spiritual worship." (Rom 12:1)

Day 5   "Jesus said to them, 'My food is to do the will of him who sent me and to complete his work.'" (John 4:34)

Day 6   "For to me, living is Christ and dying is gain." (Phil 1:21)

Day 7   "Then I saw a new heaven and a new earth; for the first heaven and the first earth had passed away, and the sea was no more. And I saw the holy city, the new Jerusalem, coming down out of heaven from God, prepared as a bride adorned for her husband. And I heard a loud voice from the throne saying, 'See, the home of God is among mortals. He will dwell with them as their God; they will be his peoples, and God himself will be with them; he will wipe every tear from their eyes. Death will be no more; mourning and crying and pain will be no more, for the first things have passed away.'" (Rev 21:1–4)

SUGGESTION FOR JOURNALING

What holds you back from surrendering yourself fully to God?

QUOTE

Over the years I have learned to trust Him. Do not be afraid! He will respect your freedom and your independence more than anyone you have ever met, because He created you to be free. He just wants more than anything that you will accept Him as your Friend. If you do, I can promise you, you will never be alone.

Joseph Girzone
Never Alone

PRAYER

> *Father, I abandon myself into your hands;*
> *do with me what you will.*
> *Whatever you may do, I thank you;*
> *I am ready for all, I accept all,*
> *Let only your will be done in me,*
> *and in all your creatures—*
> *I wish no more than this,*
> *O Lord.*

Charles de Foucauld